Lecture Notes in Computer Science 3456

Commenced Publication in 1973
Founding and Former Series Editors:
Gerhard Goos, Juris Hartmanis, and Jan van Leeuwen

T0223561

Heinrich Rust

Operational Semantics for Timed Systems

A Non-standard Approach to Uniform Modeling
of Timed and Hybrid Systems

Author

Heinrich Rust
BTU Cottbus, Software-Systemtechnik
Postfach 101344, 03013 Cottbus, Germany
E-mail: heinrich.rust@software-tomography.com

Library of Congress Control Number: 2005923604

CR Subject Classification (1998): D.2, F.1.1, D.3, D.4, F.4

ISSN   0302-9743
ISBN-10   3-540-25576-1 Springer Berlin Heidelberg New York
ISBN-13   978-3-540-25576-5 Springer Berlin Heidelberg New York

Springer is a part of Springer Science+Business Media

springeronline.com

© Springer-Verlag Berlin Heidelberg 2005
Printed in Germany

Typesetting: Camera-ready by author, data conversion by Olgun Computergrafik
Printed on acid-free paper   SPIN: 11416166   06/3142   5 4 3 2 1 0

Foreword

This monograph is dedicated to a novel approach for uniform modelling of timed and hybrid systems. Heinrich Rust presents a time model which allows for both the description of discrete time steps and continuous processes with a dense real number time model. The proposed time model is well suited to express synchronicity of events in a real number time model as well as strict causality by using uniform discrete time steps. Thus it integrates and reconciles two views of time that are commonly used apart from each other in different application domains. In many discrete systems time is modelled by discrete steps of uniform length, in continuous systems time is seen as a dense flow. The main idea to integrate these different views is a discretization of the dense real-number time structure by using constant infinitesimal time steps within each real-number point in time. The underlying mathematical structure of this time model is based on concepts of Non-Standard Analysis as proposed by Abraham Robinson in the 1950s. The discrete modelling, i.e. the description of sequential discrete algorithms at different abstraction levels, is done with Abstract State Machines along the formalisms developed by Yuri Gurevich and temporal logic. These ingredients produce a rich formal basis for describing a large variety of systems with quantitative linear time properties, by seamless integration, refinement and embedding of continuous and discrete models into one uniform semantic framework called "Non-Standard Timed Abstract State Machines" (NTASM).

On this theoretically well-founded and elegant basis Heinrich Rust discusses typical problems of time models like "zero time" and "Zeno behaviour", interleaving semantics, time bounds and composition of open systems. The semantic description of two variants of quantitative timed Petri-Nets, timed automata and hybrid automata with NTASM models shows the generality of the NTASM approach.

This book is an important contribution to the research area of time modelling formalisms. The presentation is well-balanced between theoretical elaboration and a critical discussion of the applicability of the theoretical results by means of appropriate case studies. The new temporal semantics proposed and discussed here can help theoreticians as well as practitioners in gaining better understanding of time models and in building better notations, models and tools for the formal treatment of systems where time matters.

Cottbus, January 2005   Claus Lewerentz

Preface

Time is a fascinating subject. It seems to be quite difficult to come to grips with it. Saint Augustine, in Chapter 14 of Book 11 of the Confessions, said it in this classical way:

> *What, then, is time? If no one asks me, I know what it is. If I wish to explain it to him who asks me, I do not know.*

Making our intuitive understanding of a rich phenomenon explicit, we risk being refuted, by others and by ourselves; and time is an especially rich and irreducible phenomenon. If the subject of time is dealt with in a theological or philosophical context (as Augustine did), this is especially clear, since here time is intimately connected to the concept of existence.

But also in a technical discipline like computer science, time is no simple subject. Here, the question is not what time **is**, but how it should be **modelled** in different situations. Unfortunately, the difference between these questions might seem larger than it turns out to be when we consider specific situations. A model of some phenomenon should abstract from features which are not important in the class of situations considered, while important features should be retained in the model. Thus, dealing with the question of how time should be modelled, we also have to deal with the question of what **are** the important features of time in a class of situations.

A model does not only have to be adequate for the modelled phenomena. If it is to be usable by humans it should also be adequate for their cognitive capabilities. This is sometimes used to justify striving for models that are as simple as possible (while sufficient adequacy with respect to the phenomena is retained). But cognitive simplicity is not an objective trait of a model; with familiarization, a formerly complex model might become simple for somebody working with it. If a model for some phenomenon exists which is very rich in the sense that many other models can be described as special cases of it, then using this model might sometimes be even simpler than using the special cases, and the rich model can serve as an integration platform for ideas which first were used with the more special models. In this way, some unification of concepts might be possible.

This book presents work in which a fairly novel model of quantitative time is tried out, one we hope is both general enough and simple enough to be used as an integration platform for ideas springing from different models of quantitative time. The model of time is discrete, which means that for each moment there is a well-defined next moment. The model of time is uniform, i.e., the distance between two moments is always the same; and nevertheless it is dense in the real numbers as they are used in classical mathematics, i.e., the resolution induced by the step width is so fine that any real numbered point in (classical) time is approximated by a time point of the model with vanishing error.

After you have read how this model of time is made explicit in this book, you will undoubtedly also see some drawbacks in the approach (several of them are listed in the summary at the end of the book). If you understand this list of drawbacks as a refutation of the approach proposed, then in your eyes I have fallen prey to the problem described above in the citation of Augustine. Let me confess that I myself am not yet completely sure how to interpret the drawbacks. This needs some more investigation.

Credits

A considerable number of people helped during the work which resulted in this book. Claus Lewerentz supported the work from the beginning. My colleagues, especially Dirk Beyer, discussed features of timed systems with me and helped with the presentation, as did in some phases of the work Andreas Prinz and Angelo Gargantini. Egon Börger and Dino Mandrioli gave hints regarding the exposition of ideas and the need to discuss some specific features of the formalism in more depth. The editors at Springer Verlag worked hard at correcting my English. And finally, my wife, Korinna Hiersche, made sure that I had time for this work during a parental leave, as did my son Alexander by his arrival.

Cottbus, December 2004   Heinrich Rust

Contents

Part III. Applications

List of Figures

1. Overview

This work introduces a novel approach to modelling timed systems. The main idea consists of a new model of time which is both discrete and dense in the real numbers. This allows to use a discrete base formalism for the description of timed algorithms where system behaviors can be interpreted very straight-forwardly in a timed manner without sacrificing that much precision.

Chapter 2 presents the context of our work, which is our understanding of the role of formal methods in the software development process. The main point in that chapter is that "formal methods" does not just mean the use of concepts from mathematics explicitly in software engineering, but the use of such concepts in order to deepen one's understanding of a software engineering problem and its solution, and to express this understanding unambiguously and consistently. From this contextual frame, we derive some consequences for the formalism to be developed.

Part I introduces basic concepts: Our model of time, the discrete base formalism on which we build, and a notation for a temporal logic.

Chapter 3 discusses different models of linear time and introduces a new model which avoids the main problems of classical discrete and continuous models of linear time. The main idea consists in the use of infinitesimals: The flow of time is conceptualized as a sequence of steps of identical infinitesimal length, i.e., we use an infinitesimal discretization of real numbered time.

Chapter 4 presents a short introduction to the number concept we use, which is Nelson's axiomatic approach to infinitesimality.

Chapter 5 presents a variant of abstract state machines (ASMs) as a base formalism for giving the operational semantics of discrete systems. This variant admits two kinds of composition: synchronous and asynchronous. We introduce a semantics for ASMs which is compositional for both kinds of composition, which we call "action semantics". We give reasons for using ASMs as the discrete base formalism.

Chapter 6 describes how we combine ASMs and our model of time in order to describe hybrid systems. Other applications of ASMs in the description of timed and hybrid systems specify the timing independently from the discrete changes – in our approach, the timing is derived from the discrete semantics. An approach using a classical model of time (standard timed ASMs, STASMs) is given first as a comparison; then we use our model of time (non-standard time ASMs, NTASMs) and show that the infinitesimal discretization might essentially change the semantics of an algorithm. We describe what simulation means for two algorithms given as a STASM and an NTASM, and we introduce a concept which relates the STASM interpretation of an algorithm and the NTASM interpretation of an algorithm: an algorithm is "well-behaved" if and only if each run of its STASM interpretation can be mimicked by a run of its NTASM interpretation.

Chapter 7 introduces a notation for a temporal logic which allows us to specify many properties of NTASM systems succinctly. It uses ideas from the Duration Calculus, an interval-based temporal logic, and transfers them to the infinitesimally discretized time domain.

Part II introduces basic modelling strategies for timed systems – interleaving and synchronous composition, deadlines and openness – and it describes how different magnitudes of hyperreals can be used.

Many modelling formalisms used for describing timed systems support either interleaving or synchronous composition. Our formalism supports both. Chapters 8 and 9 describe how interleaving composition and synchronous composition of timed systems are expressed without formal overheads. We point out how the typical problems of synchronous formalisms, those regarding causality and micro-steps, appear in our framework, and we discuss some specific modelling problems of interleaving and synchronous systems of NTASMs.

The concepts of deadlines, urgency and openness pose special problems in the NTASM framework, which are discussed in Chaps. 10 and 11.

Chapter 12 presents a first application: We model hardware on the gate level with timing-enhanced ASMs. We illustrate illustrated how different magnitudes of the hyperreals can be used to express in the model the fact that some delays are considered to be negligible with respect to others, but if the system is considered using a finer timescale some previously neglected delays can become considerable.

Part III describes some applications of our approach.

Chapter 13 presents an NTASM model of Fischer's real-time based synchronization protocol, and a purely discrete correctness proof made possible by our model of time.

Chapters 14 and 15 present meta-models, i.e., STASM and NTASM semantics of other modelling formalisms, in order to make it plausible that our model can express other formalisms with minimal formal overheads. Chapter 14 investigates two forms of quantitatively timed Petri nets, making explicit their differences in an operational way by supporting both variants in a common formalism. Chapter 15 discusses timed automata. In both chapters, we illustrate how the concept of well-behavedness can be lifted from the base formalism to the expressed formalism.

Chapter 16 presents a larger case study, which is inspired by real-world requirements. We describe the control program for a flexible and timing-enhanced production cell. It will become clear that the necessary timing properties are very simply expressed in our formalism, and the flexibility with respect to the abstraction level chosen comes in handy when common properties of different variants of the system are described.

Part IV presents a summary of our work.

The appendix collects the definition of some often used notation.

2. Context:
Formal Methods in Software Engineering

Before we go into the details of the formalisms which we propose for modelling some classes of real-time and hybrid systems, we describe the role we give to formal methods in software engineering and some relevant features of formal methods which seem especially useful to us. This partly is an elaboration of ideas first developed by the author in [Rus94]. This discussion will present the context for the results described later, and it will be used to derive some desiderata for the formalism to be used according to our understanding of formal methods.

2.1 The Place of Formal Methods in Software Engineering

The task in software engineering is to build computerized systems which help to solve real-world tasks, typically in groups and under economic constraints. In these tasks, three ontological spheres are important:

- The **empirical socio-physical context** in which the system to be built is to be used. This context is the application area for the system.
- The **intuitive understanding** of the task, of the computer's role in it and the way of building the system so that it can fulfill its role.
- The **expression of the intuitive understanding** which can be discussed by others or operationalized by execution on a computer.

In a typical software engineering project, the following interplay exists between the three spheres:

- The application area, i.e., the empirical socio-physical context induces the intuitive understanding of the task and its solution.
- The intuitive understanding is expressed in some way.
- Inconsistencies in the expression might be caused by ambiguities or inconsistencies in the intuitive understanding and by objective conflicts of interest in the socio-physical context, and they are opportunities for clearing up one's thoughts.
- Operationalizing program-text expressions and installing them in the application area change the latter, and this might in turn change the intuitive understanding.

Formal methods deal predominantly with the relation between the sphere of the intuitive understanding and the sphere of the expression of the understanding: They help to ensure that an intuitive understanding of something is more or less consistent by expressing it in a strictly defined notational system and checking this for plausibility and consistency. Only an expressed understanding can be exposed to public scrutiny by colleagues and customers, or to consistency checks using mathematical proofs, or to automated consistency checks using a computerized tool, e.g., a syntax checker, or to the execution of a program in order to compare the behavior of a system in the test cases with one's expectations.

2.2 The Role of Mathematics

Mathematics can play a special role in the interplay between an intuitive understanding and its expression. This is the main idea of formal methods. Dijkstra [Dij65] puts it thus: *In spite of all its deficiencies, mathematical reasoning presents an outstanding model of how to grasp extremely complicated structures with a brain with limited capacity.* For Mills [Mil75], the mathematically inspired structured programming approach has the potential that *the professional programmer of tomorrow will remember, more or less vividly, every error in his career.* Lamport [Lam97] gives a reason for the fact that mathematics is a good tool for grasping large and complicated structures: He calls it "compositionality". This means that mathematics provides one with the methods for putting a large number of "small" insights together to form a "large" and possibly more general insight.

There are also voices critical of putting too much stress on mathematics, raising important points. Gerhart and Yelowitz [GY76] give several examples of published proofs of algorithms which nevertheless contain errors. Thus, the application of mathematics in software engineering does not seem to be fool proof.

DeMillo, Lipton and Perlis [DLP79] claim that the social processes leading to belief in the truth of a mathematical theorem just do not exist for proofs of programs, since no colleague is interested in checking these proofs. Thus, it must be shown that even without social proof-checking processes, formal methods might help in some way. Naur [Nau82, Nau85] stresses that unambiguity in the informal expression of intuitive ideas is in danger of being seen as irrelevant if strict mathematization is strived for. Thus, we have to check how to avoid the danger of over-formalizing.

But how can the expression of one's intuitive understanding in a formalism, i.e., in a notation whose syntax and semantics is defined with mathematical exactness, help in sharpening the intuitive understanding? We see two typical features of formalisms at work: (1) The formalism might require decisions where the intuition is not (yet) unambiguous, and (2) the implicit inconsistencies of the intuitive understanding can be made explicit in the formalized expression by doing consistency checks. Both points are, of course, only relevant if the critical features of the intuitive understanding are not abstracted from in the used formalism. We discuss these two points.

Unambiguity of concepts is a feature of many formalisms. It results from the strictness of well-established conventions for the interpretation of elements of the formalism. This makes it plausible that formal specification alone, without any attempts to formally prove any consistencies in what one has expressed, can be helpful in clearing up one's thoughts. This point has been stressed by Hall [Hal90] and Wing [Win90].

But, of course, also formal notations must be interpreted if they are used for expressing intuitive ideas about the empirical world. The danger that ambiguities arise is just less than in everyday language since the context in which the formalized notation is used is much more restricted, and the interpretational conventions which are associated with a well-described formalism also help to resolve ambiguities. An example: If the intuition is that some algorithm computes its result quickly, this intuition must be made more precise if it is to be expressed in some formalism. For example, an O-calculus expression or an absolute time might be given, where, for both, there exist conventions for interpreting the expressions.

Explication of inconsistencies: The unambiguity of mathematical concepts makes it possible to make also very subtle inconsistencies in a larger description explicit – at least relative to the base formalism. This means that if the basic understanding is inconsistent in some features and these features are not abstracted away in the formalization, or if ambiguities in the intuitive understanding are resolved differently when different parts are expressed in the formalism, there is a good chance that the formal expression is inconsistent.

In order to be able to find such inconsistencies, the expression must have some (allegedly) redundant parts describing critical features of the intuitive understanding, or, put more simply: the same idea must be expressed twice, but not in an identical way. Examples of such consistency checks using alleged redundancy are (1) proofs are given showing the consistency of axioms and theorems in a deductive theory; (2) an operational system description fulfills a declarative one; (3) a low-level operational system description refines a high-level one; or (4) a compiler checks the type correctness of a typed programming language.

2.3 Conditions for Using Inconsistencies Productively

If inconsistencies in the formalized expression are disclosed, this is an opportunity to refine one's intuitive understanding or its translation into the formalism. It is in this way that the use of a formalism can help to deepen the intuitive understanding and can ensure that some basic quality criteria are fulfilled. There are several necessary conditions for this to work:

- Familiarity with the formalism is necessary; otherwise, it is not ensured that the interpretational conventions for the elements of the formalism are respected, and, thus, unambiguity is not necessarily ensured.
- The consistency checks which are made possible by the use of the formalism have to be performed.
- The ideas must be expressed at an abstraction level which does not abstract from the problematic features of the intuitive ideas, but it should be abstract enough to make the expression as concise as possible in order to allow meaningful consistency checks.

Consistency checks associated with formalisms can expose subtle inconsistencies in the expression. Because of this, the successful completion of a strictly defined set of consistency checks is a hard criterion for some basic quality of a formalized expression: A formalism might require that **all** theorems are proved, or that **each** expression in a program text must be type correct, etc. These objective criteria can help the software engineer to partly replace the social processes ensuring quality in mathematics (as hinted at by DeMillo, Lipton and Perlis) by individual processes.

Often, interesting consistency checks of formalisms are not recursive. Thus, consistency checking comes down to constructing proofs. Machine support for checking the proofs is helpful for bookkeeping about finished and unfinished consistency checks. Moser and Melliar-Smith [MMS90] describe how the clumsiness of the proof checkers might have the positive consequence that the ideas expressed must be quite simple in order to allow machine-checkable proofs. This indirect effect of mechanized proof checking support has obviously several good consequences: The engineer learns to strive for simplicity, which can lead to easier exposition of errors and to easier communication.

2.4 Two Sides of Machine Support for Proofs

Machine support for consistency checks has two sides: One is that the completion criterion for the consistency checks can be made more objective, even without social processes for checking the work of the software engineer in place: The computer can, partly, fulfill the role of colleagues. The other side is that the description might just be tweaked until the checker does not complain any longer, without necessarily ensuring that the description continues to correspond to the intuition. In order to define better what we understand by "Formal Methods in Software Engineering", we describe two extreme strategies of how a software engineer can react to inconsistencies made explicit by a consistency check:

- One strategy reacts to syntax errors and test failures by taking them as hints to problems with the intuitive understanding one has of the problem or its solution. Each such inconsistency is taken as an opportunity to deepen one's intuitive understanding, by first trying to really understand the inconsistency, before the expression of the understanding is changed.

– The other strategy basically considers each inconsistency as resulting from a typo which can be fixed by just changing a bit of the expression. This might lead to a trial-and-error strategy of trying to get the program text accepted by the compiler or the consistency checker and to make the tests pass.

These two strategies are possible also in the use of automated provers or proof checkers. They represent two attitudes with respect to inconsistencies: to be surprised by them and to analyze them intensely in order to get at a possible deeper cause, or to expect them and explain them away as shallow. In our eyes, only the first attitude deserves the name "formal method". Thus, we see what characterizes a method as formal less a question of using a formally defined notation or of using proof checkers, etc., but as a special state of mind when dealing with formalized descriptions. The next section explains this position.

2.5 The Essence of Formal Methods in Software Engineering

Formal methods might be used in software engineering with different goals in mind:

– Formal methods can help to **deepen one's intuitive understanding** of a problem or its solution by forcing one to be unambiguous when the understanding is expressed in the formalism and by allowing one to do consistency checks which also expose subtle inconsistencies.
– Formal methods might be used because they help in **communicating intuitive ideas**. The unambiguity induced by interpretational conventions helps with this. This is the main reason for using formalized notations for specifications of problems and solutions. Consistency proofs are not of paramount importance in this use of formal methods.
– They might be used because one believes in a **correspondence theory of truth**: If the axioms of some deductive system are true in an application area for some interpretation of the symbols, and if the deductive system is sound, the theorems of the system are also true with the same interpretation in the application area. It is possible to stay completely in the formal sphere because each possible reasoning in the formalism corresponds to a relation of facts in the application area, and this intermediate relation must not be checked: the soundness of the deductive system guarantees this.

  That a formalism can be used in this way is no triviality: For a priori unformalized application areas, the soundness of a formalism is an informal concept; it can be checked only inductively, i.e., by experience, and it depends on (informal) conventions for interpreting the symbols of the formalism in the application area.

But if the use conditions of a formalism are given in some application area, and the fulfillment of the axioms is easily checked, but the theorems are difficult to understand, then purely formal proofs can help to ensure the truth of the theorems.

For this use of formal methods, not much insight is necessary after the soundness of the proof system is inductively ensured and the interpretation of formalism elements is fixed. In this way of using formal methods, even completely automatic proof algorithms, like the currently fashionable ones based on symbolic model checking, are sensible.

We see the second and third uses of formal methods as derived from the first one. Purely formal applicability of a formalism in an application area is only sensible if the (informal) connection between the application area and the formalism is inductively ensured. The social functions of formalisms are also based on the possibility of getting a good intuitive understanding of the subject area and then expressing it for scrutiny by others or comparing it with the expressions others give of their understanding. Thus, for us, the essence of formal methods can be described in the following way:

Formal methods in software engineering consist in the use of mathematics in order to deepen one's intuitive understanding of a software-engineering problem and its solution, and in order to express this understanding unambiguously and consistently.

Thus, to apply formal methods it is not enough to use some strictly defined notation – the **goal** of such a use is important: the striving to make one's intuitive understanding unambiguous and consistent. The use of mathematics is just one of the best tools we know today that support this effort.

2.6 Specific and General Formalisms

A formalism is always specific to some application area, but this area can be chosen to be quite small or quite large. Both choices have their benefits.

A formalism optimized for a specific application area can include application-specific experiences. It can make it easy to express adequate conceptualizations of problems and solutions in the area, and it can make it difficult to express inadequate conceptualizations. The formalism can help to deepen one's understanding by guiding its expression in directions which have proved helpful in the past for the application area considered. As a relevant example, consider formalisms for concurrent systems based on interleaving (like Lamport's [Lam94a, Lam94b] and Manna/Pnueli's [MP92, MP95]) vs. formalisms for concurrent systems based on a synchronous approach (like Esterel [BdS91] or Lustre [HCP91]; compare also [Hal93]). The former make it fairly easy to model loosely connected systems and asynchronous compositions of systems, and typically they contain elements to model the fairness constraints of the systems; but each synchronization must be made explicit. The other formalisms make it fairly easy to model synchronous compositions of systems, which is often adequate for controllers or hardware systems, but they often do not deal with nondeterminism or fairness, since these are not important in the typical application areas for these formalisms.

The other strategy is to strive for more general formalisms. We will base our approach on abstract state machines (ASMs) [Gur88, Gur93, Gur95a, Gur97], which belong to this second class. ASMs started as an attempt to illustrate a strengthened Church-Turing thesis: ASMs are proposed as a formalism which can be used to express any discrete sequential algorithm on any abstraction level [Gur99] (this is the ASM thesis). This means that an activity which is conceptually done in one step can also be executed in the model in one step. This is in contrast to Turing machines, for example, where also quite simple operations might need any finite number of steps. In fact, ASMs are a formalism which is surprisingly expressive with a very simple structure. A large number of case studies have been performed which corroborate the ASM thesis [BH98].

Thus, ASMs are meant to be usable as a framework in many different application areas. One can not expect much guidance toward appropriate solutions from such a general formalism – this is the drawback of a general formalism. But one can expect that the formalism does not restrict unduly one's intuition when it is expressed in the formalism. Thus, such a formalism is meant to be a flexible tool for many application areas.

Gurevich says that sequential algorithms can be described as ASMs essentially coding free. This is to be understood as being in contrast to the Turing machine model or the register machine model of effective computation, where the data part of the algorithm has to be encoded for representation on a tape with a finite alphabet, or as a number. The claim to coding-freedom does not apply to features which in other formalisms stay implicit, like control flow, procedure calls or variable bindings: These have to be made explicit when an ASM is used to model an algorithm, and, thus, they **have** to be encoded with the simple means provided by ASMs.

No formalism can be used for **all** application areas – no formalism but perhaps one: mathematics in general, if considered as a formalism. Gurevich pleads for not restricting one's formalism when expressing one's ideas [Gur95b], in order to be able to express the ideas as faithfully as possible. This means that a given formalism should not be considered as fixed but should be used as a framework, i.e., as a collection of ideas which might be helpful, but which might also be changed or extended if this seems adequate for an application area. This is what we will do with ASMs: They are meant to be used to model primarily sequential discrete systems, even though variants have been described for concurrent and timed systems.

A problem with the framework approach for formalisms is that if the variants are too different, experience with one variant does not help much with another variant. We will use a variant of the basic sequential ASM formalism.

2.7 Goals and Consequences from the Analysis

The goal we pursue in this work is to develop a formalism for the description of quantitatively timed systems based on a linear model of time, since this is the most popular model of quantitative time. This formalism should avoid several problems of existing formalisms, which we will detail a little.

The formalism should be sufficiently general so that it can be used to express other formalisms used for the description of systems in linear quantitative time with few formal overheads, i.e., it should not be necessary to introduce additional model components only in order to allow the expression. This allows our formalism to be used for the comparison of the relative merits of other formalisms by expressing them in the same basic framework.

The formalism should be sufficiently flexible so that it can be used to express algorithms in linear quantitative time essentially coding free with respect to the data part of the algorithm. This means that we strive for a **general** rather than for a more specific formalism.

Discreteness of the time model used in the formalism is attractive because discrete algorithms are familiar to computer scientists.

We do not want to restrict the kinds of consistency checks we perform on the models expressed – any concept from mathematics is allowed. This goal results more from missing than from existing knowledge: We do not yet know enough about checking timed systems for consistency so that we could be sure that the methods we propose would suffice.

We do not want to fix an abstraction level for the algorithms to be described – it should be possible to choose this level high enough so that relevant ideas are concisely expressed, and low enough so that one does not have to abstract from the relevant ideas.

Part I

Basic Concepts

3. Models of Time and of System Behaviors

In computer science, system behaviors are often represented as a function from some time domain $\mathbb{T}$ to some state domain $\mathfrak{A}$. We will also use this approach.

We will represent states from $\mathfrak{A}$ as assignments of values from some fixed universe $\mathbb{U}$ to value carriers. We will use first-order structures to represent states, as proposed by Gurevich. In that approach, the carriers of values are "locations", which will be defined later (see Chap. 5). We denote the set of locations by $\mathbb{L}$. Then, the set $\mathfrak{A}$ of states consists of the functions $\mathbb{L} \to \mathbb{U}$ or of a subset of such functions.

The locations represent the quantities which are relevant in the system description. We will deal with systems in which in classical conceptualizations some quantities change discretely and others might also change continuously with time. We call such systems "hybrid systems".

3.1 Dense and Discrete Time Domains

For the time domain, a large number of different approaches are used in computer science. Koymans [Koy92] presents an overview of different basic principles which have been proposed for acting as the bases for models of time. To these belong linear and branching models of time, with respect to future and past; there are discrete and dense models; there are models of time admitting a metric on points in time (which we call quantitative models); and there are mere qualitative models. In this work, we focus on **linear** models of **quantitative** time. Linear models are those most often used, also in influential approaches such as Manna and Pnueli [MP92, MP95] and Lamport [Lam94a, Lam94b]. We focus on quantitative models of time because qualitative models of time are already very well investigated.

Often, quantitative time is modelled as a special group or monoid. For example, Nicollin and Sifakis [NS92] assume that time is a commutative monoid $(D, +, 0)$ with $d + d' = d \leftrightarrow d' = 0$ and where the pre-order $\leq$ defined by $d \leq d' \Leftrightarrow_{\text{def}} \exists d'' : d + d'' = d'$ is a total order. Nicollin and Sifakis see the main difference in models of time in discreteness vs. denseness. Discreteness means that if some point in time has a follower, there is a smallest follower. Denseness means that between any two different points in time, there is a third point different from both. A typical example for a discrete model of time is $\mathbb{N}_0$, and a typical example for a dense model of time is $\mathbb{R}_0^+$. The completeness property of $\mathbb{R}_0^+$ is typically **not** used in applications of the time model. A typical example for a model of time which is used in the description of hybrid systems is sequences of intervals from $\mathbb{R}_0^+$ [LSVW96]. The latter is the most advanced classical model of time for hybrid systems, and so we will use it later in the classical reference approach we use for comparison with our non-classical approach based on infinitesimals. This time model will be described in detail in Sect. 3.2.

Discrete models of time are attractive because they are so common in computer science, but there also exists a downside: The following problems in the use of a discrete time model are sometimes given [Hoo92, Jos92]:

- Independent events can occur arbitrarily near. In order to express this in the model, a dense structure is necessary.
- Reactive systems often operate in an environment which contains (piecewise) continuously changing components, and they are often modelled as functions from $\mathbb{R}$ to some state space. In order to describe a reactive system in such an environment, it is convenient to be able to use the natural time domain of the environment in the description of the context of the reactive system.
- For composition of independently specified or developed units, a common time base must be found. A dense model of time avoids this problem.
- Action refinement is difficult in a discrete model of time [Ben98].

Basically, $\mathbb{R}$ is a model of time suggested by our intuition from classical physics, which makes it attractive to use its features also for reactive systems.

The main benefits of a discrete model of time are the following:

- It is intuitively very attractive to have a well-determined next state for each state in a system behavior. This also allows us to use well-developed methods for specification, description and analysis of (untimed) discrete systems more or less unchanged for the work with timed systems. For example, simple induction can be used to prove invariants.
- When dense models of time are used, the phenomenon of Zeno-ness [AL92] has to be dealt with. This is an artifact of formalisms which have been developed for the discrete domain and are used for dense quantitative time. A system behavior is called "Zeno" if it consists of an infinite sequence of states with strictly increasing time stamps for which there exists an upper bound for the time stamps. Only dense models of time allow this artifact to occur, and it must be handled in some way, since Zeno behaviors have to be excluded from consideration: they are considered to be unimplementable. Zeno-ness is a variant of infinite activity [NS92]: This is a property of a system behavior in which in some bounded interval of real time an infinite number of discrete transitions takes place. In approaches to the description of real-time systems based on functions from $\mathbb{R}$ to some state domain, the problem underlying the Zeno-ness phenomenon occurs in this guise.

A side note: The concept of infinite activity is not the only sensible way to formalize the intuition that systems which try to do too much in too short time are not implementable. A perhaps better formalization of the idea is the more restrictive concept of unbounded activity [NS92]. As an example, consider a system in which in each time interval from n to $n+1$ (for $n \in \mathbb{N}$), exactly n discrete events take place. Such a system is not Zeno (since in each finite interval, only a finite number of discrete events take place; specifically, the number of events in an interval which is bounded from above by $n \in \mathbb{N}$ is smaller than n^2); but it shows unbounded activity in the sense that for each bound $n \in \mathbb{N}$, there is an interval of length 1 so that more than n discrete events take place in that interval (for example take the interval from $n+1$ to $n+2$). While this system is not Zeno, it can nevertheless not be considered implementable; thus, boundedness of activity seems to be a more appropriate abstract concept of implementability of a system with respect to the amount of activity in finite intervals of time.

3.2 Interval Sequences and Subclasses of Hybrid Systems

The typical way of representing system behaviors of real time or, more generally, hybrid systems is as sequences of (mostly closed) intervals over $\mathbb{R}$. Each such interval represents a (possibly) continuous change of some system quantity; the transition from the end point of one interval to the start point of the next interval represents a discrete transition. The typical way to model time in this framework is the following:

- If infinitely many discrete transitions take place, time is modelled by infinitely many intervals $[l_i, u_i]$ for $i \in \mathbb{N}_0$ with
  - $l_i, u_i \in \mathbb{R}_0^+$ (a dense, even complete model of time is used),
  - $l_0 = 0$ (time starts at zero),
  - $l_i \leq u_i$ (each interval spans the time distance $u_i - l_i$; point intervals are allowed and represent states which are immediately left as soon as they are assumed),
  - $u_i = l_{i+1}$ (a discrete transition takes no "real" time), and
  - the sequence of u_i diverges (this requirement ensures that Zeno behaviors do not occur). This requirement avoids the artifact of a system in which an infinite number of discrete transitions takes place in a finite span of time.
- If only $n \in \mathbb{N}_0$ discrete transitions take place, the time is represented by $n+1$ intervals, the first n of which are of the form $[l_i, u_i]$, and the last is of the same form or of the form $[l_n, \infty)$. The conditions on l_i and u_i, for the i's for which they exist, are as for the first case (of course, without the non-Zeno requirement). The second form of the last interval represents the infinite time span in which no discrete transition takes place.

The fact that point intervals are allowed means that instantaneous transitions from some state just entered can be modelled. This abstraction is very common for synchronous programming languages (e.g., [BdS91, BG92, Hal93]).

Systems modelled in interval sequence time are often modelled as transition systems with two types of transitions: There are discrete transitions which take no time, and there are time transitions which might take time. We will describe in Sect. 6.1.1 a variant of this approach.

Hybrid system behaviors are described by associating a state from $\mathfrak{A}$ with each element of each interval. Depending on the type of hybrid system, the kind of change during the intervals is somehow restricted. The different kinds of restrictions typically distinguish between **discretely changing** system components which can only be changed in discrete transitions and keep their value during intervals, and (possibly) **continuously changing** system components, which can change both in discrete transitions and during intervals. Typical restrictions for the changes during the intervals are the following:

- The only system quantity allowed to change continuously might be the time (which we denote by the symbol now). Abadi and Lamport [AL92] call this restriction convenient, perhaps because it fixes the values of all quantities for each interval element.
- Another approach is to allow any number of (continuously changing) clocks, all of them running with the same speed (equal to 1) all the time, but which might be reset from time to time. This is the idea used for timed automata [AD94]. All other quantities are discrete.
- A third approach is to associate a speed with each continuously changing quantity, where the quantities representing the speed only change discretely. Sometimes these systems are called "linear", but we prefer to call them PCD systems (for piecewise constant derivative). The formalism on which HyTech [HHWT95] is based uses this approach. Because of the linearity of all continuously changing quantities, the values at the interval end points suffice to represent the values at all intermediate points.
- A fourth approach describes the system development during interval time spans very generally by "trajectories" [Zei76, Chap. 9] [LSVW96] [Lyn96, Chap. 23]. These trajectories have to obey some general conditions like additivity (a trajectory leading to some state and a trajectory leaving from the same state can be concatenated to another trajectory with a length which is the sum of the lengths of the components) or time determinacy (the state assumed by the system at a point inside an interval is completely determined by the start state of the interval and the time span which has been spent since the start state of the interval), but apart from this they can be chosen quite freely. Not even continuity is required when this approach is used.

All these variants have in common that the changes during time intervals do not count as "activity" in the sense of finite or infinite activity in bounded time intervals. For this, only the discrete transitions are relevant. System changes which are represented in intervals are meant to describe what can change just by the flow of time, needing no extra "system activity".

The interval-sequence approach to modelling hybrid systems of different kinds is quite flexible, but it also has some drawbacks:

– A fairly complicated, non-uniform model of time is used.
  It would be nice to have a uniform model of time also for the description of hybrid systems.
– Discrete transitions take no time at all. This contrafactual assumption is a helpful abstraction in some situations, employed successfully in the application of synchronous languages; but it leads to problems with causality in the definition of such languages (see [HG92] for an analysis of the general problem, and consider the different attempts to get at a satisfying semantics for ESTEREL [BG92, Ber99] or for StateCharts [Har87, vdB94]).
  It would be nice to have a model of time which can express both causality and instantaneity of transitions in an intuitive way.
– Composition of independently developed deterministic systems is a problem: If in two such systems a discrete transition takes place at the same real-numbered moment, we do not know which takes place before the other, if they take place synchronously, or if there is just some partial overlap between the transitions. This is because transitions belonging to the same moment are only in a relative order if they belong to the same system behavior. A typical way to deal with this is by using nondeterminism to express the missing knowledge about the relative orders of the transitions. For deterministic systems, this artifact might be inconvenient.
  It would be nice to be able to use, if needed, an absolute ordering for discrete transitions taking place at the same point in real time.

The last three points mentioned three goals to be fulfilled by our model of time, which will be a discrete model. In addition, we want to avoid the problems of common discrete models of time mentioned earlier. We will reach our goals by using infinitesimals.

3.3 The Main Idea: Use of Infinitesimals

Our idea is to investigate a model of time which allows us to model hybrid systems and seems at least to solve the problems of interval sequences for PCD systems. We will use the multiples of some infinitesimal as the time domain, or, expressed in another way, we use simply the natural numbers, only scaled by some infinitesimal number. This is a discrete and uniform model of time, giving to each transition an absolute position, which is nevertheless dense in the real numbers, and which allows us to model both causality (by representing causes by states and/or transitions which come earlier than their effects) and instantaneity (by infinitesimal time spans) if the behaviors are considered at the level of the real numbers. A system model based on this time model can approximate behaviors defined in the reals with infinitesimal exactness and allows action refinement. Also phases of continuous change can be described with step-by-step actions of some underlying discrete formalism, which makes a simple induction principle possible for proving invariants.

The main motivation to investigate the use of infinitesimals as the base of the time domain is concisely given in the preface of [ACH97]:

> The nonstandard framework allows many informal ideas (that could loosely be described as idealization) to be made precise and tractable. For example, the real line can (in this framework) be treated simultaneously as both a continuum and a discrete set of points; and a similar dual approach can be used to link the notions infinite and finite, rough and smooth.

Our initial hope was to be able to use well-established discrete techniques for analysis of discrete systems in order to understand systems with continuously changing components. During the investigation, another concept arose as important: Time as multiples of an infinitesimal allows us to investigate the problems of the discretization of a solution based on the abstraction of zero-time discrete steps independently from the question of a minimal step width. The concept of well-behavedness as defined and investigated in later chapters is the formalization of this idea.

One technical problem of the interval-sequence approach is that discrete transitions lead to several states being associated with the same point in "real" time. There are temporal logics which are based on the idea that at most one state is associated with each point in time. Gargantini et al. [GMM99] use such a logic. The interval-sequence approach contradicts the intuition that a system development can be adequately described by a function from a time domain to a state domain (of course, this could be repaired by a more complicated time domain, e.g., using $\mathbb{R} \times \mathbb{N}$, which is unattractive because of other reasons). Gargantini et al. use, for system specification, a temporal logic which uses the temporal operator $\mathrm{DIST}(P,t)$ for a predicate P and a real number t; if interpreted at a time x of a system development, this operator expresses that at time $x + t$ the predicate P holds. This operator is obviously best suited to models of system behaviors in which at most one state is associated with each moment of time. For interval-sequence models of system behaviors this is not the case, which makes the use of the operator difficult. Gargantini et al. propose to use a time model based on infinitesimals for solving the problem. A zero-time transition of the interval-sequence approach is replaced by an infinitesimal-time transition which takes strictly positive time. Gargantini et al. claim that this approach allows a simpler axiomatization than the zero-time approach; the reason is that a system behavior associates at most one state with an element of the set used for representing time. The main idea explored in the current work is based on the same reasoning.

Note that it might seem inconvenient for some applications that the time step width is fixed[1]. We discuss this question in Chap. 12.

---

[1] This was pointed out by Dino Mandrioli in a personal communication.

We generally require that models be written so that they are correct independently of the exact value of the step width used; the only allowed assumption will be that the step width is smaller than (or equal to) some design step width of the model.

While the approach to modelling the time domain using a scaled version of $\mathbb{N}$ might look extraordinarily simple, this does not mean that all modelling problems disappear. The only point we can hope for is that the formalism chosen does not induce many extra complications, in addition to those present in the application area modelled. Many problems which can appear using classical models of quantitative time will reappear in some guise, for example the problem of classical formalisms that a model might be too unrealistic because it allows an infinite amount of activity in a finite interval of time. In the formalism looked at here, such a model is not possible, since in any finite interval of our model of time, there are only a finite number of steps possible; but it might happen that the number of steps performing some work is *unlimited*, which is a concept similar in some respects to the intuition of infinity. Thus, the exact formalization of some problem might not apply to our model, so that at first sight the problem of the classical approach seems to be solved; but a (not necessarily very deep) analysis will typically show that this is not the case; the problem reappears and has to be formalized in some other way, but this can sometimes be done in a far simpler way (as an example, see the redefinition of "receptivity" in Chap. 11).

So, what kind of simplifications can in general be expected from our new model of time, if compared to a classical $\mathbb{N}$-based or a classical interval-sequence-based approach? We give some hints:

– **Combination of independently developed models not complicated by differing time scales.** Since modellers can only specify an upper bound for the allowed time step width for their models, independently developed models can be combined by just choosing, as an upper bound for the combination, the smaller one of the two.
  But why can the same requirement for models not be used in a classical approach using $\mathbb{N}$ as the time domain? Here, the requirement regarding modelling a system independently from the step width used seems too harsh.

– **Case distinctions avoided in analyses of system runs.** Using classical interval sequences as the time domain, the modeller of a system typically has to decide for each situation the system can be in if the next step is an instantaneous discrete step or a time step, and, if the latter, of what length the time step is. Because of this, some case distinctions are typically necessary when a run of such a system is analyzed. If time proceeds as the natural numbers do, simple induction will typically suffice.

– **Combination of independently developed models not in need of a complicated semantics.** If independently developed systems are combined, forming now subsystems of a larger system, during the computation of a behavior of the larger system it must be determined which subsystem wants to do the shortest step, and all systems must perform a step of such a length; thus, formalizing and preparing systems for parallel composition might become quite involved.

In systems driven by a global synchronous clock, which is an idea applicable to systems using equidistant models of time, no such problems occur.

3.4 Summary

Some problems of classical approaches to model time discretely in a quantitative way and some benefits of using a discrete model of time are mentioned. We present interval sequences as the most advanced classical approach to modelling time quantitatively for the description of hybrid systems, and we discuss some drawbacks of this model. Finally, we give a short first exposition of the main idea of this work: time is discretized with an unspecified but constant non-zero infinitesimal step width. This allows us to combine the flexibility of the interval-sequence approach while avoiding its drawbacks, and combines this with the merits of a discrete model of time.

4. Infinitesimals

Infinitesimals, i.e., numbers which are in some respect like zero and in some other respect unlike zero, have been used in mathematics since the beginning of the calculus. Robinson [Rob96] gives an overview of the use of infinitesimals in the history of the calculus: Leibniz uses infinitely small numbers in the development of the calculus without admitting their existence; he considers them to be useful fictions. De l'Hospital seemed to believe in the existence of infinitesimals, and he formulated Leibniz' principles in a way which made the main inconsistency stand out – that infinitesimal quantities are sometimes treated as being equal to zero, and sometimes as being not equal to zero. At the end of the 18th century, the inconsistency led to different approaches to avoid infinitesimals: Lagrange tries to base the calculus on Taylor expansions, and D'Alembert uses the concept of limit, an idea already used by Newton, and related to the Method of Exhaustion, attributed to Archimedes. D'Alembert seems to have made the approach popular on the continent. At the beginning of the 19th century Cauchy, the founder of modern analysis, strangely enough reverts again to infinitesimals (in some sense, by using variables "tending to zero"), e.g., in the definition of continuity where he says that a function is continuous for some argument value if changing the argument value infinitesimally, the function value also only changes infinitesimally. Starting with Weierstrass' approach to analysis, talking of infinitesimal quantities was just considered a shorthand description for an ϵ-δ-definition or argument. At the end of the 19th century, different approaches for dealing with the infinite were developed. Cantor's set theory was developed in that time, as was du Bois-Reymond's theory of orders of magnitudes. In the 20th century, Skolem represented infinitely large natural numbers by functions tending to infinity; nevertheless, neither Cantor nor Fraenkel believed in the possibility of basing analysis on infinitesimal quantities.

So basically, the properties of infinitesimals could not be made precise for nearly 300 years and their use led to contradictions. In the 1950s, the logician Abraham Robinson used model-theoretic means to develop a non-standard model of analysis [Rob96]. The existence of non-standard models of arithmetic had already been shown by Skolem in the 1930s [Sko34], and Robinson built on Skolem's ideas for the real numbers. Robinson's approach was to extend the field of real numbers in a similar way as the real numbers can be constructed from the rational numbers by considering equivalence classes of Cauchy series of rational numbers. Robinson used a logical apparatus in order to determine which results of classical mathematics carries over to the new model. Introductions to Robinson's approach to infinitesimals and applications can for example be found in [LR94] and [ACH97].

Already Robinson hoped for some axiomatic approach to infinitesimals to be found. Nelson [Nel77] developed such an approach, using ideas based on those of Robinson to construct a consistency proof of his axioms relative to Zermelo-Fraenkel set theory with the Choice axiom (ZFC). See [Rob88] for another introduction to this theory. Nelson extends the ZFC-formalization of mathematics by three more axioms (more precisely, axiom schemes), describing the properties of a new predicate for mathematical objects (which are all sets in ZFC). This new predicate is called "standard", abbreviated as "st", which can be likened to the intuitive concept "classical". Thus, the mathematical objects x for which $st(x)$ holds are meant to represent the objects intuitively known from classical mathematics, while the non-standard objects are meant to represent new objects.

Nelson's approach is a conservative extension of classical mathematics, i.e., all classical theorems remain valid in the new axiomatization. This makes Nelson's approach so attractive in contrast to Robinson's: The latter needs quite some logical apparatus in order to determine which theorems can be transferred to the newly constructed domain; Nelson's approach is simpler to use. Because of this, we base our approach on Nelson's rather than on Robinson's theory.

Nelson's three axioms are commonly called "idealization", "standardization", and "transfer", and his approach is often called "internal set theory" (IST).

Note that we collected the notations used in the appendix.

4.1 The Axiom of Idealization

The axiom of idealization guarantees the existence of non-standard entities.

Let $B(x, y)$ be a classical formula (i.e., it does not contain the predicate "st") with free variables x and y (and possibly other free variables). Then:

$$(\forall^{\text{st fin}} z\, \exists x\, \forall(y \in z)\, B(x, y)) \leftrightarrow (\exists x\, \forall^{\text{st}} y\, B(x, y))$$

The x on the right hand side is the "ideal" object the existence of which is asserted. This is typically a non-standard object.

Let $B(x, y) \Leftrightarrow_{\text{def}} x, y \in \mathbb{R}^+ \wedge x < y$. Since for any finite set of positive real numbers, there is a positive real number smaller than all of them (just take half of the minimal element of the set), the axiom of idealization guarantees the existence of positive real numbers strictly smaller than all standard positive real numbers. In a similar way, it can be proved that there are natural numbers larger than all standard natural numbers. Another consequence of the axiom is that for a set X, every element of X is standard if and only if X is a standard finite set, and by contraposition, that any infinite set contains non-standard elements.

4.2 The Axiom of Standardization

What needs most adaptation from the side of the user of IST is that the new predicate "st" and derived predicates are not necessarily set-forming. This means that the standard elements of some set do not necessarily form a set. For example, there is no set containing exactly the standard natural numbers, and there is no set containing exactly the non-standard reals. The axiom of standardization defines how subsets can nevertheless be formed using non-classical predicates.

Let $C(z)$ be a predicate (classical or not) containing the free variable z (and possibly others). Then:

$$\forall^{\mathrm{st}} x \exists^{\mathrm{st}} y \forall^{\mathrm{st}} z (z \in y \leftrightarrow z \in x \wedge C(z))$$

Since by transfer of set-extensionality, two standard sets are equal if they have the same standard elements, the set y defined in the axiom is unique. It is denoted as $^S\{z \in x : C(z)\}$. The axiom says that any predicate can be used to define a standard subset y of some standard set x, but that only the standard elements of x are filtered by the predicate. A non-standard element z of x might be in y without fulfilling $C(z)$, and it might not be in y though it fulfills $C(z)$.

4.3 The Axiom of Transfer

The axiom of transfer is used to describe the idea that whatever holds for **all standard** objects, holds for **all** objects.

Let $A(x, t_1, \ldots, t_k)$ be a classical formula with free variables $x, t_1, \ldots, t_k$, and no other free variables. Then:

$$\forall^{\mathrm{st}} t_1 \ldots \forall^{\mathrm{st}} t_k (\forall^{\mathrm{st}} x A(x, t_1, \ldots, t_k) \rightarrow \forall x A(x, t_1, \ldots, t_k))$$

The axiom of transfer guarantees that all theorems of classical mathematics remain valid if they are restricted to standard objects. The contraposition of the transfer axiom can be used to show that any object uniquely defined in classical mathematics is standard, e.g., the sets $\mathbb{R}$ and $\mathbb{N}_0$ and the numbers 0, 1 and π. This axiom also implies that standard sets are characterized by their standard elements. This justifies to understand "standard" intuitively as "classical".

4.4 More Structure Discerned in Classical Objects

Nelson's approach to non-standard mathematics leaves all of classical mathematics (as based on ZFC) intact, i.e., the properties of $\mathbb{N}$ or of $\mathbb{R}_0^+$ are exactly those of classical mathematics: Classical induction is used for proving a classical property of every natural number, standard or non-standard. The new predicate only allows us to discriminate more structure in these well-known sets.

Of special importance for us is the additional structure given to $\mathbb{R}$ in the new theory. Let us first define some basic concepts.

Definition 4.4.1. *A number $x \in \mathbb{R}$ is* **infinitesimal** *if and only if* $\forall^{st} y \in \mathbb{R}^+ : |x| < y$

A number $x \in \mathbb{R}$ is **limited** *if and only if* $\exists^{st} y \in \mathbb{R} : |x| < y$

A number $x \in \mathbb{R}$ is **appreciable** *if and only if it is limited and not infinitesimal.*

Note that the only classical infinitesimal number is zero, but, via the idealization axiom, it can be shown that non-zero infinitesimal numbers exist. A limited number can be understood as being of the same "magnitude" as classical numbers: unlimited numbers are those whose absolute value is larger than that of all classical numbers; thus, they are very large indeed.

Simple consequences from these definitions are: Zero is the only standard infinitesimal. Reciprocal values of non-zero infinitesimals are unlimited. The product of an infinitesimal and an appreciable number is infinitesimal, and the product of an appreciable and an unlimited number is an unlimited number. The product of an infinitesimal and an unlimited number can be infinitesimal, appreciable or unlimited, depending on the orders of magnitude of the two numbers. Each standard real is limited.

We already stressed that the new predicate "st" is in general not set-forming. This means that we can not use it to single out the standard elements from the natural numbers or from the reals as a set, and we can not define the set of infinitesimal reals, the set of limited reals or the set of appreciable reals. Rather, for selecting elements from a set using a non-classical predicate, we have to use the standardization axiom. The standard set containing the standard elements of the reals which are infinitesimal is the singleton set containing zero. The standard set containing the standard elements of the reals which are limited is just the set of reals.

The concept "unlimited" might seem to be related to that of "infinite", but in fact, they are quite different. A set is finite if there is no injection of it into a proper subset, or equivalently: if there is a bijection with a set $\{i \in \mathbb{N}_0 \mid i < n\}$ for some $n \in \mathbb{N}_0$. Thus, each set with exactly $n \in \mathbb{N}_0$ elements is finite – also if n is unlimited. It follows that the properties of being finite and of being limited have to be distinguished.

This also calls for a change of formalization of the intuitive concept of effectivity. Classically, a function is considered to be effectively computable if its value can be computed for each input argument in a finite number of effective steps. Since the finite natural numbers also include unlimited ones, this formalization might not be adequate in the non-standard framework. The formal notion corresponding best to the intuition of effectivity is to replace "finite" by "standard finite", which is for natural numbers equivalent to "limited".

Let us be more specific. For a standard Turing machine with a standard input, there exists a finite number $n \in \mathbb{N}_0$ so that after n steps, we can decide if the Turing machine will ever halt: Just take an unlimited n. If the Turing machine did not halt in the first n steps, it did not halt for any standard number of steps, and since the Turing machine and its input are standard, we can apply the transfer principle: If a standard Turing machine with a standard input does not halt after any standard number of steps, it will not halt at all. Thus, it can be decided in a finite number of steps if a standard Turing machine with a standard input halts – but this can not be decided in a limited number of steps.

Another important fact of IST is that each limited real number x is in infinitesimal distance from some unique standard real number:

Proposition 4.4.1. *Let x be a limited real number. Then there is a unique standard real number, which we denote by ${}^o x$, with $x \simeq {}^o x$.*

${}^o x$ is called the **standard part** or the **shadow** of x. Many theorems of non-standard analysis are formulated in terms of the standard part of a limited number. The operation of taking the standard part can be understood as an abstraction operation on limited real numbers: using this abstraction means ignoring infinitesimal distances between limited real numbers.

Note that ^{o}, as introduced above, is not a function, since its domain and range are not sets. But for limited x, the standard set ${}^S \{y \in \mathbb{R} \mid y \leq x\}$ can be formed by standardization, all elements are limited (all **standard** elements are real numbers not greater than x, and, thus by transfer, **all** elements are real numbers not greater than x), and, thus, has a supremum, which allows us to define:

$$ {}^o x =_{\mathrm{def}} \sup{}^S \{y \in \mathbb{R} \mid y \leq x\} $$

Since in the formalism of non-standard analysis, not all predicates are set-forming, we can not use the term "set" for the collection of elements for which some predicate is fulfilled. If some term is needed, we call such a collection a "class"; for example, we can talk about the class of standard real numbers. Sometimes, it is convenient to use predicate symbols from set-theory also with a class C. In this case, this means the corresponding predicate; for example, if C is the class of standard real numbers and C' is a class corresponding to some other predicate, $x \in C$ means that x is a standard real number, and $C \to C'$ means that being a standard real number implies fulfilling the predicate of C'.

4.5 Real-Time Systems
with Constant Infinitesimal Steps

Let dt be a strictly positive infinitesimal, and let $\mathbb{T} =_{\mathrm{def}} dt * \mathbb{N}_0$ denote the multiples of dt: This is the model of time in our approach to describing real-time systems. dt will be called the step width of $\mathbb{T}$. Obviously, this time model consists basically just of the natural numbers; they are only scaled by the infinitesimal dt.

The field $\mathbb{R}$ is Archimedean, i.e., for $0 < a < b$, there is a natural number n such that $n * a \geq b$. This also holds for infinitesimal a and non-infinitesimal b; in that case, n must be unlimited. This means that a discrete system described with our model must perform an unlimited natural number of steps until an appreciable time has been spanned. Nevertheless, this number of steps is finite: the smallest such n is $\lceil \frac{b}{a} \rceil$.

Such an unlimited number of steps can not be effectively performed step by step; this is a major problem of our approach.

A nice property of our discrete model of time is that for each classical predicate which is fulfilled for some element of $\mathbb{T}$, there is a smallest such element, i.e., a first moment at which the predicate is fulfilled. This is in contrast to $\mathbb{R}_0^+$, where there is no first moment in time at which "now $>$ 1" holds. For non-classical predicates, this existence of a smallest element fulfilling the predicate is not guaranteed.

There are enough moments between any two standard reals for any standard number of discrete transitions to be modelled:

Theorem 4.5.1. *Between any two standard non-negative reals, there is an unlimited number of elements of $\mathbb{T}$.*

Proof. Let dt be the step width of $\mathbb{T}$. Since dt is infinitesimal, also $\sqrt{dt}$ is infinitesimal, and $n = \lfloor \frac{\sqrt{dt}}{dt} \rfloor$ is unlimited. Let x_1, x_2 be standard non-negative reals with $x_1 < x_2$. With $m = \lceil \frac{x_1}{dt} \rceil$, the set $\{(m + i) * dt \mid 1 \leq i \leq n\}$ is a subset of $\mathbb{T}$ and all of its elements lie strictly between x_1 and x_2.

Corollary 4.5.1. $\mathbb{T}$ *is dense in the standard non-negative reals.*

$\mathbb{T}$ seems to solve several problems of the interval-sequence approach to modelling hybrid systems:

- $\mathbb{T}$ is uniform.
- $\mathbb{T}$ is dense in the standard reals and allows any standard number of discrete transitions between any two standard moments in real numbered time.
- $\mathbb{T}$ is discrete.
- Discrete transitions in $\mathbb{T}$ are absolutely ordered.

But it generates new problems:

- Simulation is non-trivial. Though time is discrete, and each point in time is transgressed after a finite number of steps, the system can not be simulated step by step, since for appreciable time spans, an unlimited number of steps is necessary.
- The base formalism is too expressive. E.g., if we allow predicates "standard" and "rational" in the definition of the step function, we could define a timed system characterizing the standard rational points in time.
- While in a system description based on the time domain $\mathbb{T}$, Zeno runs can not occur, unlimited activity can take place, and it has to be avoided that this artifact compromises the real-world validity of proofs. We will discuss this at the end of Sect. 6.2.

4.6 Summary

This chapter gives a very short historical overview of the use of infinitesimals in mathematics. We present Nelson's approach of conservatively extending ZFC, discussing the three axiom schemes proposed by him. Then we describe that this theory allows us to discern additional structure in $\mathbb{R}$, most importantly infinitesimal, limited/unlimited and appreciable numbers, and finally, we describe some important properties of our model of time.

5. Operational Semantics of Discrete Systems

Different approaches exist for the description of discrete concurrent and reactive systems. Often used examples are automata models (including hierarchical and parallel automata like Harel's StateCharts [Har87]), formalisms for the description of concurrent and reactive systems (including Lamport's Temporal Logic of Actions [Lam94a, Lam94b] or Manna and Pnueli's Fair Transition Systems [MP92, MP95]), different versions of Petri nets [Rei86], or even models used in theoretical computer science like Turing machines [Tur37]. We use abstract state machines (ASMs) [Gur88, Gur93, Gur95a, Gur97]. Abstract state machines are proposed as a formalism for operationally describing sequential discrete algorithms on any abstraction level [Gur99]. The latter means that one intuitive step of the modelled algorithm corresponds to one step of the formal algorithm. This is typically not possible in the common models for effective computation used in theoretical computer science like Turing machines or register machines, since in these models, inputs, system state and output of the algorithms must be encoded with very basic means, and the single steps which are allowed by these models are also of a very simple kind. Thus, in these models, algorithms can only be encoded on a quite low abstraction level. This means that these models are not adequate for high-level modelling of algorithms. Abstract state machines are meant as a remedy for this, as a model of computation which is both simple enough to be attractive for being used in theoretical computer science, and powerful enough to be used for modelling realistic systems and algorithms. In this way, they are hoped to help bridge the gap between theoretical computer science and more practice oriented branches of the discipline.

5.1 Action Systems

Abstract state machines are a specific formalism for the definition of action systems. We first introduce the ideas behind this approach to the definition of discrete systems.

We fix a set $\mathbb{L}$ of locations and a universe $\mathbb{U}$, which is a set of values.

Definition 5.1.1. *We represent* **states** *of a system as elements of* $\mathfrak{A} = \mathbb{L} \to \mathbb{U}$, *and the set of state changes, which we call* **actions** *and which we denote by* $\mathbb{A}$, *as partial functions from the locations to the universe. The partial function with empty domain is called the vacuous action and is written* v.

A system is defined by giving, for each state, the set of actions possible in that state:

Definition 5.1.2. *A (nondeterministic)* **action system** *is defined as a function in $\mathfrak{A} \to \mathcal{P}(\mathbb{A})$, i.e., a function which, for each state, defines a set of actions which the system can perform in that state.*

Consider an action system f. Note that we allow that $f(q)$ might be empty. This formalizes that the system f can not perform a step from state q. If $f(q) = \{v\}$, this formalizes that f can only perform the vacuous action in state q, which represents a step which does not change anything.

A linear system behavior is defined by a start state and a sequence of actions, which might be generated by an action system.

Definition 5.1.3. *A start state $q \in \mathfrak{A}$ and a sequence of actions $\boldsymbol{a} \in \mathbb{A}$ defines a sequence of states $\boldsymbol{q} \in \mathfrak{A}$ in which $\boldsymbol{q}(0) = q$ and $\boldsymbol{q}(i+1) = \boldsymbol{q}(i)[\boldsymbol{a}(i)]$ for $i \in \operatorname{dom} \boldsymbol{a}$. A* **run** *of an action system $f : \mathfrak{A} \to \mathcal{P}(\mathbb{A})$ from some state q is a sequence of actions $\boldsymbol{a}$ so that in the associated sequence of states $\boldsymbol{q}$ with start state q, $\boldsymbol{a}(i) \in f(\boldsymbol{q}(i))$ for all $i \in \operatorname{dom} \boldsymbol{a}$.*

The concept of an action system is different from the more often used transition system. A transition system is a subset of $\mathfrak{A} \times \mathfrak{A}$ describing the possible state transitions of the system. The action system represents explicitly, for each state change in which some locations do not change their value, if this is just because there was no update for the location performed, or because the value written into the location was just identical to the value in the location before the transition. This additional information is needed for the definition of parallel composition.

An action system f defines, in a canonical way, an associated transition system $\{(q, q') \in \mathfrak{A} \times \mathfrak{A} \mid \exists (a \in f(q)) : q' = q[a]\}$. Similarly, it defines in a canonical way an associated labeled transition system, i.e., a transition system in which each transition is an element of $\mathfrak{A} \times \mathbb{A} \times \mathfrak{A}$, by $\{(q, a, q') \mid a \in f(q) \wedge q' = q[a]\}$. When we talk about an action system and then about a transition system or a labeled transition system, these are the mathematical structures derived from the action system.

A state q' is said to be reachable from a state q, or, equivalently, a state q is said to reach a state q' in a given transition system, if there is a sequence of transitions in the system which leads from q finally to q'. Via the canonical transition system, the concept of reachability can also be applied to action systems.

Now we are prepared to describe the specific formalism we use for the definition of action systems.

5.2 Abstract State Machines

Gurevich uses first-order structures to encode the state of an algorithm, which includes inputs and outputs. This provides the flexibility to describe the state with the level of detail which is necessary on the abstraction level for which one heads; this, at least, is a believe corroborated by a large number of case studies [Bör98] and by a speculative argument in [Gur99]. Since ASMs are primarily meant to replace less flexible models of effective computation, the steps of ASMs should be effective. Gurevich uses **rules** to describe transitions. We will interpret them as functions from states to action sets, i.e., as action systems. The exact semantics will be given later.

Before we introduce the syntax of rules, we first present our notations for first-order structures. $\mathbb{S}$ denotes the vocabulary and $\mathbb{U}$ the universe of values. Each vocabulary element $s \in \mathbb{S}$ is interpreted as a function from $\mathbb{U}^{s_a}$ to $\mathbb{U}$, where s_a denotes the fixed arity of s. Constants are represented as 0-ary functions, predicates are represented as functions yielding Boolean values for each argument tuple (the Boolean values tt and ff are assumed to belong to $\mathbb{U}$), and partial functions are represented by using an element $\perp \in \mathbb{U}$ as the value of the function for argument tuples for which the function is meant to be undefined. The set $\mathbb{L}$ of locations is the set $\{(s, t) | s \in \mathbb{S} \land t \in \mathbb{U}^{s_a}\}$, and the set $\mathfrak{A}$ of states is the set of functions $\mathbb{L} \to \mathbb{U}$. Thus, a state $q \in \mathfrak{A}$ defines, for each $s \in \mathbb{S}$, a function from $\mathbb{U}^{s_a}$ to $\mathbb{U}$ by fixing the value of $(s, (u_1, \ldots, u_{s_a}))$ for each argument s_a-tuple to the function which is represented by s.

When we say that two vocabularies are compatible, we mean that for symbols occurring in both of them, the arity is the same.

ASMs describe dynamical systems by changes to the first-order structures. In ASMs, neither the vocabulary nor the universe is assumed to change during a system behavior – only the interpretation of vocabulary elements can change. The change at a single location is described by an **update** $(l, u) \in \mathbb{L} \times \mathbb{U}$ which represents that the value of the location l is set to the universe element u. An update (l, u) is called **trivial** in a state if the current value of l in the state is already u. An ASM allows several locations to change at once, which is semantically represented by an **action**, which is a set of updates in which the location-components of the updates are all different. We denote the set of actions by $\mathbb{A}$. ASMs also allow nondeterminism. This is expressed by **action sets**, where each element action represents one possible resolution of the nondeterminism in the step.

In the original definition of ASMs, syntactical elements are provided which express the import of new elements from some infinite subset of the universe, the "reserve", which is unused, i.e., for which all functions but equality are undefined. The reserve is used to model generation of new elements for an algorithm. We will not use the special syntax, but we will use the assumption that there is some way of generating new elements, for example when we model processes or events by agents.

In the definition of some rules, also variables will be used. These are elements from a set $\mathbb{V}$, disjoint from $\mathbb{S}$ (in order to be able to distinguish syntactically 0-ary vocabulary symbols from variables). Variables are interpreted by variable assignments $\mathbb{V} \to \mathbb{U}$. The context in which rules with free variables are interpreted consists of a function in $(\mathbb{V} \cup \mathbb{L}) \to \mathbb{U}$, combining a variable assignment and a state. We call such a function an **extended state** and will denote individual extended states typically by p, q or decorated versions of these letters.

5.2.1 Some Introductory Examples of ASM Rules

Intuitively, an ASM formalization of an algorithm consists in presenting a rule which defines, for each state of the state space of the algorithm, which alternatives exist for changes (i.e., in general ASM algorithms can be non-deterministic); and each such change can consist of changes of values of any number of locations.

The simplest rules are SKIP and HALT. An execution of the former changes nothing, while an execution of the latter is not possible: it represents a deadlock of the algorithm.

Another very simple rule is the assignment, consisting of the description of a location at the left hand side, and a term whose value is to be put into the location at the right hand side. An example is the following ASM rule for a modulo 1000 counter:

```
ctr := (ctr + 1) mod 1000
```

This looks just like an assignment statement in some programming language. The semantics is only different from the programming language semantics insofar as we typically assume that the ASM rule defining an algorithm is executed repeatedly; thus, the rule above defines an algorithm which increments the value of ctr until it becomes 999, and then it starts at 0 again.

A counter which counts up to 1000 and stops then can be described with a selection rule scheme and HALT:

```
IF ctr = 1000
THEN HALT
ELSE ctr := ctr + 1
```

We now present a rule which performs a sequential search for an element x in an array A from the element at index startidx up to but not including the element at index endidx. A flag found is set accordingly. A flag stop is used to signal if the algorithm should stop; it is assumed to be initially false.

```
IF stop
THEN HALT
ELIF startidx >= endidx
THEN || found := false
     || stop := true
ELIF A(startidx)=x
THEN || found := true
     || stop := true
ELSE startidx := startidx + 1
```

Remember that repetition is implicit. The vertical bars denote a parallel execution of subrules. In the example, this means that if the range to be searched is empty, found is set to false and stop is set to true, and in the case that the element looked for has been found, the flags found and stop are both set to true.

In order to express the search algorithm conceptually as one step, we might use an EXISTS-term:

```
found := (∃ i:(startidx <= i AND i < endidx AND A(i)=x))
```

These very simple examples are only meant to set the scene so that the exact definitions of terms and rules which follow are more easily understood. We will later present more involved examples.

5.2.2 Terms

Definition 5.2.1. *Values are denoted by* **terms**. *Terms are interpreted in extended states; they have the following forms and interpretations:*

- **Variable.** *A variable $v \in \mathbb{V}$ is a term. The value of v in the extended state q is $q(v)$.*
- **Selection term.** *For three terms t, t_1 and t_2, $(t \; ? \; t_1 : t_2)$ is a term in state q. If $q(t)$ is Boolean, its value is $(q(t) \; ? \; q(t_1) : q(t_2))$, otherwise its value is $\perp$. We will also use the notation IF t THEN t_1 ELSE t_2, and we use ELIF, as in programming languages, for abbreviating occurrences of other selection terms in the ELSE branches of containing selection terms.*
- **LET term.** *For a variable symbol v and two terms t_1 and t_2, the value of LET $v = t_1$ IN t_2 in the extended state q is $q[v \mapsto q(t_1)](t_2)$, i.e., t_2 is evaluated in an extended state in which variable v has the value described by t_1 in q. We will also use a variant with values for several variables behind the LET keyword.*
- **Symbol term.** *A 0-ary vocabulary element $s \in \mathbb{S}$ is a term. The value of s in the extended state q is $q((s, ()))$. If s is an n-ary vocabulary element with $n > 0$ and $t_1, \ldots, t_n$ are terms, then $s(t_1, \ldots, t_n)$ is a term. Its value in the extended state q is $q((s, (q(t_1), \ldots, q(t_n))))$.*
  In both cases, s is called the **head symbol** *of the term.*
- **EXISTS term** *and* **FORALL term.** *The expressions $(\forall x : t)$ and $(\exists x : t)$, where x is a variable and t is a term evaluating to a boolean for all values of x in the context of the expression, represent an infinite conjunction and an infinite disjunction, respectively, with a component for each value of x.*

An extended state is defined as a function only from locations and variables to values, but as already seen in the definition of the meaning of $s(t_1, \ldots, t_n)$, we will use it also as the induced function from terms to universe values.

Sometimes, we use a vertically aligned prefix notation and indentation for avoiding parentheses for associative functions and their arguments, typically for the Boolean functions AND and OR, which are often translated to ∧ and ∨. E.g., the following notation denotes the term AND(t1,AND(t2,OR(t3,t4))):

∧ t1
∧ t2
∧ ∨ t3
   ∨ t4

Vertical alignment of partial terms at the same level and indentation makes it clear how such a term is to be interpreted.

5.2.3 Rules

Transitions of ASMs are described by **rules**, which we interpret as functions from extended states to action sets, i.e., as the functions $((\mathbb{V} \cup \mathbb{L}) \to \mathbb{U}) \to \mathcal{P}(\mathbb{A})$. For closed rules, i.e., rules without free variables, the variable assignment part will be irrelevant. This is the type of rule we will typically consider. Closed rules are also called **programs**. Rules with free variables will only occur in the definition of the semantics of other rules.

With a rule r, we associate two functions on extended states. $\llbracket r \rrbracket^d$ is a Boolean function which describes if the effect of r is defined in an extended state q. The semantics $\llbracket r \rrbracket$ of r is an action system, i.e., it is a function describing the possible effects of executing r in an extended state q in which r is executable, i.e., it returns the set of actions from which one is understood to be nondeterministically chosen. In an application, a rule may never be applied in an extended state in which its effect is undefined.

We will have rule schemes allowing the synchronous composition of two rules. In order to describe the consistency of two such rules, we need a function describing the locations occurring in some action:

Definition 5.2.2. $\mathrm{loc} : \mathbb{A} \to \mathbb{L}$ *is the function yielding all locations occurring in the updates of an action:* $\mathrm{loc}(a) = \{l \in \mathbb{L} \mid \exists u \in \mathbb{U} : (l, u) \in a\}$

Definition 5.2.3. *We call a rule r **enabled** in some extended state q if the action set $\llbracket r \rrbracket(q)$ is not empty.*

We now describe the rules, the conditions under which they are defined, and their semantics:

Definition 5.2.4. *Rule alternatives:*

— *Let r be* SKIP. *This is the do-nothing rule. It is always defined, and its effect is to change nothing.*

$$\llbracket r \rrbracket^d(q) = tt$$

$$\llbracket r \rrbracket(q) = \{\{\}\}$$

— *Let r be* HALT. *This rule can be used to signal an error condition, if executed. It is always defined, and a computation stops if this is the only applicable rule.*

$$[\![r]\!]^d(q) = tt$$

$$[\![r]\!](q) = \{\}$$

— *Let r be* $s(t_1, \ldots, t_{s_a}) := t$, *where* $s \in \mathbb{S}$ *and* $t, t_1, \ldots, t_{s_a}$ *are terms over the extended vocabulary* $\mathbb{S} \cup \mathbb{V}$. *This represents an assignment, i.e., there is just one action with just one update in which the location denoted by the left-hand side gets the value denoted by the right-hand side. All terms are evaluated in the current extended state.*

$$[\![r]\!]^d(q) = tt$$

$$[\![r]\!](q) = \{\{((s, (q(t_1), \ldots, q(t_{s_a}))), q(t))\}\}$$

— *Let r be* IF t THEN r_1 ELSE r_2, *where the term t, the condition, evaluates to a Boolean, and r_1 and r_2 are rules. This is the conditional rule, equivalent to r_1 if the condition evaluates to "true", and equivalent to r_2 if the condition evaluates to "false".*

$$[\![r]\!]^d(q) = q(t) \in \{tt, f\!f\} \wedge (q(t) \; ? \; [\![r_1]\!]^d(q) : [\![r_2]\!]^d(q))$$

$$[\![r]\!](q) = (q(t) \; ? \; [\![r_1]\!](q) : [\![r_2]\!](q))$$

The syntax IF t_1 THEN r_1 ELIF t_2 THEN r_2 ... ELSE r_n *is interpreted as expected.*

— *Let r be* $r_1 \mid \mid r_2$, *where r_1 and r_2 are both rules. This represents synchronous execution of rules r_1 and r_2 and is allowed only in states in which the locations possibly updated by r_1 and r_2 are disjoint. We call such a pair of rules **compatible** in such states. Thus, we even disallow consistent parallel updates, in contrast to Gurevich's original definition.*

$$
\begin{aligned}
[\![r]\!]^d(q) = \\
\wedge \quad & [\![r_1]\!]^d(q) \\
\wedge \quad & [\![r_2]\!]^d(q) \\
\wedge \quad & \forall(a_1 \in [\![r_1]\!](q), a_2 \in [\![r_2]\!](q)) : \mathrm{loc}(a_1) \cap \mathrm{loc}(a_2) = \{\}
\end{aligned}
$$

$$[\![r]\!](q) = \{a_1 \cup a_2 \mid a_1 \in [\![r_1]\!](q) \wedge a_2 \in [\![r_2]\!](q)\}$$

— *Let r be* r_1 OR r_2, *where r_1 and r_2 are both rules. This represents nondeterministic selection between the alternatives given by r_1 and r_2.*

$$[\![r]\!]^d(q) = [\![r_1]\!]^d(q) \wedge [\![r_2]\!]^d(q)$$

$$[\![r]\!](q) = [\![r_1]\!](q) \cup [\![r_2]\!](q)$$

$$\llbracket r \rrbracket^d(q) =$$
$$\land \quad \forall(u \in \mathbb{U}) : q[x \mapsto u](t) \in \{tt, f\!f\}$$
$$\land \quad \forall(u : q[x \mapsto u](t)) : \llbracket r_1 \rrbracket^d(q[x \mapsto u])$$
$$\land \quad \forall(u, u' : q[x \mapsto u](t) \land q[x \mapsto u'](t))$$
$$u \neq u' \to \mathrm{loc}(q[x \mapsto u]) \cap \mathrm{loc}(q[x \mapsto u']) = \{\}$$

$$\llbracket r \rrbracket(q) = \{ \textstyle\bigcup_{u : q[x \mapsto u](t)} a_u \mid a_u \in \llbracket r_1 \rrbracket(q[x \mapsto u]) \}$$

*Note that a step of the FORALL-rule is not necessarily effective, even if for
each allowed value of the variable x which fulfills t, r_1 is effective, since (1)
there might be an infinite number of values for x which make t true, or (2)
the set of values for x which fulfill t might be not effectively computable. In
Sect. 5.3, we will define a variant of this rule which avoids these problems.*

- *Let r be* CHOOSE $x : t$ IN r_1, *where x is a variable, t is a term evaluating
to a Boolean for all values of x, and r_1 is a rule. This denotes the nondeterministic choice between the instances of r_1 for values of x such that t is
true, and such that r_1 is enabled for this value of x.*

$$\llbracket r \rrbracket^d(q) =$$
$$\land \quad \forall(u \in \mathbb{U}) : q[x \mapsto u](t) \in \{tt, f\!f\}$$
$$\land \quad \forall(u : q[x \mapsto u](t)) : \llbracket r_1 \rrbracket^d(q[x \mapsto u])$$

$$\llbracket r \rrbracket(q) = \textstyle\bigcup_{u : q[x \mapsto u](t)} \llbracket r_1 \rrbracket(q[x \mapsto u])$$

*Note that as for the FORALL-rule, the CHOOSE-rule is not necessarily
effective, even if for each allowed value of the variable x which fulfills t, r_1 is
effective, since the set of values for x which fulfill t might be not effectively
computable. We will define a variant also of this rule which avoids these
problems.*

In order to avoid some parentheses, we also use the following syntax to
denote that rules R_1 to R_n are to be executed synchronously:

```
|| R₁
|| ...
|| Rₙ
```

The || signs are aligned, so that if R_i spans several lines and all lines of R_i
are indented appropriately, it is clear where the next synchronous statement
begins.

Like for synchronous composition, we also use a syntax with vertically
aligned OR prefixes to denote that rules R_1 to R_n are to be executed alterna-
tively:

```
OR R₁
OR ...
OR Rₙ
```

We observe some relations between the rules:

Proposition 5.2.1. *The following properties hold for the rules defined above:*

— SKIP *is a neutral element with respect to synchronous composition, and* HALT *is a neutral element with respect to nondeterministic choice.*
— *The* FORALL *rule is a generalization of synchronous composition; if the predicate term does not evaluate to tt for any value of the variable, then the rule is equivalent to* SKIP.
— *The* CHOOSE *rule is a generalization of nondeterministic choice; if the predicate term does not evaluate to tt for any value of the variable, then the rule is equivalent to* HALT.
— *The* OR *combinator and the* || *combinator are both associative and commutative.*

There are two idioms which might be plausible interpretations of the partial IF statement "IF t THEN r". One is r_1 =IF t THEN r ELSE SKIP, the other is r_2 =IF t THEN r ELSE HALT. r_1 is sensible if the main way of combining rules is by synchronous composition, r_2 would be sensible if the main way of combining rules is by nondeterministic choice. We will avoid the abbreviation.

An ASM is formally defined like this:

Definition 5.2.5. *An* **ASM** *is a universe, a vocabulary of symbols, und a rule in which the symbols are used with the correct arities.*

If the universe is implied, a rule alone can define an ASM, by choosing the symbols occurring in the rule as the symbols of the ASM.

5.3 Effectivity

Gurevich's basic definition of sequential ASMs [Gur99] does not include HALT, the nondeterministic rules and the FORALL rule. We allow them here, but we note that for the CHOOSE rule and for the FORALL rule, our definition in this generality deviates from the goal of describing just effective steps, since in order to determine for which values of the variable the predicate is true, typically an infinite amount of work is necessary (all values in $\mathbb{U}$ have to be checked for the variable), and an infinite number of locations might be changed in a FORALL step. Gurevich proves that his set of rules and rule schemes (which Börger calls 'basic ASMs' [BS03]) suffices to describe sequential algorithms (by assuming some plausible formalization for "bounded work").

We will use a special notation which combines the convenience of the notation of FORALL and CHOOSE rules with effectiveness. We assume that the vocabulary $\mathbb{S}$ contains a subset of unary predicate symbols $\mathbb{F}$ which are interpreted as finite sets which are given in an effective manner (those elements $u \in \mathbb{U}$ are assumed to belong to the set described by $F \in \mathbb{F}$ in an extended state q for which $q((F, (u))) = tt$). We call the interpretations of elements of $\mathbb{F}$ **effective sets**. To be specific, assume that for an effective set, there is an enumeration procedure of the elements of the set which signals when it has enumerated all elements of the set. With this convention, we use the following additional forms of rules and terms:

Definition 5.3.1. *(Effective variants of rules)*

- **Effective FORALL-rule.** *Let r be* FORALL $(x : F) : t$ DO r_1*, where x is a variable, $F \in \mathbb{F}$ is a symbol of an effective sub-universe of $\mathbb{U}$, t is a term evaluating to a Boolean for all values of x so that $F(x)$ is true, and r_1 is a rule. The semantics is basically that of* FORALL $x : F(x) \wedge t$ DO r_1*, there is only one conjunct added to $\llbracket r \rrbracket^d$, which is that F denotes a finite effective set. If t is* true*, the rule may be abbreviated as* FORALL $(x : F)$ DO r_1*.*
- **Effective CHOOSE-rule.** *Let r be* CHOOSE $(x : F) : t$ IN r_1*, where x is a variable, $F \in \mathbb{F}$ is a symbol of a finite effective sub-universe of $\mathbb{U}$, t is a term evaluating to a Boolean for all values of x so that $F(x)$ is true, and r_1 is a rule. The semantics is, similar to the previous case, basically that of* CHOOSE $x : F(x) \wedge t$ IN r_1*, and again there is only the conjunct added to $\llbracket r \rrbracket^d$ that F denotes a finite effective set. If t is* true*, the rule may be abbreviated as* CHOOSE $(x : F)$ IN r_1*.*
- *We extend the (Boolean)* **terms** *by two effectively computable expressions $(\forall(x : F) : t)$ and $(\exists(x : F) : t)$, in both of which x is a variable, $F \in \mathbb{F}$, and t evaluates to a Boolean for all values of x such that $F(x)$ is true. We interpret these two expression in extended states in the standard way: The $\forall$ term is true if t evaluates to true for all values of x so that $F(x)$ evaluates to true, and the $\exists$ term is true if t evaluates to true for at least one value of x so that $F(x)$ evaluates to true.*

If an ASM rule does not contain occurrences of rules with unrestricted quantification, each step described by it is effective whenever the application of the program is defined in a state.

Note that the application of a rule to some state is only well-defined if the symbols are used in the rule with the same arity as in the state, and if the classification of the symbols is respected, e.g., if static symbols are not updated by the rule (classification of symbols is described in Sect. 5.4). It is simple to check if this is the case; in the sequel, we will silently assume that these consistency criteria are fulfilled. For a given rule R, we will talk about a **state** q **for** R, or a **state** q **compatible with** R in order to make explicit that q contains the necessary symbols with the proper arities and, possibly, further restrictions allowing the application of R.

5.4 Classes of Symbols

In order to make some coding conventions explicit and to describe some systems more concisely, the function symbols of an ASM are classified into several classes; we assume that these properties of symbols are also recorded in the vocabulary, and that for two compatible vocabularies, the properties are the same for symbols occurring in both.

– Symbols can be classified as **static**. These denote functions whose locations are not intended to be updated during a run. The latter makes it possible to use a static symbol slightly incorrectly to denote also its interpretation. There are other plausible reasons for defining a symbol as static in an ASM. One is that its interpretation must not change, which would allow trivial updates to locations of the symbol. Another is to call all symbols static which do not change their value (or are not updated) in any run of a given system, i.e., to define the concept semantically. We choose to call a symbol static if it is denoted by the designer as such, which allows design errors to be detected.
– Symbols can be classified as **dynamic**. These are symbols which may occur as the head of terms on the left-hand side of assignments, and they represent dynamically changing components of the modelled system.
– Finally, symbols can be classified as **derived**. Derived symbols are interpreted as functions whose values can be computed from the static and dynamic functions in the system. Thus, their interpretations do not need to be represented explicitly in the system – they can be derived from the state.

The meaning of a derived n-ary symbol s is defined by a term t with at most n free variables, where each argument position $i \in \{1, \dots, n\}$ is associated with a variable symbol v_i.

When the value of a term function $s(t_1, \dots, t_n)$ with a derived n-ary symbol s is to be determined, the values of the t_i are determined and an extended state is used for the evaluation of t which maps each v_i to the value of t_i.

We define syntactically a directed dependency graph between derived symbols by saying that there is an edge between s and s' if $s' \neq s$ and s' occurs in the defining term of s. We require that there are no infinite paths in this graph, which excludes indirect recursion.

Direct recursion is allowed, but only if it is well-defined. We require that when $s(t_1, \dots, t_n)$ is a direct recursive occurrence in the definition of the value $s(v_1, \dots, v_n)$ (where $v_1, \dots, v_n$ denotes the variables used as formal parameters in the definition of the derived symbol s), there is a well-ordered domain O and a function $f : \mathbb{U}^n \to O$ so that $\forall_{v_1, \dots, v_n} (P \to f(t_1, \dots, t_n) < f(v_1, \dots, v_n))$ is a tautology, where P expresses the conditions for the recursive invocation (we stole this approach to ensuring well-definedness of function declarations from the proof support system PVS [ORSvH95]).

Derived symbols can not be written to, but they change their value when a dynamic symbol occurring directly or indirectly in the defining term of the symbol changes its value. The definition of the semantics of rules only encodes the effects of updates on dynamic symbols. The change of the meaning of a derived symbol is implicit.

We will generally assume that together with a vocabulary, the definitions of all derived symbols of the vocabulary are given. And we assume that when we say that two vocabularies are compatible, we assume that the definitions of derived symbols occurring in both are identical.

5.5 Interaction with the Environment

In order to model open systems, i.e., systems interacting with an environment, or in order to express features which can not be well described in an operational way, Gurevich proposes to fix a subset of the locations which are to be used as inputs from the environment. The behavior of the environment is not necessarily described as a rule, i.e., operationally; rather, any mathematical concept may be used to restrict the behavior of the environment – typically, the admissible environments will be described in some declarative way.

Somehow it must be ensured that such locations are not written to concurrently by the system described operationally and its environment, since any semantic resolution of such a form of access would be *ad hoc*. Gurevich proposes in [Gur95a] that the system and the environment take turns in changing the state. Another approach would be to simply disallow write access of the operational system to the locations written to by the environment. In this work, I propose that the environment and the system operate synchronously (in order not to introduce a new concept), but that both obey some protocol so that they do not write to the same location in the same step. Gurevich's proposal is a special case of this approach where the protocol would say that in each even step, the system may take a turn and change any location, while in each odd step, the environment may take a turn. The read-only proposal also is a special case of our approach. Additionally, our approach lends itself nicely to further refinement, i.e., if part of the declaratively described environment task should be re-described in an operational way as a rule, this rule can then just be combined with the system rule with the synchronous combinator, and the access protocol used by the environment rule and the system rule have to ensure that the compatibility condition holds for the two rules.

The drawback of our approach is that there is no default write access protocol for the interaction of system and environment; thus, we have to describe this protocol explicitly, operationally for the system component, and typically declaratively for the environment, when open systems are described.

5.6 Gurevich's Thesis

As already mentioned, variants of ASMs are proposed as a formalism for describing algorithms on any abstraction level. Gurevich claims specifically that each sequential algorithm can be mimicked step-by-step by an ASM. This is a sharpened version of the Church-Turing thesis that, e.g., Turing machines are a universal model to express any computable function. Gurevich's thesis relates, like the Church-Turing thesis, an informal concept (that of sequential algorithm) and a formal concept (the ASM). Because of the informal element, the thesis can not be proved in the mathematical sense, but one can strive for speculative arguments by trying to make the intuition behind the informal concept precise, and one can try to collect empirical evidence for the thesis.

One formulation of the thesis which one sometimes find for this is that an intuitive algorithm can be described as an ASM basically without coding. In order to avoid misunderstandings, we want to describe shortly in which sense we accept this claim and in which sense the claim might be misunderstood so that it would be false.

The claim that not much coding is used when an algorithm is described as an ASM is plausible if an ASM description is compared to a Turing machine description or a register machine description. This is because the possible configurations of algorithms can nicely be modelled as first-order structures, and algorithms doing finite work in each step can nicely be modelled by an ASM program. In order to use a Turing machine for solving a problem algorithmically, one has to encode the inputs, outputs and states of the algorithm as tape configurations and states of the finite control component. In comparison to this and other common models of effective computation used in theoretical computer science, intuitive ideas can be expressed more directly in the formalism of ASMs, because the data types and step operations allowed by ASMs are very flexible.

5.6.1 Elements of Programming Languages

But there are also features of algorithms which are implicit in some descriptions and must be made explicit when abstract state machines are used. Examples are features of common programming languages, like the control state, which is implicit, for example, in while-languages; or recursion; or different visibility ranges of variables, etc. ASM rules provide only very basic means to describe algorithms, e.g., for control structures. More complicated features of common programming language must be encoded. Let us investigate two of these features a bit more:

- Non-determinism is explicit by systems described by ASM. Only openness (which might allow a non-deterministic environment) or an occurrence of a CHOOSE or OR rule can make a system non-deterministic. Thus, implicit non-determinism of other formalisms must somehow be coded explicitly when an ASM model of the system is described.
- All state-components of the system must represented explicitly, i.e., must be assigned to some locations. Typical state elements which are implicit in other formalisms are the control state (which is one or a set of positions in a program text), and elements like timers in real-time languages which are

used to determine minimal and maximal waiting times. Note that it is very convenient not to be forced to think about a name for each configuration a system might be in – but in order to reason about the dynamic system behavior, one typically has to introduce some naming scheme for the control locations or sets of control locations of a program described with implicit control flow (see [MP92] for an example).

5.6.2 Operationality

Another type of restriction of the ASM model is that ASMs describe systems operationally rather than declaratively. This is, for example, in contrast to temporal logic with which a system can be described at a higher abstraction level. For example, a system might be described by requiring that every possible run fulfill the formula $\Box(x = 0 \rightarrow \Diamond x = 1)$ of linear temporal logic (meaning that every state in which $x = 0$ holds is followed by some state in which $x = 1$ holds). This kind of declarative system characterization is at a too high level of abstraction for ASMs, since ASMs can relate only states of system behaviors in which one state is the direct follower of the other. Tableau-based approaches exist for encoding the semantics of a formula of some temporal logic by a characteristic automaton, i.e., somehow operationally, but this expression of temporal formula as automata is exactly the kind of low-level encoding which is to be avoided if systems are to be described at their natural abstraction level.

Note that this observation does not contradict Gurevich's claim. Algorithms are supposed to perform their task step by step, i.e., operationally. From the claim that a formalism is expressive enough for modelling algorithms on any abstraction level, it does not follow that it must be expressive enough to model also declarative specifications of properties of algorithms concept-by-concept. Note that the original ASM approach allows some "cheating" by (1) modelling the system as an open system, (2) assigning a subtask which is not easily described operationally to the environment, and (3) specifying the environment declaratively.

5.6.3 No Complications Induced by Formalism

Sometimes, a formalism is proposed for some application area with the claim that it does not induce complications in excess of those inherently contained in the application area. The hope in such a case is that the factual problems of the application area can be isolated and do not mix with technicalities which just arise from the use of a given formalism. For de Roever [dR98], one condition for this claim to hold is that the formalism is compositional, i.e., that a complicated analysis of a system or a problem can be performed by doing a number of simple analyses and putting the results together. Lamport [Lam97] argues in this respect for the use of all of mathematics, instead of the use of some artificially restricted sub-language.

But for restricted application areas, restricted formalisms might be appropriate, if the restrictions are more seen as a form of guidance for the modeller than as a strict prohibition to use any concept not already contained in the formalism. Also ASMs are in many applications used not so much as a strictly defined model, but as a framework providing some inspiration. For example, Gurevich [Gur99] leaves explicitly open the question as to in which way the set of admissible states and of initial states is defined. For the specification of sequential algorithms, ASMs are a formal model which does not require the software engineer to specify more structure than is strictly necessary on the abstraction level chosen, i.e., it is claimed that with respect to step-wise execution of an algorithm, the ASM formalism does not induce any excess complications. As already mentioned, for features of algorithms which can not be expressed directly in the operational ASM formalism, Gurevich proposes to let the environment solve the partial task, where the properties of the environment may be specified using any idea from all of mathematics, or more specifically: also declarative specifications are admitted in the description of the environment. In this way, the inherent restriction to operationality in ASMs is partly suspended.

As discussed in Sect. 2.6, a very generally usable formalism will not give much guidance to the software engineer: If a formalism can express all intuitive ideas likewise concisely and directly, then this holds *a fortiori* for silly ideas. In an extreme way this also holds for "all of mathematics", which Lamport proposes to use. Thus, it is helpful for a general formalism to describe at least conventions and idioms which have proved helpful for specific application areas. This is also true for ASMs. For example, a convention has been developed for defining the operational semantics of programming languages, e.g., using a constant representation of the parsed syntax tree of the program in the (memory) state as guidance for mimicking the control flow of the program.

5.7 Comparison to Other Formalisms for Discrete Systems

To highlight the reasons for choosing ASMs as the basic discrete formalism on which we base our approach to modelling real-time systems, we describe some features which distinguish it from other possible choices:

5.7.1 Updates vs. Transitions

We use a formalism based on updates rather than one based on transitions because transition based semantics are not compositional for the operator expressing synchronous execution of several steps.

Several popular base formalisms for the description of discrete systems are based on transitions, i.e., a possible step of the system is described by a binary relation on states, or equivalently by a function from states to state sets. Examples are Lamport's Temporal Logic of Actions (TLA, [Lam94b]) and Manna and Pnueli's Fair Transition Systems (FTS, [MP92]). These formalisms are designed for expressing concurrency which is based on interleaving and they allow the expression of fairness constraints (see Chap. 8). ASMs do not provide fairness concepts in the basic semantics, but there is no problem with defining them in the ASM context.

We use ASMs rather than transition systems since we need an operator for synchronous composition, and we want to be able to "close" a system. We want to express the following: "If no synchronously running process changes the value of location ℓ, it keeps it value (by default), but it is allowed that a synchronously running process changes its value." This is the normal semantics of an assignment in a programming language with respect to locations which are not assigned to in the assignment. The transition system semantics can not express this: Transition-based approaches do not allow us to distinguish between quantities which keep their value in a step by default and quantities which keep their value because of a trivial but explicit assignment.

This means that transitions are too abstract a concept to express synchronous composition of assignments. A semantics of a formal language, i.e., a function relating a meaning to each phrase of the language, is called **compositional** if it represents enough information from the syntax in order to define the meaning of composition operators only via the meanings of the components [Mos90]. In this sense, a transition semantics of a discrete system is non-compositional for the synchronous composition of assignments, since it is too abstract. An update semantics, i.e., a semantics which describes the meaning of a step just by its effect on those locations which are explicitly set to some value, contains the necessary details.

5.7.2 State Based vs. Event Based Systems

We use a formalism representing states explicitly rather one representing events explicitly.

There is probably no very deep reason for this decision. We just feel more comfortable with states than with events as the basic concept for describing system behaviors, but this is probably by chance.

Process algebras (like CSP or CCS [Hoa85, Mil89]) describe discrete systems in a way making the events of the system explicit and defining the states of a system implicitly via the possible event sequences of a system. In the state based approach, events are described as classes of state pairs.

One reason for using a state-based approach is the fact that one can use many concepts from formal logics to characterize both states and events in a quite direct way.

We can model event based systems as ASMs quite directly by writing an operational interpreter for process algebra terms, e.g., by representing explicitly each active agent, and by representing for each agent the set of events it offers, and by modelling the interleaving of agents and the nondeterministic selection of an event of the selected agent by explicit CHOOSE rules.

Bolognesi and Börger [BB03] describe an approach combining features from ASMs and from process algebras. They define an extension of ASMs in which both the concept of an evolving process description and the concept of an evolving state is used. Börger[1] points out that process algebra events can, in the ASM context, just be interpreted as special cases of update sets; in this way, the conflict between state-based and event-based approaches to system description can be resolved by a special interpretation of some features of ASMs.

5.7.3 Structured vs. Unstructured States

We use structured representations of states rather than unstructured in order to be able to express each global configuration of the modelled system at any abstraction level.

States of finite automata typically described in books on automata theory have no internal structure [HU79]. This is adequate if the automata are looked at a very high level of abstraction. If more details of situations are to be represented explicitly, more structure is needed.

The several decades of experience with first-order structures makes the assumption plausible that the global state of a dynamical system at any fixed moment can on any abstraction level be described by such a structure. Thus, the level of detail to be represented of a situation can probably be tuned exactly to one's wishes if first-order structures are used.

5.7.4 Explicit vs. Implicit Nondeterminism

We use a formalism in which nondeterminism is typically made explicit in order to distinguish potentially nondeterministic systems and necessarily deterministic systems syntactically.

In ASMs, nondeterminism can only be introduced by special syntax, or by environment assumptions. Both forms of the introduction of nondeterminism make it fairly explicit, and since nondeterminism seems to be a complicated concept to deal with and not necessary for many applications, it is nice to be able to define easily a fragment of the notation where the steps are all deterministic.

This is in contrast to constraint based or logical formalisms where determinism must typically be defined semantically.

---

[1] Personal communication.

5.7.5 Operationality vs. Declarativity

We use an operational formalism in order to make it easy to describe effective and non-contradictive systems.

ASMs are designed for making it easy to describe systems operationally: declarative components of a system description are not treated explicitly, i.e., ASMs do not provide specific notation and semantics for defining system properties declaratively. While ASMs do not exclude declarative components of system descriptions, they are refined for operational descriptions of algorithms, i.e., of systems which proceed step by step, each step being effective, and where some effort is made to make it clear that a system description is non-contradictive. In more declarative formalisms, less stress is laid on effectivity and the avoidance of contradictions.

It is reported that also non-experts in mathematics or theoretical computer science feel comfortable with the formalism. We believe that this has to do with the fact that the operational base idea of ASMs, i.e., to describe dynamical systems by (effectively) guarded assignments and to combine such systems by synchronous execution and non-deterministic choice, is simple to understand.

5.8 Summary

This chapter details the reasons for using a variant of ASMs as the base formalism for our approach. We introduce the concept of "action system" as a semantical basis for ASMs. Our introduction of ASM term and ASM rule syntax is rather standard; semantically, we use a variant from the standard by disallowing concurrent updates of a location in a step if they update to the same value, and by interpreting a CHOOSE rule with a false range for the variable as deadlock. Environment interaction in our variant of ASMs is defined so abstractly that refinement is made easy, but synchronisation has to be made explicit. In the discussion of Gurevich's thesis, we deal with possible misunderstandings which the claim to coding-freedom of expressions of algorithms as ASMs might induce. Finally, the basic ideas used in ASMs are compared to decisions taken in other formalisms, and, where possible, reasons are given why we follow the ASM approach.

6. Defining Hybrid Systems with ASMs

We will define hybrid systems using the most important ideas from ASMs. First we define a classical approach to modelling hybrid systems, and then we define a novel, non-standard approach of modelling hybrid systems.

6.1 ASMs for the Definition of Classical Hybrid Systems

6.1.1 Standard Time ASM Rules and Hybrid Transition Systems

In order to be able to compare the approach based on infinitesimals to a classical approach, we first develop a method for describing algorithms needing a quantitative model time with ASMs in a classical way. We use the interval sequence approach to model time in this classical approach to model hybrid systems.

ASMs are basically proposed as a formalism for the description of discrete systems. There are different approaches extending the use of ASMs to the description of systems containing also continuously changing quantities. Examples are given in [GM95, GH96, BS97b, BS97a]. In these approaches, the continuously changing quantity is the time. The timing of the rule, which describes the discrete changes, is defined independently from the rule. Our approach is different: here, the rule also defines the timing of discrete changes.

While the investigation of the use of ASMs for the definition of hybrid systems defined with an interval sequence time model is not the main focus of this work, it will provide some insights into a problem of using a dense model of time and a reference formalism for classical hybrid systems. We use the following definition:

Definition 6.1.1. *A* **standard time ASM rule** *(STASM rule) is a rule in which the nullary symbol* now *is treated as a static symbol.*

We consider an STASM rule R as defining discrete and continuous transitions. We do this analogously as for normal ASMs, by understanding R as a function from states to actions; the only special point is the handling of updates to now. We denote this function, the hybrid semantics of an STASM rule R, as $[\![R]\!]^h$. The discrete transitions are those of standard ASMs, we just make explicit that the value of now does not change. Continuous transitions are those in which time is spent, represented by changes of **now**. A rule allows time to be spent as long as it admits the vacuous action v, which has thus a special role in our approach.

Definition 6.1.2. *The hybrid semantics* $[\![R]\!]^h$ *of an STASM rule* R *is an action system, i.e., a function of* $\mathfrak{A} \to \mathcal{P}(\mathbb{A})$, *defined as*

$$
[\![\mathbf{R}]\!]^h(\mathfrak{q}) = \left(
\begin{array}{l}
\{a[now \mapsto q(now)] \mid v \neq a \in [\![R]\!](q)\} \\
\cup \\
\{\{now \mapsto q(now) + l\} \mid \\
\quad l \in \mathbb{R}^+ : \forall(l' : 0 \leq l' < l) \\
\quad\quad v \in [\![R]\!](q[now \mapsto q(now) + l'])\}
\end{array}
\right)
$$

$[\![R]\!]$ and $[\![R]\!]^h$ differ only with respect to updates of **now**. Since in R, **now** is not updated, there occur no updates of **now** in actions of $[\![R]\!](q)$, which means that the updates we add can not lead to inconsistencies. In $[\![R]\!]^h$, we make explicit that in discrete steps, **now** does not change its value, and that there are additional time actions in which only **now** changes its value. These time steps can be as long as $[\![R]\!]$ admits the vacuous action; they may lead into states in which $[\![R]\!]$ does not admit the vacuous action.

Note that we never allow zero-time time transitions, since l must be strictly positive. Note also that a discrete transition is assumed to take no time, since **now** can not be changed during a discrete transition. Note also that the only dynamical symbol of the vocabulary which changes during a time transition is **now**. This means that other continuously changing quantities must be modelled differently. For this, derived symbols involving the symbol **now** directly or indirectly will be used. We will call **now** and the derived symbols using **now** directly or indirectly in their definition **continuous** symbols, since their values are the only ones which can change in the course of a time transition.

The time transitions fulfill some conditions sometimes required from time transitions of hybrid systems [LSVW96]:

Proposition 6.1.1. *(1) A transition system defined by an STASM rule R is forward and backward time deterministic, i.e., if p reaches q and q' by time transitions of the same length, then $q = q'$, and if p and p' both reach q by time transitions of the same length, then $p = p'$.*

(2) The time transitions defined by an STASM rule R are closed under concatenation, i.e., if p_0 reaches p_1 by a time transition and p_1 reaches p_2 by a time transition, then p_0 reaches p_2 by a time transition.

Both facts follow directly from the definition.

An STASM rule R and an associated vocabulary $\mathbb{S}$ define a set of interval sequences in the obvious way. In the start state, **now** has the value 0. To points in time x between the end points of a continuous transition, we assign the state $q[now \mapsto x]$. True system activity is only assumed to take place during discrete transitions.

In order to illustrate the idea, we describe some simple examples:

- A saw-tooth function increasing like time and jumping from 1 back to 0 as soon as 1 is reached can be modelled by a derived nullary function t and a dynamic nullary function s encoding the time of the last reset. t is defined by $t =_{\mathrm{def}} now - s$. The rule defining the transitions is "IF $t = 1$ THEN s:=now ELSE SKIP", and the system starts with $s = 0$.
- We can express more complicated hybrid systems by using more complicated static functions of the reals which are applied to some term involving now. As a simple example, the sine function of time can just be defined via a derived nullary function symbol s and a static unary function sine, where the term defining the value of s in each state is sine(now). With these definitions, the following rule increments a counter each time the sine function reaches its maximum 1:

```
IF s=1 ∧ lastcounttime ≠ now
THEN || count := count + 1
     || lastcounttime := now
ELSE SKIP
```

The partial condition involving lastcounttime (which is assumed to be initialized with the undefined value at system start) is necessary because of the time model in which time does not increase in discrete steps; since with the incrementation of count, the time does not change, the incrementation would have to be performed infinitely often if it would not be blocked from execution by the additional condition which ensures that for each value of now, it is performed at most once. We discuss this variant in Sect. 6.1.2.
- PCD systems can be defined by an STASM rule and associated derived symbols in which each derived continuous symbol s is defined by a term which is linear in now for all direct and indirect occurrences of now in the term.

Note that we did not restrict the static functions of the reals usable in the definition of derived symbols. This means that we can model quite general hybrid systems by STASM rules and associated definitions of derived symbols.

6.1.2 Infinite Activity

Above, we described a rule which counts the maxima of the sine function. The similarly looking rule IF s=1 THEN count:=count+1 ELSE SKIP, which might look like a counter for moments at which s equals 1, leads to a system which up to time 1 can only let time pass and then, time can not increase any longer, since discrete actions take no time in our model, which means that after s has become equal to 1 for the first time, the discrete incrementation step is performed again and again, and time can not flow on. This is a variant of infinite activity, since there is a finite span of time, specifically: each finite interval containing time 1, in which this system shows an infinite amount of activity. This problem can occur in models in which discrete steps take no time and in which steps might be urgent, i.e., in which discrete steps might imply that they be taken before any time passes.

6.1.3 Hesitation and Urgency

There is another difficulty of our formalization, which is specific to dense models of time. As an illustration, consider the rule "IF x=0 ∧ now>1 THEN x:=x+1 ELSE SKIP". Starting at time 0 with x=0, when will the update "x:=x+1" take place? At time 1, it is too early; the condition is not fulfilled. And at any real (or rational) time larger than 1, it is too late, since by denseness of the model of time, there was an earlier time at which the condition was fulfilled, and when it thus should have been taken. The consequence is that in a state with time 1, the rule admits neither a time step nor a discrete step, which means that the rule is equivalent to **HALT** in such a state; but it is a fairly implicit **HALT**.

This is one of the artifacts of the given approach to the description of hybrid systems. In a discrete model of time which is isomorphic to $\mathbb{N}_0$, each non-empty subset of the moments has a smallest element, which implies that for each standard predicate of time, there is a specific first moment at which the predicate becomes true. For dense models, this is not the case, which means that we can get in trouble if the condition of an action characterizes a set of times without a first element, and the semantics requires that some action be performed as early as possible.

We characterize the problem in the following way:

Definition 6.1.3. *Let R be an STASM rule and q be a state for R in which $q(\texttt{now})$ is a real number. We say that R **hesitates in** q if and only if $[\![R]\!](q) = \{v\}$ and $\exists(x \in \mathbb{R} : x > q(\texttt{now})) \, \forall(y \in \mathbb{R} : q(\texttt{now}) < y < x) \; : \; v \notin [\![R]\!](q[\texttt{now} \mapsto y]) \neq \{\}$.*

The first condition ensures that R can only let time pass in q. The second condition ensures that R **must** do a discrete step before any non-zero time has been spent, which implies:

Proposition 6.1.2. *If an STASM rule R hesitates in q, then $[\![R]\!]^h$ can do only zero-time steps.*

The condition $v \notin [\![R]\!](q) \neq \{\}$ is called **urgency** of R in q. It expresses that from q, no time may pass before R does a discrete step.

6.2 ASMs with Infinitesimal Step Width

The approach of using a constant infinitesimal step width for the description of real-time systems based on a discrete formalism can be used in the ASM framework very easily by requiring that there is a static nullary sym-

bol dt interpreted as a strictly positive infinitesimal, that there is a dynamic
nullary symbol now initialized to 0, and that the rule now:=now+dt is executed synchronously with each step of the system. We admit more generality
and require that there is a time rule R_{time} which is executed synchronously
with the system rule and which increments now by dt in every step, but which
might also do some more timing-related work. A time-only step of the system
is then one which can be explained by R_{time} alone, and all other steps are
discrete steps of the system.

In order to reason about ASMs with infinitesimal step width, it is helpful
to restrict the occurrence of non-standard objects in the ASM state space. In
order to do this, we will introduce yet another distinction between symbols:
There are symbols which are always interpreted as standard objects, and there
are symbols which may also be interpreted as non-standard objects. We will
simply call the first kind of symbol **standard symbol**, and the other **non-
standard symbol**, even though the interpretation of a non-standard symbol
may also be a standard object.

Definition 6.2.1. *An interpretation of a set of symbols is* **standardly correct** *if standard symbols are interpreted as standard objects.*

Note that not all locations of standard symbols are required to have standard values. For example, the standard static symbol + used for addition has
a non-standard value at location $(+, (0, dt))$ for strictly positive infinitesimal
dt. In order to determine standardness of the interpretation of a symbol, all
locations associated with the symbol must be considered. Note also that a
standard function will always yield standard results for standard arguments.

We will use a syntactical criterion on rules which is sufficient to ensure
that a rule will not move from a standardly correct state into a standardly
incorrect state:

Definition 6.2.2. *An ASM rule R is a* **non-standard ASM rule** *if the
following conditions are fulfilled:*

(1) All FORALL-rules and CHOOSE-rules in R are effective.
*(2) Non-standard symbols may only occur in assignment rules which assign
     to a location of a non-standard symbol, or in the conditions of IF rules.*

Non-standard ASM rules lead from standardly correct states to standardly
correct states:

Proposition 6.2.1. *Consider a standardly correct interpretation q of a vocabulary and a non-standard ASM rule R of the same vocabulary. Then each
follower of q according to R is standardly correct.*

Proof. Assume by contradiction that a standard symbol s has no standard
interpretation after the step. Since the precursor state was standardly correct,
s was interpreted as a standard object in that state, i.e., some location of s
must have changed. Since in assignments to locations of s, only standard
symbols and variables can have been involved, and standard symbols could

do no harm, it must have been a variable occurring in an assignment to a location of s which must have been associated with a non-standard value in the extended state which was the context of the assignment. Variables are only introduced by CHOOSE and by FORALL, and since all these rules are effective in a non-standard ASM rule, and no non-standard symbols can occur there, we have a contradiction.

Note that an unrestricted FORALL- or CHOOSE-rule would have allowed us to bind a non-standard value to a variable by a construction like FORALL x:x=dt DO.... Note also that we might have allowed such constructs if in the body of the FORALL- or CHOOSE-rule considered, only assignments to non-standard symbols occur; but we believe that we do not need that flexibility.

Normally, we will assume that the vocabulary of the non-standard ASM considered contains non-standard symbols now and dt, and that the rule does something like this:

```
|| now := now + dt
|| R
```

Here, R represents the activity of the system in addition to the flow of time, and R_{time} equals now:=now+dt, which is the standard case.

We will give a special name to rules which fulfill this condition:

Definition 6.2.3. *A non-standard ASM rule R in which* now *and* dt *are non-standard nullary symbols,* now *dynamic and* dt *static, in which* dt *is interpreted as a strictly positive infinitesimal, and which can be described as $R'\|R_{\text{time}}$, where R_{time} ensures that if* now *is a real, it is guaranteed to be incremented by* dt *in a step by the rule, is called a* **non-standard time ASM rule***, or NTASM rule.*

When we consider an NTASM rule R, R_{time} will commonly denote its timing part. Typically, it can be assumed to be equal to now:=now+dt, but other possibilities exist. See Sect. 10.3 for an example in which the time rule is responsible for incrementing a simulation time in addition to the real time.

The fact that now is updated in each step of a system modelled by the timing part of an NTASM rule implies, by the consistency requirement for the synchronous composition in ASMs, that no other assignment in a real time system modelled in this way may write to now: The progress of time is thus ensured to be independent of the rest of the system.

An NTASM rule shows neither infinite activity nor hesitation: in a finite interval of length l, at most $\lceil \frac{l}{dt} \rceil$ discrete steps take place, which is an integer, i.e., finite; and since we do not admit non-standard predicates in rules, there is a specific first moment at which some predicate is true, if it ever is. Thus, the two artifacts described for the STASM semantics are avoided. For the second, it might be a matter of taste if it seems adequate to assume that time is not dense; but *with* an adequate taste, the dissolution of this artifact is real. For the first, the dissolution of the artifact sounds better than it is, since NTASM systems might show a similar artifact: unlimited activity in limited intervals of time. We discuss this in a bit more detail.

6.2.1 A Note on Zeno-ness in NTASMs

At the end of Sect. 3.1 on dense and discrete time domains we mentioned the artifact of Zeno-ness (discussed by Abadi and Lamport [AL92]) which occurs in some declarative formalisms based on dense models of time. Zeno behaviors do not exist in NTASMs. But a problem very similar to Zeno-ness can occur in NTASMs: A modelled system might show unlimited activity in limited intervals of time. This is typically not admitted as result of an adequate abstraction from a real system, in contrast to the abstraction to model very short reaction times of the system by infinitesimals. The occurrence of unlimited activity in a limited time interval can be a hint to a modelling error, but it can also be understood as an artifact of the formalism, and can lead to the same problems which Abadi and Lamport identify for Zeno-ness:

– It might make a proof system based on this semantics incomplete in spite of the fact that only non-realistic runs of a modelled system do not fulfill the property to be proved.
– It might make a system description or a specification inconsistent in the sense that it only admits behaviors showing unlimited activity.
  This would have the consequence that specifications which avoid the first problem by simply using a limited-activity-requirement into the antecedent are just vacuously true.

Thus, it can be expected that the check that an NTASM admits system behaviors with limited activity is part of the verification task for many systems.

In interleaving-based concurrent systems, a similar problem is being dealt with by fairness constraints: They are used to express which system behaviors can be considered as so unrealistic that they should be excluded from consideration. The temporal logics typically used for the specification of properties of interleaving systems are capable of expressing fairness constraints, so that this artifact can be dealt with explicitly in the specification. In Chap. 7 we develop a notation for a temporal logic which allows us to express that in limited intervals of time, only limited activity occurs.

6.3 Simulation of an STASM by an NTASM

In this section, we will define a concept which allows us to compare the standard semantics of an STASM rule and the non-standard semantics of a related NTASM rule. Since we consider STASM rules and their semantics as a variant of the classical way to define hybrid systems, they can serve as comparison point for the specific possibilities and problems of systems described as NTASMs.

In order to do this, we will define a concept which helps to express that for some STASM rule R and some time rule R_{time}, $[\![R]\!]^h$ and $[\![R||R_{\text{time}}]\!]$ are in close correspondence. This will be in the form of a simulation relation asserting that each run of the STASM can be simulated with infinitesimal precision by the NTASM.

We hope that we can make the concept we propose fairly plausible and we will describe some sufficient conditions which may be fulfilled by R so that the correspondence property between the hybrid semantics and the discrete semantics holds. A rule for which the NTASM semantics simulates the STASM semantics will be called "well-behaved"; this means that it can be interpreted both as an STASM rule and as the non-time (i.e., discrete) component of an NTASM rule basically in the same way.

What conditions should $[\![R||R_{\text{time}}]\!]$ and $[\![R]\!]^h$ fulfill so that we might say that the first action system simulates the second? We propose to make this concept relative to a set of start states $\mathfrak{A}_0$. We partition the actions into discrete actions and time actions.

Definition 6.3.1. Time actions of an STASM *are those which only update* now.

Time actions of an NTASM *are those which can be explained by the time rule alone.*

For both STASMs and NTASMs, **discrete actions** *are the non-time actions.*

For a run $\boldsymbol{a}$ of an action system from some state, the **discrete steps** *are the positions of discrete actions in $\boldsymbol{a}$.*

The idea is the following: We require that for each run of $[\![R]\!]^h$ starting in a state in $\mathfrak{A}_0$, there is a corresponding run of $[\![R||R_{\text{time}}]\!]$ starting from the same state so that

- there is a time-order preserving bijection of the discrete actions of $[\![R]\!]^h$ and those of $[\![R||R_{\text{time}}]\!]$ in which related actions occur at approximately the same time and update the same locations to approximately the same values (ignoring locations different from now updated by the time rule of the NTASM rule), and
- that for each time action of $[\![R]\!]^h$, there is a (possibly empty) sequence of time actions in the run of $[\![R||R_{\text{time}}]\!]$ of approximately the same time span.

Note that for all time steps in $[\![R]\!]^h$ but a (possibly existing) last one, the first requirement implies the second. These requirements imply that the NTASM can mimic each run of the STASM with infinitesimal precision.

Let us be more precise: We define first a distance measure on action sets and the parts of action sets for which we need it:

Definition 6.3.2. *For a fixed ASM, d denotes a function from pairs of some elements (of different types) to $\mathbb{R}_0^+$ with, for universe elements u and u' of the ASM,*

$$d(u, u') = \begin{cases} 0 \ \textit{if } u = u' \\ 1 \ \textit{otherwise if } u \notin \mathbb{R} \vee u' \notin \mathbb{R} \\ min(1, |u - u'|) \ \textit{otherwise} \end{cases}$$

For two pairs of a location and a value (ℓ, u) and (ℓ', u') of the ASM, d is defined by

$$d((\ell, u), (\ell', u')) = \begin{cases} 1 \ \textit{if } \ell \neq \ell' \\ d(u, u') \ \textit{otherwise} \end{cases}$$

For two actions a and a' of the ASM, $d(a, a')$ is defined by

$$d(a, a') = \begin{cases} 1 \ \textit{if there is no bi-total relation of } \operatorname{dom} a \textit{ and } \operatorname{dom} a' \\ \min_R \max_{(x,y) \in R} d((x, a(x)), (y, a'(y))) \ \textit{otherwise} \end{cases}$$

where R ranges over the bi-total relations of $\operatorname{dom} a$ and $\operatorname{dom} a'$.

The definition for actions is also used to define $d(q, q')$ for states q and q' of the ASM, where states are understood as mappings from locations to values.

For two action sets A and A' of the ASM, $d(A, A')$ is defined by

$$d(A, A') = \begin{cases} 1 \ \textit{if there is no bi-total relation of } A \textit{ and } A' \\ \min_R \max_{(x,y) \in R} d(x, y) \ \textit{otherwise} \end{cases}$$

where R ranges over the bi-total relations of A and A'.

For element pairs for which d is defined, it is a distance metric.

Proposition 6.3.1. *d is a distance metric (i) on pairs of universe elements, (ii) on pairs of updates, (iii) on pairs of actions or states, and (iv) on pairs of action sets.*

Proof. To show that $d(x, x')$ is a distance metric, we have to show for all x, x', x'' so that pairs of these are in the domain of d: (a) $d(x, x') \geq 0$, (b) $d(x, x') = d(x', x)$, (c) $d(x, x') = 0 \leftrightarrow x = x'$, and (d) $d(x, x') + d(x', x'') \geq d(x, x'')$.

For each of the cases (i)...(iv) of the proposition, (a) and (b) are obvious, (c) follows from a simple distinction of the different cases and (d) can be inferred by contradiction, where for cases (iii) and (iv) it is used that the composition of bijections is a bijection.

Note that the maximal value of 1 for d expresses that the arguments are very different. The definition requires that a necessary condition for actions to be similar is that the same sets of locations are updated by the actions, i.e., we do not even allow infinitesimal differences in positions of the value-tuple part of a similar locations.

Now we can define the simulation relation:

Definition 6.3.3. *Consider an STASM rule R and an NTASM rule R' with a common vocabulary $\mathbb{S}$, and consider a set $\mathfrak{A}_0$ of states over $\mathbb{S}$. Then we say that R' **simulates R infinitesimally for standard runs with finite activity from $\mathfrak{A}_0$** (abbreviated: $R' \triangleright_{\mathfrak{A}_0} R$) if and only if the following condition holds:*

For any standard run with finite activity $\boldsymbol{a}$ of $[\![R]\!]^h$ from any standard state $q_0 \in \mathfrak{A}_0$, there is a run $\boldsymbol{b}$ of $[\![R']\!]$ from the same state q_0 so that there is a monotone bijection f from the discrete steps in $\boldsymbol{b}$ to the discrete steps in $\boldsymbol{a}$ so that for all standard i in the domain of f, $d(\boldsymbol{b}(i), \boldsymbol{a}(f(i))) \simeq 0$; and if there is a last element of $\boldsymbol{a}$ and it is standard, then there is a last element of $\boldsymbol{b}$ and $d(\boldsymbol{b}(\max \operatorname{dom} \boldsymbol{b}), \boldsymbol{a}(\max \operatorname{dom} \boldsymbol{a})) \simeq 0$.

*We say that R' **strongly simulates R infinitesimally for runs from $\mathfrak{A}_0$** (abbreviated: $R' \triangleright^s_{\mathfrak{A}_0} R$) if the condition above holds even with all standardness assumptions removed.*

The definition expresses the idea that R' can mimic the standard part (resp. all) of each standard run of R with infinitesimal precision, at least if the standard run of R does not perform an infinite number of discrete steps in a finite interval of time. A consequence is that for each standard state reachable by R, there is an infinitesimally neighbouring state reachable by R'. This definition does not allow action refinement, i.e., each discrete step of the standard system is simulated by exactly one step of the non-standard system.

A consequence of the definition is that for each standard state reachable by R, there is an infinitesimally distanced state reachable by R':

Proposition 6.3.2. $R' \triangleright_{\mathfrak{A}_0} R$ *implies that for each standard state q reachable by R from $\mathfrak{A}_0$ in a standard run, there is a state q' reachable by R' so that $d(q, q') \simeq 0$.*

Proof. Reachability of standard q by R in a standard run means that there is a standard finite run $\boldsymbol{a}$ of R from some $q_0 \in \mathfrak{A}_0$ which leads to q. We consider a run $\boldsymbol{b}$ of R' from q_0 which simulates $\boldsymbol{a}$. Such a run exists by $R' \triangleright_{\mathfrak{A}_0} R$. By induction on the number of discrete transitions in $\boldsymbol{a}$, we conclude that the states reached by corresponding discrete transitions in the runs $\boldsymbol{a}$ and $\boldsymbol{b}$ from q_0 are infinitesimally distanced, which completes the proof for runs ending in a discrete action. For runs ending in a time action, we know that only now is updated in the last actions, and by definition of simulation, it is updated to infinitesimally neighbouring values.

6.4 Well-Behaved Rules

The simulation definition now enables us to define when an ASM rule R can be interpreted both as the definition of an STASM and of an NTASM, and that the NTASM interpretation encompasses the STASM interpretation. We call such a rule well-behaved:

```
IF now-lastEventTime = 1
THEN || clock := clock+1
     || lastEventTime := now
ELSE SKIP
```

Fig. 6.1. A non-well-behaved rule modelling a discrete clock.

Definition 6.4.1. *An ASM rule R is called* **well-behaved** *for start states $\mathfrak{A}_0$ if R is an STASM rule, $R||$now:=now+dt *is an NTASM rule, and for any strictly positive infinitesimal value of the static symbol* dt, $(R||$now:=now+dt$) \rhd_{\mathfrak{A}_0} R$.

Well-behavedness of a rule is meant to express that it admits any infinitesimal discretization of time. As an example, the rule given in Fig. 6.1 is not well-behaved: the discrete version only works if dt divides 1. The problem can be traced back to the equality comparison in the IF-condition.

As might be expected, well-behavedness, i.e., the fact that a rule admits infinitesimal discretization, can be guaranteed by a form of continuity. An especially simple sufficient condition for well-behavedness of rules is the following:

Proposition 6.4.1. *Consider the STASM rule $[\![R]\!]$ as a function of its locations, and consider the topologies induced by the metric d (defined above) on the universe and the range of $[\![R]\!]$. If $R||$now:=now+dt *is an NTASM rule and $[\![R]\!]$ is continuous in all states for all its locations, then it is well-behaved for all start states.*

Proof. We have to show that for each standard run of $[\![R]\!]^h$ from some standard state, there is a simulating run of $R||$now:=now+dt from the same state. We use the abbreviation $R' = R||$now:=now+dt.

First, we show that from neighbouring states, each standard step of $[\![R]\!]^h$ can be mimicked by $[\![R']\!]$. Consider states q, q' with $d(q, q') \simeq 0$, q standard.

- By continuity of $[\![R]\!]$, $d(q, q') \simeq 0$ implies for standard q $d([\![R]\!](q), [\![R]\!](q')) \simeq 0$, which implies that for each standard discrete action of $[\![R]\!]^h$ from q, there is an infinitesimally neighbouring discrete action of $[\![R']\!]$ from q'.
- If $[\![R]\!]^h$ admits a standard time step of length l from q, this means that $\upsilon \in [\![R]\!](q[now\mapsto q(now) + l'])$ for all l' with $0 \le l' < l$. By continuity, this implies $\upsilon \in [\![R]\!](q'[now\mapsto q'(now) + l' + \delta])$ for infinitesimals δ and for all l' with $0 \le l' < l$, which means that $[\![R']\!]$ can do a sequence of time steps from q' which together mimic the time step of $[\![R]\!]^h$ from q infinitesimally.

A (standard) induction on the number of discrete steps of $[\![R]\!]^h$ completes the proof.

Unfortunately, continuity in all locations is far too strong a requirement to be helpful in practice. For example, we can not model a discrete clock counting the time units with the rule in Fig. 6.2, where we assume that we start with

```
IF now-lastEventTime >= 1
THEN || clock := clock+1
     || lastEventTime := now
ELSE SKIP
```

Fig. 6.2. A well-behaved rule modelling a discrete clock.

now=clock=lastEventTime=0. For example, the semantics of the rule is not continuous for location now in states in which now=1. More generally, requiring that a rule is continuous in all its locations for all its states means that by the flow of time, an action dissimilar to some continuously possible one can not become possible, since creation of an action which is not similar to an already existing action will always lead to an discontinuity. Since v is an action dissimilar to any other action, this is a fairly strong restriction.

Fortunately, complete continuity is not necessary for well-behavedness:

Proposition 6.4.2. *The rule of Fig. 6.2 is well-behaved for start states with* now=lastEventTime=clock=0.

Proof. Let us call the discrete clock rule R, and let us use the name R' for $R||now := now + dt$.

A system behavior of $[\![R]\!]^h$ has alternating phases: at integer times $n > 0$, the rule must do a discrete step updating clock and lastEventTime to n; and between integer times, it can only let time pass. More precisely: Let a be a run of $[\![R]\!]^h$ from a start state. For all $n \in \mathbb{N}$, the nth discrete action in a, if it exists, updates both clock and lastEventTime to n, and the time steps before the first and between these discrete action sum up to length 1, and the time steps after the last discrete action, if they exist, sum up to a length ≤ 1.

Let us now consider the runs of $[\![R']\!]$. Only time can pass up to the point in time which is the first multiple of dt which is ≥ 1. Let us call this time $1 + \delta$, where δ is a non-negative infinitesimal smaller that dt. At that time, clock is set to 1 and lastEventTime is set to $1 + \delta$. Then, it again takes $1 + \delta - dt$ time units until the next discrete step is taken, when clock is set to 2 and lastEventTime is set to $2 + 2\delta$. An induction shows that the nth discrete step starts from a state at time $n + n\delta$, and it sets clock to n and lastEventTime to $n + n\delta$.

Obviously, for standard $n \in \mathbb{N}$, the nth discrete steps of the two systems take place in infinitesimally distanced states and are infinitesimally distanced (limited n implies infinitesimal $n\delta$). Each standard time step of the standard system of length l can obviously be mimicked infinitesimally by a sequence of $\lfloor \frac{l}{dt} \rfloor$ steps of the non-standard system, or by a sequence of dt-steps leading up to the next discrete step, for the standard time steps preceding discrete steps.

For standard states reached during runs of $[\![R]\!]^h$, $[\![R]\!]$ is right-continuous in the location of now. This implies that it does not hurt much if the function is evaluated an infinitesimal later. Additionally, the only other location which is affected by the discretization error of now is lastEventTime, but this location is only read in a term in which the errors of now and lastEventTime cancel each other out.

Note that the distance between corresponding discrete steps of the standard and the non-standard system defined by the discrete clock rule increases with time. There is an unlimited number n of discrete steps so that the corresponding states and steps will not be infinitesimally distanced. This has to do with the fact that the infinitesimal discretization error sums up in the rule described.

A rule in which the discretization error does not sum up in this way is called **strongly well-behaved**. Here, we require that the infinitesimal simulation does not only work for the standard parts of standard runs of $[\![S]\!]^h$:

Definition 6.4.2. *An ASM rule R is called* **strongly well-behaved** *for start states $\mathfrak{A}_0$ if R is an STASM rule, $R\|$now:=now+dt is an NTASM rule, and for any strictly positive infinitesimal value of the static symbol* dt, $(R\|$now:=now+dt$) \triangleright^s_{\mathfrak{A}_0} R$.

From the proof above, we conclude:

Corollary 6.4.1. *The rule of Fig. 6.2 is not strongly well-behaved for start states with* now=lastEventTime=clock=0.

A strongly well-behaved rule is analyzed in the proof of the following proposition:

Proposition 6.4.3. *The rule in Fig. 6.3 is strongly well-behaved.*

```
IF now-clock >= 1
THEN clock := clock+1
ELSE SKIP
```

Fig. 6.3. A strongly well-behaved rule modelling a discrete clock.

Proof. In the STASM semantics, discrete transitions take place exactly at times $n \in \mathbb{N}$ when clock is equal to $n - 1$. In the NTASM semantics of the rule, for each $n \in \mathbb{N}$ there is a non-negative infinitesimal $\delta_n < $ dt so that the nth discrete step is taken at time $n + \delta_n$. Obviously, strong simulation holds.

The assumption that the step width of the simulating system is an infinitesimal is, for real systems, a helpful abstraction; in reality, noticeable time discretization errors might arise. The distinction between well-behaved and strongly well-behaved rules helps to check if these discretization errors accumulate during the run time of a system.

6.5 Summary

This chapter introduces a way to use ASMs to define classical timed systems based on an interval-sequence model of time (the STASM model). This is done in order to have a reference for comparison with the infinitesimal-step-width based approach. We encode the flow of time **in** the rule, not by an extra formalism. This makes it necessary to discuss some artifacts of the chosen formalization: infinite activity and hesitation. Then we introduce an ASM-based way to define timed system for the infinitesimal-step-width model of time (the NTASM model), we discuss syntactical restrictions for the rule defining the algorithm and describe the tasks of the timing rule R_{time}. We describe in which guise the (classical) Zeno-ness artifact appears in our formalism. Finally, we compare the STASM and the NTASM interpretations of the same algorithm, given by an ASM rule, by defining simulation and well-behavedness: The fact that the effects of infinitesimal discretization of time does not hurt is formalized by the concept of (strong) well-behavedness of an ASM rule, which is formalized by the fact that the NTASM interpretation can simulate each behavior of the STASM interpretation.

7. A Notation for a Temporal Logic

If Gurevich's thesis is valid, ASMs can be used to model any sequential algorithm on any abstraction level. But algorithms are defined in an operational way, and they operate step by step. Often, a higher abstraction level than this is wanted for describing properties of systems. Temporal logics of different kinds are proposed for this in computer science (see [Pnu77] for the introduction of the concept into computer science, and [MP92, Lam94b] for several well-developed approaches).

A well worked-out temporal logic consists of three components. One is a concise notation for the specification of important temporal system properties. Normally the semantics of this notation is presented as a set of operator definitions, reducing formulas of the logic to formulas of some first-order logic. A second component is a proof system, i.e., a collection of axioms and proof rules which allows the derivation of the validity of a formula without recurrence to the semantic definitions of the operators of the logic. And a third component are proof techniques and heuristics for using the proof system. This chapter will not present a logic in this sense; we will only describe a concise specification notation for important system properties.

When a system is specified with a temporal logic, this is by using a formula for characterizing a set of system behaviors. Behaviors are typically modelled as functions from a time domain $\mathbb{T}$ to a domain of states $\mathfrak{A}$. States are often modelled as assignments from a fixed set of locations, often formalized by a finite set of symbols, into a fixed universe. As time domains, linear and tree-like domains are most popular, where trees represent nondeterminism more directly and in more detail. Both dense and discrete domains are used. As already discussed in Chap. 3, we use a discrete model of linear time.

The operators of a temporal logic are typically defined by a first-order predicate logic to be interpreted in positions of runs of the systems to be specified. The reasons why they are used instead of their definitions are the reasons why definitions are typically introduced elsewhere in mathematics: (1) Using these operators, specifications can be written in a shorter form, and (2) they make important concepts explicit by using a specialized notation for them.

The conciseness of temporal logic notations results from the fact that the defined operators allow references to points in time and the most important relations between them to be made implicit. The approaches of Manna and

Pnueli and of Lamport mentioned at the beginning of the chapter use logical formulas which are interpreted over positions in infinite state sequences, i.e., the structure over which such a formula is interpreted is an element of $(\mathbb{N}_0 \to \mathfrak{A}) \times \mathbb{N}_0$.

We consider situations in which quantitative properties of the model of time are important, and in which not only the states are relevant, but also the updates resp. the actions which led into a state. It is convenient to use an interval-based temporal logic for these situations, and to use an interpretation context in which the sequence of actions connecting the states is explicit. In [Mos85], an interval based logic for discrete time is defined; our operators are more similar to the "Duration Calculus" of [CHR91] which is defined for a dense model of time.

7.1 Semantic Domain

We will represent a system development as a pair (q, a) from $\mathfrak{A} \times \mathbb{A}$. Such a pair defines in a canonical way a **transition system run**, which is a function q from $\mathfrak{A}$ by the following inductive definition:

$q(0) = q$
$q(i + 1) = q(i)[a(i)]$, for all i where $a(i)$ is defined

q is the sequence of states defined by the start state q and the action sequence a. For finite sequences a, q is just one element longer than a. When we use a function q, it will always be clear from context which q and a are used for its definition.

7.2 Interval Terms and Focused Predicates

There are two categories of terms of our logic: interval terms and focused predicates. Interval terms are interpreted over intervals in a system behavior, and focused terms are interpreted over positions in a system behavior. As interpretation contexts, we use elements from $\{(q, a, I) \in \mathfrak{A} \times \mathbb{A} \times \text{intervals}(\text{dom } q)\}$ for interval terms and elements from $\{(q, a, i) \in \mathfrak{A} \times \mathbb{A} \times \text{dom } q\}$ for focused terms.

We will define the syntax of terms of our logic as variants of terms of ASMs as described in Chap. 5. Predicates are simply Boolean terms.

We will use two syntactic categories, each defined as variants of terms in ASMs. Together with their syntax, we will now define their semantics.

Definition 7.2.1. Interval terms *are to be interpreted over elements of* $\{(q, a, I) \in \mathfrak{A} \times \mathbb{A} \times \text{intervals}(\text{dom } q)\}$. *They are defined as terms of ASMs with the restriction that no dynamic symbols occur in them, and with the extension that there are two more forms of terms (and sub-terms) allowed (where dynamic symbols in focused predicates are again admitted):*

- **Count terms** *are of the form #p, where p is a focused predicate (see below).*
- *The two-argument Boolean* **chop operator** $p_1; p_2$ *takes two interval predicates.*

Disallowing dynamic symbols makes interpretation over the interval unambiguous. Count terms are interpreted as the (natural) number of positions in the interval under consideration which fulfill the formula p; as defined below, focused predicates are interpreted over positions in state sequences. A chop term is interpreted as true if and only if the interval under consideration can be split into two subintervals so that p_1 holds in the first and p_2 holds in the second. We define the semantics formally further down.

Definition 7.2.2. Focused predicates *are interpreted over elements of* $\{(q, \boldsymbol{a}, i) \in \mathfrak{A} \times \mathbb{A} \times \operatorname{dom} \boldsymbol{q}\}$. *They are extensions of state predicates of the underlying ASM. We allow the following additional forms of terms in a focused predicate:*

- *A* **bar term** $p_1" | p_2$ *is a predicate, where p_1 and p_2 are interval predicates. If one of the interval predicates is just* **true**, *it can be dropped, yielding a term of the form $p|$ or $|p$.*
- *For a rule R without free variables, the* **rule predicates** enabled(R), hasChoice(R), taken(R), takenAlone(R) *and* takenVacuously(R) *are focused predicates.*

Focused predicates are defined at positions in state sequences. A bar term is true at a position if just before that position, an interval ends which fulfills p_1, and at that position, an intervals starts which fulfills p_2. The vertical bar represents the position just in front of the focus. Rule predicates are true if in the state and step defined by the position under consideration, the rule is enabled, taken, etc.

The formal definition of the semantics of interval terms and focused terms is the following:

Definition 7.2.3. *The semantics* $[\![t]\!]_{(q,\boldsymbol{a},I)}$ *of an interval-term t is defined inductively:*

- *If the top-level structure of the term is that of a first-order term without dynamic symbols, just take the meaning of this term in q, applying the interpretation function $[\![\cdot]\!]_{(q,\boldsymbol{a},I)}$ to the components of the top-level structure.*
- $[\![\#p]\!]_{(q,\boldsymbol{a},I)} =_{\text{def}} |\{i \in I \mid [\![p]\!]_{(q,\boldsymbol{a},i)}\}|$
- $[\![p_1; p_2]\!]_{(q,\boldsymbol{a},I)} \Leftrightarrow_{\text{def}}$
  $$\exists (k \in I \cup \{\min(I) - 1\}) \ : \ [\![p_1]\!]_{(q,\boldsymbol{a},\{i \in I \mid i \leq k\})} \wedge [\![p_2]\!]_{(q,\boldsymbol{a},\{i \in I \mid i > k\})}$$

The semantics of focused terms $[\![t]\!]_{(q,\boldsymbol{a},i)}$ *is defined for positions in state sequences:*

- *State symbols s in a focused predicate are just interpreted by* $[\![s]\!]_{(q,\boldsymbol{a},i)} = [\![s]\!]_{\boldsymbol{q}(i)}$.

- *The semantics of a bar term is defined as*

$$[\![p_1|p_2]\!]_{(q,a,i)} \Leftrightarrow_{\mathrm{def}}$$
$$\exists(k \in \mathbb{N}_0) : [\![p_1]\!]_{(q,a,\{n\in\mathbb{N}_0:k\leq n<i\})}$$
$$\wedge\exists(k \in \mathbb{N}_0 \cup \{\omega\}) : [\![p_2]\!]_{(q,a,\{n\in\mathbb{N}_0:i\leq n<k\})}$$

- *Rule predicates are defined by interpreting the rule function of the state $q(i)$. Since the rules are assumed to be closed, i.e., there are no free variables in them, we take the liberty of applying the function induced by a rule to a state, not an extended state: the values of variables are irrelevant for closed rules.*
  - $[\![\mathrm{enabled}(R)]\!]_{(q,a,i)} \Leftrightarrow_{\mathrm{def}} \exists a \in [\![R]\!](q(i))$
  - $[\![\mathrm{hasChoice}(R)]\!]_{(q,a,i)} \Leftrightarrow_{\mathrm{def}} \exists a, a' \in [\![R]\!](q(i)) : a \neq a'$
  - $[\![\mathrm{taken}(R)]\!]_{(q,a,i)} \Leftrightarrow_{\mathrm{def}} \exists a \in [\![R]\!](q(i)) : a \subseteq a(i)$
  - $[\![\mathrm{takenAlone}(R)]\!]_{(q,a,i)} \Leftrightarrow_{\mathrm{def}} \exists a \in [\![R]\!](q(i)) : a = a(i)$
  - $[\![\mathrm{takenVacuously}(R)]\!]_{(q,a,i)} \Leftrightarrow_{\mathrm{def}} \exists a \in [\![R]\!](q(i)) : a = \{\}$

Note that rule predicates are all interpreted as existence of an action in the set of actions allowed by a rule in a step from state number i. "enabled" requires that some action is possible. "hasChoice" expresses that in the current state, the rule has a choice, i.e., two different actions are possible. "taken" just requires that part of the effect in the step is consistent with a step of the rule. "takenAlone" requires that the whole effect of the step can be accounted for by the rule. "takenVacuously" means that the rule admits an empty action in state i. It is typically used in negated form, in conjunction with "taken", and it is used to characterize steps in which a rule really does some work.

7.3 Abbreviations

We assume that we have the usual arithmetical predicate and function symbols available in the static ASM vocabulary, with their usual interpretation.

Definition 7.3.1. *We will use the following abbreviations:*

- $\ell =_{\mathrm{def}} \#\mathtt{true}$: ℓ *is the cardinality of elements of the interval under consideration. For an infinite interval, we write $\ell = \aleph_0$.*
- $[\,] \Leftrightarrow_{\mathrm{def}} (\ell = 0)$: *True for the empty interval.*
- $\{p\} \Leftrightarrow_{\mathrm{def}} (\ell = \#p)$, *for a focused predicate p: p is an invariant of the current interval, which is possibly empty.*
- $[p] \Leftrightarrow_{\mathrm{def}} \{p\} \wedge \neg[\,]$, *for a focused predicate p: p is an invariant of the current interval, and that interval is nonempty.*
- $\mathrm{first} \Leftrightarrow_{\mathrm{def}} \neg([\mathit{true}]|)$
- $p\mathcal{U}q \Leftrightarrow_{\mathrm{def}} (p; q; \mathtt{true})$, *for interval predicates p and q: This is similar to the "until" operator of classical temporal logic, if interpreted over an interval of infinite length.*

- $p \mathcal{W} q \Leftrightarrow_{\text{def}} p \vee (p; q; \text{true})$, *for interval predicates p and q: This is similar to the "weak until" operator of classical temporal logic.*
- $\Diamond p \Leftrightarrow_{\text{def}} (\text{true}; p; \text{true})$, *for an interval formula p: this expresses that in the current interval, there is a subinterval fulfilling p.*
- $\Box p \Leftrightarrow_{\text{def}} \neg\Diamond\neg p$ *for an interval formula p: this expresses that in the current interval, all subintervals fulfill p.*
- $\circ p \Leftrightarrow_{\text{def}} (\ell = 1; p)$ *for an interval formula p: this expresses that p is valid starting with the second position of the current interval.*
- $\text{takenNonvacuously}(R) \Leftrightarrow_{\text{def}} \text{taken}(R) \wedge \neg\text{takenVacuously}(R)$. *This predicate expresses that an R-step has taken place, and that this step was not equivalent to a* SKIP.

There are two rule predicates which are used to detect if a rule is taken in some step: "taken" and "takenNonvacuously". This deserves some comment. Typically, "taken" is more helpful if the system to be described is modelled in an interleaving fashion, since in that case, non-execution of a rule is typically encoded by a HALT. In systems which are combined by synchronous execution, non-execution of a rule is typically encoded by a SKIP, which is excluded from consideration by "takenNonvacuously".

7.4 Examples of Valid Formulas

In this work, we will not develop a calculus for our logical notation. We will present some possible candidates for axioms, of which some match those given in [CHR91] for the Duration Calculus. We will present them as semantical propositions, to be proved by replacing the defined symbols by their definitions.

Definition 7.4.1. *We write $\models P$ for an interval predicate or a focused predicate P which is tautologically true, i.e., which holds in each model.*

Proposition 7.4.1. *Let P, Q be any focused predicates. Then:*

$$\models \#\text{false} = 0 \tag{7.1}$$

$$\models \#P \geq 0 \tag{7.2}$$

$$\models \#(P \vee Q) - \#(P \wedge Q) = \#P + \#Q \tag{7.3}$$

For all $a, b \in \mathbb{N}_0$,

$$\models (\#P = a + b) \leftrightarrow (\#P = a); (\#P = b) \tag{7.4}$$

These facts can be proved just by filling in definitions.

The following proposition describes some facts involving non-standard concepts.

Proposition 7.4.2.

$$\models \left(\begin{array}{c} \mathrm{limited}(\ell * dt) \wedge \neg\, \mathrm{limited}(\#P) \\ \rightarrow \\ \forall^{st} n \in \mathbb{N}_0 : \Diamond(\mathrm{infinitesimal}(\ell * dt) \wedge \#P \geq n) \end{array} \right) \tag{7.5}$$

$$\models \mathrm{limited}(\ell) \rightarrow \mathrm{infinitesimal}(\ell * dt) \tag{7.6}$$

The first fact says that if something is true for an unlimited number of moments in a limited time span, than there is a concentration of such moments in an infinitesimal time span. It follows from simple non-standard reasoning. For the second fact, remember that the step width dt is assumed to be infinitesimal.

The following proposition collects some facts about rule predicates:

Proposition 7.4.3.

$$\mathrm{taken}(R) \rightarrow \mathrm{enabled}(R) \tag{7.7}$$

$$\mathrm{hasChoice}(R) \rightarrow \mathrm{enabled}(R) \tag{7.8}$$

$$\mathrm{takenVacuously}(R) \rightarrow \mathrm{taken}(R) \tag{7.9}$$

$$\mathrm{takenAlone}(R) \rightarrow \mathrm{taken}(R) \tag{7.10}$$

The facts are obvious consequences of the definitions.

Just recurring to the facts in Proposition 7.4.1 and standard and nonstandard arithmetics, we can deduce:

Proposition 7.4.4. *Let P, Q be focused predicates. Then:*

1. $\models \#\neg P = \ell - \#P$
2. $\models \{P \rightarrow Q\} \rightarrow \#P \leq \#Q$
3. $\models \{P\}; \{P\} \leftrightarrow \{P\}$

7.5 Fairness, Limited Activity and Other Example Specifications

Our notation allows us to specify succinctly weak and strong fairness and limited activity with respect to a rule R:

Definition 7.5.1. *A rule R is treated **weakly fair** in an interval if the following formula is true:*

$$\mathrm{wf}(R) =_{\mathrm{def}} \Box \left(\{\mathrm{enabled}(R)\} \wedge \ell = \aleph_0 \rightarrow \#\,\mathrm{taken}(R) = \aleph_0 \right)$$

*A rule R is treated **strongly fair** in an interval if the following formula is true:*

$$\mathrm{sf}(R) =_{\mathrm{def}} \Box \left(\#\,\mathrm{enabled}(R) = \aleph_0 \rightarrow \#\,\mathrm{taken}(R) = \aleph_0 \right)$$

A rule R shows **limited activity** *in an interval if the following formula is true:*

$$\mathrm{la}(R) =_{\mathrm{def}} \square \, (\mathrm{limited}(dt * \ell) \to \mathrm{limited}(\#\,\mathrm{takenNonvacuously}(R)))$$

An interval shows **limited activity** *if in each interval of limited time length, all but a limited number of state transitions are time-only steps, where the effect of a time-only step is described by a rule R_{time}:*

$$\square \, (\mathrm{limited}(dt * \ell) \to \mathrm{limited}(\#\neg\,\mathrm{takenAlone}(R_{\mathrm{time}})))$$

Often, the time rule is just `now:=now+dt`, but in general, also dynamical symbols different from `now` might be changed just by the flow of time. The context will make it clear what kinds of changes are admitted in a pure time step if the limited-activity specification is used.

The fairness definitions have wrong antecedents in finite intervals, i.e., they are only meaningful if interpreted over infinite intervals, as can be expected.

Other example specifications are:

– "A p-state is followed by a q-state between x and y time units." Let p and q be characterized by focused predicates:

$$\square \left(\wedge \begin{array}{ll} [p]; \{\neg q\}; [q] & \to \quad dt * \ell > x \\ ([p]; \mathrm{true}) \wedge dt * \ell > y & \to \quad \circ\lozenge[q] \end{array} \right)$$

– "Each cr-phase takes only a limited number of steps."

$$\square([cr] \to \mathrm{limited}(\ell))$$

– "After a new input has been provided, the computation of the corresponding output only takes negligible time." We use two focused predicates "inputProvided" and "outputReady" to characterize the respective states.

$$\square \left(\begin{array}{c} [\mathrm{inputProvided}]; \{\neg\mathrm{outputReady}\}; [\mathrm{outputReady}] \\ \to \\ \mathrm{infinitesimal}(dt * \ell) \end{array} \right)$$

7.6 On Accountability of a Step to Some Rule, and an Application to Synchronous Systems

We note a fact about accountability of the effect of a step to some rules:

Proposition 7.6.1. *For pairwise compatible rules $R_0, \ldots, R_n$ without free variables, $[\![\mathrm{takenAlone}(R_0 || \ldots || R_n)]\!]_{(q,a,i)}$ implies that we know exactly which rules are accountable for some part of $a(i)$: There is just one partition of $a(i)$ as $\cup_{0 \le j \le n} a_j$ with $\forall_{0 \le j \le n} a_j \in [\![R_j]\!](q(i))$.*

Proof. If a_j contains an update of a location l, compatibility of $R_0, \ldots, R_n$ implies that no rule but R_j can update l in state $q(i)$, and takenAlone($R_0 \| \ldots \| R_n$) implies that each location updated is updated by some R_j.

The last proposition guarantees that for synchronously combined systems for which we know all top-level components, we can attribute all non-SKIP system activities as defined by "takenNonvacuously" unambiguously to the subsystems. The proposition is only valid under the assumption that synchronously executed rules do not update the same location, not even in a consistent fashion. Perhaps this justifies our deviation from Gurevich's original definition which admitted consistent updates of a location by synchronously executed rules.

As an example application, consider a synchronous system with the following properties:

- The computation of a reaction takes only a limited number of steps.
- Rule R is enabled only during the computation of a reaction.
- Starts of a computation of a reaction have a non-infinitesimal time distance.

Then, R is only limitedly active.

The first property above is an abstraction which is intimately correlated with the basic assumption of synchronous systems, which is that the computation of a reaction only needs negligible time (where we interpret "negligible" as "infinitesimal"). The second property is a technical assumption, and the third property encodes another basic assumption of synchronous systems, which is that the time distance of sequential inputs from the environment is non-negligible.

Formally:

Theorem 7.6.1. *Let cr be a state predicate describing if the system is currently computing a reaction.*

Assume that R is at most enabled during the computation of a reaction:

$$\models \text{enabled}(R) \rightarrow cr \tag{7.11}$$

Assume that each phase of computing a reaction needs only a limited number of steps:

$$\models \Box([cr] \rightarrow \text{limited}(\ell)) \tag{7.12}$$

Assume that any interval in which at least two reaction computations start is longer than infinitesimal:

$$\models \Box(\#((\neg\text{true} \vee [\neg cr])|[cr]) \geq 2 \rightarrow \neg\text{infinitesimal}(dt * \ell)) \tag{7.13}$$

Formulas 7.11, 7.12 and 7.13 imply that R is limitedly active:

$$\text{la}(R) \tag{7.14}$$

We structure the proof into several lemmata:

Lemma 7.6.1. *With the abbreviation* $\uparrow cr =_{\text{def}} ((\neg\text{true} \lor [\neg cr]) | [cr])$, *Formula 7.13 implies* $\square(\text{limited}(dt * \ell) \rightarrow \text{limited}(\# \uparrow cr))$.

Proof. The first fact in Proposition 7.4.2 implies

$$\text{limited}(\ell * dt) \land \neg\,\text{limited}(\# \uparrow cr) \rightarrow \Diamond(\text{infinitesimal}(\ell * dt) \land \# \uparrow cr \geq 2)$$

Formula 7.13 contradicts the consequence, which means that the antecedent is false, which is propositionally equivalent to

$$\text{limited}(\ell * dt) \rightarrow \text{limited}(\# \uparrow cr)$$

Since the interval is arbitrary, this proves the lemma.

Lemma 7.6.2. *Formula 7.12 implies*

$$\square(\text{limited}(\# \uparrow cr) \rightarrow \text{limited}(\#cr))$$

Proof. Formula 7.12 implies $\square([cr] \rightarrow \text{limited}(\#cr))$. We prove the lemma by induction, relativized to standard elements of $\mathbb{N}_0$, on $\# \uparrow cr$.

Induction start: An interval with zero or one rising cr-edges can be described as $\{cr\}; \{\neg cr\}; \{cr\}; \{\neg cr\}$. There are $a, b \in \mathbb{N}_0$ with $(\{cr\} \land \ell = a); \{\neg cr\}; (\{cr\} \land \ell = b); \{\neg cr\}$. Since both a and b are limited, also $a + b$ is limited, which implies $(\{cr\}; \{\neg cr\}; \{cr\}; \{\neg cr\}) \rightarrow \text{limited}(\#cr)$.

Induction step: Let $n \in \mathbb{N}_0, n \geq 2$ be standard, i.e., limited. Then $(\# \uparrow cr = n + 1) \rightarrow (\# \uparrow cr = n); (\# \uparrow cr = 1)$. The number of cr-states in each subinterval is limited by the induction hypothesis; thus, also the sum is limited.

Note that normal induction, i.e., induction which is not relativized to the standard elements of $\mathbb{N}_0$, can not be used to prove some non-classical predicate for all $\mathbb{N}_0$.

Lemma 7.6.3. *Proposition 7.4.3 and formula 7.11 imply*

$$\square(\text{limited}(\#cr) \rightarrow \text{limited}(\text{taken}(R)))$$

Proof. The second fact of Proposition 7.4.4, the first fact of Proposition 7.4.3 and formula 7.11 imply that there are at most as many states in which R is taken as there are cr states. For natural numbers, if the larger one is limited, so is the smaller one.

Now we can do the proof of Theorem 7.6.1:

Proof. Consider an arbitrary interval. The antecedent of $\text{la}(R)$ is $\text{limited}(dt * \ell)$. Apply Lemmas 7.6.1, 7.6.2 and 7.6.3 in that order.

7.7 Summary

In order to be able to succinctly describe properties of systems based on the infinitesimal-step-width approach to modelling timed systems, a novel notation for a temporal logic is developed. It uses two types of terms: **focused** terms are interpreted over positions in a system behavior, and **interval** terms are interpreted over intervals. The logic is similar to the Duration Calculus with respect to its operators. An extension is the "bar term" in which two interval terms are combined into a focused term, and another extension are rule predicates. Another specialty of our approach is that the semantic domain over which the formulas are interpreted contains not just the state sequence of a system behavior, but the sequence of **actions** which lead to the state sequence. The notation is rich enough to express important predicates of other temporal logics. Important concepts of reactive systems can be formalized: weak and strong fairness and limited activity. An application of the notation to a problem of modelling synchronous systems in our time model is given, which proves limited activity of a synchronous system.

Part II

Modelling Strategies

8. Concurrency and Reactivity: Interleaving

A system is called concurrent if it is considered at an abstraction level where during its run-time, there are moments when several subsystems are active. For real-time systems, this is a typical case. For non-quantitative linear time, the interleaving approach and the synchronous approach are the most important modelling strategies. Since real-time models build on non-quantitative models and since we investigate a linear-time model, we will investigate how these two strategies are expressed in the ASM formalism and, more specifically, as NTASMs.

We will call the subsystems of concurrent system "processes", and algorithms in concurrent systems will typically be called "protocols". A very typical example are mutual exclusion protocols which ensure that a non-shareable resource is only used by one process at a time, and that a process which wants to access the non-shareable resource will get access to it eventually. Concurrent systems are contrasted to **sequential systems** in which one subsystem finishes its task, producing some outputs, before the next takes the outputs of its predecessor as inputs. A concept intimately related to concurrence is the distinction between reactive and transformational systems [HP85]: **Reactive systems** are systems which listen to their environment and which react on it depending on their state, and where this cycle is performed repeatedly, while **transformational systems** are systems which, after having read their inputs at the start, are not influenced by the environment until they have computed their final result (i.e., they just **transform** an element of a set of inputs into some output), and then they finish. When larger systems are put together from subsystems, transformational systems are typically combined by some kind of sequential composition, resulting in sequential systems; and reactive systems are typically combined by some kind of parallel composition, resulting in concurrent systems. Thus, reactive systems might be called the "open" counterpart of concurrent systems, in the sense that for the case of a concurrent system, we assume that the whole system is given, i.e., there is no relevant unknown environment, while for the case of a reactive system, we assume that we do not know the whole system.

Concurrent systems occur in several variants. One are **distributed systems**, in which the abstraction is adequate that the steps of the reactive systems running in parallel are not necessarily totally ordered, but a partial order between the steps is assumed which expresses a causality relation between the steps [Gur95a], or additionally an exclusion relation is assumed between the steps which expresses that if some step occurs in a system run, other steps may not occur in that run (event structures, [Win88]). In this work, we deal with quantitatively timed systems, which means that each step will be assigned to a moment in real-numbered time. This implies that the abstractions used for distributed concurrent systems are not adequate in our context; thus, we will not go into the details of the models for distributed systems.

For modelling concurrent rsp. reactive systems with a totally ordered model of time, two main approaches can be found. One is the **interleaving** approach, to be described in the rest of this chapter, and the other is the **synchronous** approach, to be described in Chap. 9. We will describe the two variants with their respective application areas, their strong points, their weaknesses, and their expression in our model.

8.1 The Interleaving Approach to Concurrency

When concurrency is expressed by interleaving, system behaviors are modelled as sequences of steps so that in each step of the whole system, only one subsystem (also called "process") performs a step. Thus, the set of possible runs of the whole systems consists of interleavings of the steps of the processes (see [MP92, MP95, Lam94b] for popular models of concurrency based on interleaving).

Typically, not all interleavings of process steps are allowed: fairness restrictions are used to exclude interleavings which are assumed to violate conditions given in the real world. In order to understand the fairness restrictions, we shortly describe the intuition behind the interleaving idea.

At first sight, the interleaving approach might seem to be appropriate for the description of concurrent processes which are executed on a single processor. In this situation, at most one process can do a step in each moment – the steps represent atomic actions of the processes. Restrictions on the interleavings of steps of the different processes which are admitted by an interleaving semantics correspond to properties which an implicit scheduler is assumed to fulfill which determines how the processes are executed. Such properties are called **fairness constraints**. There is a large number of different variants of fairness constraints, but two variants are especially common, which are called **weak fairness** and **strong fairness** (see [Fra86] for an overview).

In order to define fairness constraints, the concept of enabledness of a transition and the concept of a transition being taken is used. Typically, the set of possible state transitions which a process can perform is defined as a set of functions $\tau : \mathfrak{A} \to \mathcal{P}(\mathfrak{A})$, where $\tau(q)$ represents the possible effects of performing the (in general nondeterministic) transition τ in state q.

Definition 8.1.1. *If $\tau(q)$ is nonempty, then τ is defined to be **enabled** in q. If for all q, τ is disabled or $\tau(q)$ is a singleton, τ is called **deterministic**. Otherwise, i.e., if for some q, $\tau(q)$ has more than one element, τ is called* **nondeterministic**.

Note that a process might be nondeterministic even though all its transitions are deterministic, because there might be states in which several transitions with different allowed follower states might be enabled.

In an ASM model of a concurrent system in which each τ is in each state either disabled or deterministic (which is a typical case), we can model each τ by a rule of the following form:

```
IF <guard> THEN <parallelAssignments> ELSE HALT
```

`<guard>` is a term which evaluates to a Boolean. It determines if the statement is enabled. `<parallelAssignments>` is a number of assignments which are performed in parallel. We call rules of this form "guarded assignments". They are the ASM representation of the basic transition descriptions of Dijkstra's "guarded command" language [Dij75].

Now let us define what it means for a transition τ to be taken in a system run.

Definition 8.1.2. *Consider a run of a system, i.e., a function $\sigma : \mathbb{N}_0 \to \mathfrak{A}$. We say that τ is* **taken at position** *$i \in \mathbb{N}_0$ of σ if $q_{i+1} \in \tau(q_i)$.*

Note that in general, several transitions might be considered to be taken at some position i of σ, but in many applications it is typically unambiguous which transition is taken for any position in a run.

Definition 8.1.3. *In a run σ, a transition τ is treated* **weakly fair** *if there is no moment so that in σ from that moment on, τ is enabled all the time without being taken, and τ is treated* **strongly fair** *in σ if there is no moment so that from that moment on, τ is infinitely often enabled without ever being taken.*

In Chap. 7, formalizations of the concepts of a rule being taken or a rule being treated fairly have been introduced. Obviously, they fit these definitions.

In interleaving based models of concurrent systems, weak fairness is typically used to ensure that independent processes are treated with some minimal amount of fairness: no transition of a process which is willing to work all the time from some moment on can be discriminated against by the scheduler forever. For communication or coordination statements, this kind of fairness is too weak: The enabledness of this kind of statements depends on the state of concurrent processes. If τ toggles from enabledness to disabledness ever and ever again, e.g., because some concurrent processes enter and leave their critical sections all the time, and the scheduler "asks" τ if it wants to work only at moments at which it is disabled, it will never be scheduled. In order to ensure that also in such scenarios, τ will be scheduled, τ must be treated strongly fair. Note that for transitions which can only be disabled by being taken, weak fairness and strong fairness are equivalent. Manna and Pnueli [MP92] use the terms strong and weak fairness in the sense just described.

An ASM model of a concurrent system with finitely many rules modelled by fair interleaving can express the nondeterminism by the following construct:

$\text{OR}_{R \in \text{Rules}} \ R$

The indexed OR notation abbreviates a nondeterministic choice between the finite set of rules in Rules, which are used to denote the set of rules describing the transitions of the system. The fairness constraints can not be expressed in the basic ASM notation; they have to be expressed semantically, by describing which of the alternative rules have to be treated with which kind of fairness constraint.

8.2 Some Remarks on Fairness

Manna and Pnueli [MP92] call fairness the difference between nondeterminism and concurrency. Unconstrained nondeterminism does not adequately describe concurrent systems, since it allows too unrealistic runs, or more specifically: unfair runs.

If it was not for fairness, the set of all the transitions T of some process might be combined to one of the form $\lambda(q) : \cup_{\tau \in T} \tau(q)$, but since different transitions of a process might have to be treated with different kinds of fairness, a process is typically described by a set of transitions rather than by just one transition. As mentioned, this requirement applies only to formalisms in which liveness properties are to be specified and proved. If a formalism is only used for safety properties, the whole process can be represented by just one transition. In Gurevich's proposal to extend the ASM formalism to the description of distributed systems [Gur95a], fairness constraints are not dealt with, but they can easily be incorporated into the model, by describing each process not with only one rule but with a (finite) set of rules, where each single rule can be associated with a fairness constraint.

The fairness concepts discussed here are no quantitative concepts. If two transitions τ and τ', which are to be treated weakly fair, are continuously enabled in a run, a weakly fair scheduler might on average schedule τ a thousand times more often than τ', or it might even become more and more discriminating against τ' in time. Thus, these fairness concepts are quite minimal, not intended to be implemented as such, but meant as minimal constraints on an implicit scheduler of a concurrent system which nevertheless suffice to prove important properties of many protocols. If a protocol is proved to be correct if the scheduler can be assumed to fulfill the minimal fairness types just described, then it is also expected to be correct for realistic schedulers, which typically can be assumed to fulfill the minimal properties.

Fairness as defined here is admittedly no effective concept. This idea can be made formal by showing that fairness is equivalent to unbounded nondeterminism [Fra86].

8.3 Properties

We now proceed to describe how properties of concurrent systems are formalized, and we describe a classification of properties which is especially relevant for interleaving-based concurrency.

Definition 8.3.1. *A* **property** *is a set of system behaviors, i.e., for some fixed state space* $\mathfrak{A}$, *a subset of* $\mathbb{N}_0 \to \mathfrak{A}$.

We say that a concurrent system has a property P if all system behaviors belong to P.

Often, two basic kinds of properties are distinguished of concurrent systems described with an interleaving approach. These are called safety properties and liveness properties.

A safety property intuitively claims that something bad does not happen: The idea is that in each system behavior not belonging to a safety property, there is a precise moment at which something bad has happened. This is formalized in the following way:

Definition 8.3.2. *A property P is a* **safety property** *if for each state sequence σ not belonging to P, there is a moment $i \in \mathbb{N}_0$ so that no state sequence σ' which is identical with σ up to moment i belongs to P.*

See [AS85] for a topological characterization of safety and liveness properties. We cite some results.

Proposition 8.3.1. *In the Baire topology on $\mathbb{N}_0 \to \mathfrak{A}$, which is induced by the metric $d(\sigma, \sigma') = (\sigma = \sigma'\,?\,0\,:\,\frac{1}{1+\max\{i \in \mathbb{N}_0 \mid \forall j < i: \sigma(j) = \sigma'(j)\}})$, safety properties are the closed sets.*

Let us now proceed to the characterization of liveness properties. Intuitively, these are properties so that whatever happens in a system behavior in a finite time, there is an extension of the finite prefix which belongs to P.

Definition 8.3.3. *A subset P of $\mathbb{N}_0 \to \mathfrak{A}$ is a* **liveness property** *if for each finite sequence of states, there is an element $\sigma \in P$ so that the finite sequence of states is a prefix of σ.*

With the topology as defined in Proposition 8.3.1, we have:

Proposition 8.3.2. *Liveness properties are the dense sets of the Baire topology on $\mathbb{N}_0 \to \mathfrak{A}$.*

This follows directly from the definition of liveness properties.

Since each set of elements can be defined as the intersection of some dense and some closed set of a topology, we can deduce with Alpern and Schneider:

Theorem 8.3.1. *Each property of $\mathbb{N}_0 \to \mathfrak{A}$ can be defined as the intersection of a safety property and a liveness property.*

Typical safety properties are invariants. A typical liveness property is termination of a process. It can be shown that in order to prove that a system fulfills some safety property, we do not need the fairness restrictions. Fairness constraints are only necessary in order to prove liveness properties. Not to use fairness constraints makes for a simpler theory, which makes it plausible that some approaches to modelling concurrent systems only deal with safety properties. The basic ASM formalism, which does not include safety notions, can describe enough features of a system to derive its safety properties, but not its liveness properties.

8.4 Interleaving NTASM Models

As a general framework for modelling interleaving-based concurrent systems as an NTASM, we associate a rule with each concurrent agent in the following manner:

Definition 8.4.1. *An* **interleaving NTASM model** *of a concurrent system consists of the following components:*

- *A set of (sequentially executing)* **agents,** *represented by an effective set. We characterize agents by the unary predicate symbol* `Agent`*. The agent set may be static or dynamic. The latter case allows us to model that agents are generated or destroyed in the course of a computation.*
- *A finite static set of* **rule identifiers.** *Each rule identifier r is associated with a rule, which we denote by R_r.*
- *A mapping from agents to rule identifiers. We use a unary function* `rule` *from agents to rule identifiers to represent this mapping.*
- *A set of fairness requirements for agents, in the form of two unary predicates* `wf` *and* `sf` *characterizing the agents which are to be treated weakly fair and strongly fair, respectively.*

Typically, an agent will, during the time it exists, be associated to the same rule, and its value in the fairness-defining functions `wf` and `sf` also does not change. We can assume that an agent exists as long as the `rule` mapping associates a rule with it. Destruction of an agent is modelled by the agent being removed from `Agent` and from the domains of `rule`, `wf` and `sf`.

We can describe the operational part of the interleaving semantics by a rule scheme which represents a scheduler of a non-fair interleaving system:

Definition 8.4.2. *An* **interleaving NTASM model scheduler** *is a rule of the following form:*

```
||  now := now + dt
||  OR SKIP
    OR CHOOSE (a:Agent) IN
        OR IF rule(a)==r₁ THEN R_{r₁} ELSE HALT
        OR ...
        OR IF rule(a)==rₙ THEN R_{rₙ} ELSE HALT
```

The list of OR-*prefixed statements inside the* CHOOSE *has one line for each rule identifier* r_i *and each associated rule* R_{r_i}.

We will assume that execution of R_{r_i} *is in no state equivalent to* SKIP. *This is in order to ensure that we can recognize unlimited activity of the interleaving scheduler in an interval.*

Note that the CHOOSE construct in the definition selects only one of the enabled agents, by the definition of the semantics of CHOOSE. Note also that each rule R_{r_i} might contain occurrences of the unbound variable a, which it can use to refer to the agent for which it works.

The fairness requirements are used in the semantics of an interleaving NTASM model to restrict the set of its runs.

Definition 8.4.3. *An infinite sequence* σ *of states is a run of an interleaving NTASM model if the following conditions are fulfilled:*

- *Each step of* σ *is a step of the same interleaving NTASM model scheduler.*
- *For each agent* a, *if from some point in the sequence on, the rule associated with rule identifier* rule(a) *is enabled continuously and* wf(A) *holds continuously, the rule is taken infinitely often.*
- *For each agent* a, *if there is an infinite number of states in the sequence so that* sf(a) *holds and the rule associated with rule identifier* rule(a) *is enabled, the rule is taken infinitely often.*

Note that fairness constraints can be expressed "almost operationally" if we allow infinitely branching non-determinism [Fra86]. We feel that a declarative specification of fairness at the level of runs is simpler.

This definition allows us, for example, to model the Fair Transition Systems which Manna and Pnueli use as the semantical basis of their approach to concurrency [MP92, MP95]. The only restriction is that we require the basic steps, the transitions of Manna and Pnueli, which are represented by ASM rules, to be effective.

8.5 On the Appropriateness
of the Interleaving Abstraction

The idea of a uniprocessor scheduling transitions from a set of processes in a fair manner seems to be the most natural interpretation of the interleaving approach to concurrency, but also distributed systems are commonly described with an interleaving semantics. Two steps s and s' which are unrelated in the partial order of steps of the total system, i.e., for which it is not determined which is performed before the other or if they are performed synchronously, give rise to a partition of the set of interleavings into two subsets: One in which s takes place before s', and another in which s' takes place before s (sometimes, it is allowed that the transitions are performed synchronously, in which case a third subset would have to be defined). Non-causality between two steps is expressed in the interleaving linear time model by the existence of two runs so that in one, s precedes s' and in the other, it is the other way round. In the interleaving approach, the a priori plausible idea to also allow runs in which the two steps are taken synchronously is not admitted.

The decision to allow only interleavings of the transitions of processes and to disallow synchronous or overlapped execution of such steps makes for fewer global transitions of the concurrent system composed of the processes: The set of transitions of the system is just the union of the transitions of the subsystems. If also synchronous execution of transitions of concurrent processes was admitted, this would in general lead to a number of global transitions which is exponential in the number of processes. Many proof techniques of properties of a concurrent system use a case distinction over all global transitions. This makes the interleaving approach attractive.

The decision to model a concurrent system by interleaving introduces nondeterminism (which is restricted by fairness constraints). While this fair nondeterminism is in some cases an appropriate abstraction, e.g., if the steps of the runs of a concurrent system are best modelled as a partial order, there is also a large class of applications in which this is not the case. For example in hardware systems, there is an abstraction level at which it is best assumed that the processes of the concurrent systems work in perfect synchrony. If such systems are modelled with an interleaving semantics, nondeterminism is introduced which is not present in the original concurrent system, and the synchronization between the processes must be encoded explicitly. While this should be possible, the interleaving approach introduces a complexity into the model which is only necessary because the interleaving models do not provide the appropriate means for modelling the synchronous composition of subsystems. In order to model such systems, the synchronous approach can be used, which is described in Chap. 9.

8.6 Summary

For linear-time concurrent systems, two composition strategies are often chosen: interleaving and synchronous composition. This chapter discusses important concepts of the interleaving approach and describes how it can be used in the current framework.

9. The Synchronous Approach to Concurrency

Synchronous systems are concurrent systems in which the components proceed in a lockstep fashion. An early investigated model of synchronous systems are cellular automata [vN66, Vol79], where the synchronously working components, which are called "cells" in this context, communicate according to some regular interconnection scheme, so that each cell only communicates with its neighbors. This abstraction is appropriate in applications in which the signal travel time in the system is not negligible. A more general model of synchronously working systems assumes a broadcasting communication, i.e., it assumes that an output of a component is instantaneously visible to each other component. In this section, we will investigate such a model of synchronous systems.

9.1 Reactive Systems as Mealy Automata

The synchronous approach to reactive systems can in principle be characterized very simply: A reactive system is just an input-enabled nondeterministic Mealy automaton. This is a variant of an I/O automaton [LT87].

Definition 9.1.1. *An **I/O automaton** is a tuple $(\mathfrak{A}, \mathfrak{A}_0, I, O, \delta)$ where:*

- *$\mathfrak{A}$ is a set of states.*
- *$\mathfrak{A}_0 \subseteq \mathfrak{A}$ is the set of initial states.*
- *I is the set of inputs.*
- *O is the set of outputs, disjoint from the inputs.*
- *$\delta : (\mathfrak{A} \times I) \to \mathcal{P}(\mathfrak{A} \times O)$ is the step function.*

*An I/O automaton is **input-enabled** if for all $(q, i) \in \mathfrak{A} \times I$, $\delta(q, i)$ is non-empty.*

*An I/O automaton is **deterministic** if $\mathfrak{A}_0$ is a singleton and for all $(q, i) \in \mathfrak{A} \times I$, $\delta(q, i)$ is a singleton.*

*A **Mealy automaton** is an I/O automaton in which $\mathfrak{A}$, I and O are finite.*

The elements of $\delta(q, i)$ are the possible effects of an input i in state q: If $(q', o) \in \delta(q, i)$, then the system can go from state q under input i to state q' and output o to the environment. We call (q', o) a possible reaction for

(q, i). Input-enabledness of an I/O automaton means that in each state there is a follower state for each input. Note that deterministic I/O automata are input-enabled.

The behavior of an input-enabled I/O automaton is interpreted in the following way: The system starts in a state $q \in \mathfrak{A}_0$ and waits for some input. After some time, input $i \in I$ arrives, and instantaneously, the system selects a possible reaction (which always exists, because of input-enabledness), moves to the state part of the reaction and outputs the output part of the reaction. Then it starts waiting again for the next input.

The instantaneous computation of the reaction on some input is called a macro-step. Typically, this macro-step is implemented by a sequence of micro-steps. If an I/O automaton is implemented as a real system, the selection of a reaction takes some time, and, thus, it is an abstraction to assume that the reaction takes its effect instantaneously when an input arrives. For a given application, the **synchrony hypothesis** is the claim that this abstraction is appropriate: The time needed for macro-step of the implemented I/O automaton is negligible in comparison to the reaction times of its environment.

Applications for which the synchrony hypothesis holds are typically not well described by interleaving concurrency. One reason is that the inherent nondeterminism of interleaving systems is only restricted by fairness, and the fairness types defined are not well suited to model that the reaction to some input be immediate – at least one would need a specific interpretation. A way to extend fairness based formalisms is to define a subset of the transitions as urgent, which means that they must be executed as soon as they are enabled (or before any non-urgent transition is taken, since in general, several transition might be enabled in some state, and only one transition can be taken in a step of an system based on interleaving concurrency). Such an approach could combine synchrony and interleaving.

In applications which are typical for synchronous systems, there is not much need for interleaving; rather, they are deterministic and have a fixed structure, and since they have a finite number of states, inputs and outputs, they are Mealy automata. Hardware systems and process controllers are typical examples. The formalism used for describing such applications does not have to deal with nondeterminism and fairness. The problem lies elsewhere: It consists of describing a Mealy automaton with large sets of states, inputs and outputs in a way which allows the structure to be dealt with in a compositional way. This means that it should be specified, designed, understood, analyzed, optimized, debugged, possibly also compiled, etc., by dealing with the elements of some partition of the synchronous system and putting together the partial work results in order to construct the work result for the entire system.

Basically, it is only the transition function δ which has to be defined. Thus in synchronous systems, the task of defining a reactive system can be reduced to defining one macro-step of the system, which is just some transformation of inputs (the current state and the input event) into some results (the next state and the output reaction). Thus, what is needed for defining a synchronous reactive system is exactly what Harel and Pnueli [HP85] call a transformational system. This might be considered as a contradiction in terms, since reactive systems and transformational systems are considered to be disjoint classes. This contradiction dissolves if we admit that a system can be transformational at one level of abstraction and reactive on another. Synchronous systems can be considered as reactive systems either at a **higher** abstraction level than that of a single macro-step – where the synchronous system describes a **sequence** of macro-steps which are reactions on inputs from the environment, fitting exactly the definition of a reactive system–and also if we consider a **lower** abstraction level – where a single step of the synchronous system is computed as the effect of the **work of concurrent modules**, each reacting on inputs from other modules, as will be discussed further down in more detail, and where each such module also fits nicely the definition of a reactive system.

Let us consider synchronous systems on the abstraction level where they are transformational. Classical techniques for describing functions in a manageable way are:

1. Hierarchy: Use step-wise refinement [Wir71] to develop a detailed design or an implementation from a high-level, i.e., more abstract design, representing also the higher design levels as procedures or functions explicitly in the implementation.
2. Modularity: Decompose a unit of a higher abstraction level into smaller units, called modules [Par72]. The task of a higher-level module is split into sub-tasks which are dealt with by several lower-level modules, which possibly interact in performing their work.

The only difference between the classical approach to the definition of a transition function and the approach often used for synchronous systems is that in order to compose modules into higher-level units, classical approaches typically used only deterministic selection, repetition and an operator for sequential composition, while the different approaches used for synchronous systems use additionally some kind of parallel (or concurrent) composition of submodules. The latter also makes necessary some kind of communication mechanism for submodules, which for many synchronous formalisms can be understood as a shared-variable approach. This means that a partial result computed by some module is instantaneously available to all other modules which monitor the location of the result. Halbwachs [Hal93] calls this approach "broadcasting", since it is a form of one-to-many communication not involving any synchronization on the part of the sender[1].

---

[1] Neither the classical nor the synchronous approach to describing transformational systems uses explicit nondeterministic selection, and where nondeterminism is introduced in the use of a synchronous formalism, this is typically considered to be a designer error (most synchronous formalisms do not admit nondeterminism).

There are many different proposals for modularly describing Mealy automata. ESTEREL [BdS91, BG92, Ber99] is an imperative programming language. STATECHARTS [Har87] is a graphical formalism, based on some extensions of finite automata, for operational system specification; ARGOS [Mar89, Mar90] can be considered as a version of StateCharts with a cleaned-up semantics. LUSTRE [HCP91] is a functional stream-processing language. Signal [LBBG85, LGLL91] is a stream-processing language with a constraint-programming flair. The system description language of the model-checking tool SMV is a synchronous language [McM93]. VERILOG [TM95, Gor95] and VHDL [LMS86] are hardware description languages. Halbwachs [Hal93] gives an overview of some synchronous formalisms proposed for programming. In order to get some order into this zoo of synchronous formalisms, we investigate some concepts which are important for several of the formalisms in a general setting.

9.2 Composing I/O Automata

On the abstraction level of I/O automata, the composition of two synchronously proceeding systems can not be expressed conveniently. We use more structure for the sets of inputs, outputs and state. We model $\mathfrak{A}$, I and O as functions from sets of set-specific locations to some universe $\mathbb{U}$:

Definition 9.2.1. *A* **structured I/O automaton** *is a tuple* $(\mathbb{U}, \mathbb{L}^Q, \mathbb{L}^I, \mathbb{L}^O, \mathfrak{A}_0, \delta)$, *where*

- $\mathbb{U}$ *is a universe of values,*
- $\mathbb{L}^Q$ *is a set of state locations, defining the set of states* $\mathfrak{A} = \mathbb{L}^Q \to \mathbb{U}$,
- $\mathbb{L}^I$ *is a set of input locations, defining the set of inputs* $I = \mathbb{L}^I \to \mathbb{U}$,
- $\mathbb{L}^O$ *is a set of output locations, defining the set of outputs* $O = \mathbb{L}^O \to \mathbb{U}$,
- $\mathbb{L}^Q$, $\mathbb{L}^I$ *and* $\mathbb{L}^O$ *are pairwise disjoint,*
- $\mathfrak{A}_0 \subseteq \mathfrak{A}$ *is the set of initial states,*
- $\delta : ((\mathbb{L}^Q \cup \mathbb{L}^I) \to \mathbb{U}) \to ((\mathbb{L}^Q \cup \mathbb{L}^O) \to \mathbb{U})$ *is the transition function.*

We call $\mathbb{L}^Q \cup \mathbb{L}^O$ *the set of* **controlled locations**. *The values of these locations have to be determined in a macro-step. In contrast, the values of input locations are only read during a macro step.*

We call $\mathbb{L} = \mathbb{L}^Q \cup \mathbb{L}^I \cup \mathbb{L}^O$ *the set of* **locations**.

In the obvious way, a structured I/O automaton defines an I/O automaton. The concepts of input-enabledness, determinacy, and Mealy automata are transferred from I/O automata.

In order to be combined in parallel, two structured automata must fulfill a compatibility condition:

Definition 9.2.2. *Two structured I/O automata are* **compatible** *if they are defined over the same universe, the set of state locations of each is disjoint from the locations of the other, and the sets of output locations are disjoint.*

Note that compatibility implies that at most one automaton controls a given location, and that output locations of one automaton may be input locations of the other. It is over these common locations that the automata can communicate when they are combined.

We are now prepared to define synchronous composition of structured I/O automata:

Definition 9.2.3. *Let P_1 and P_2 be two compatible structured I/O automata. Then their synchronous composition $P = (P_1 \| P_2)$ is defined by*

- $P.\mathbb{L}^Q = P_1.\mathbb{L}^Q \cup P_2.\mathbb{L}^Q_2,$
- $P.\mathbb{L}^I = (P_1.\mathbb{L}^I \cup P_2.\mathbb{L}^I) - (P_1.\mathbb{L}^O \cup P_2.\mathbb{L}^O),$
- $P.\mathbb{L}^O = P_1.\mathbb{L}^O \cup P_2.\mathbb{L}^O,$
- $P.\mathfrak{A}_0 = \{q_1[q_2] \mid q_1 \in P_1.\mathfrak{A}_0, q_2 \in P_2.\mathfrak{A}_0\}$
- *For all $q \in P.\mathfrak{A}, i \in P.I,$ $\delta(q[i])$ is defined as*

$$\{q'[o] \mid q' \in P.\mathfrak{A}, o \in P.O,$$
$$(q'[o] \downarrow P_1.\mathbb{L}) \in P_1.\delta(q[i[o]] \downarrow (P_1.\mathbb{L}^Q \cup P_1.\mathbb{L}^I)),$$
$$(q'[o] \downarrow P_2.\mathbb{L}) \in P_2.\delta(q[i[o]] \downarrow (P_2.\mathbb{L}^Q \cup P_2.\mathbb{L}^I))\}$$

The input locations of the combination of the two automata are those inputs of either automaton which are not controlled by the other automaton. As the set of possible results of processing input i in state q, we admit all mappings from state and output locations to universe elements which are consistent with possible results of both combined automata.

Unfortunately, the synchronous composition operator just described does not fulfill a condition which is important for synchronous systems: The composition of deterministic systems should be deterministic. We investigate the problem and a solution for structured Mealy automata.

Proposition 9.2.1. *There are compatible deterministic structured Mealy automata with non-deterministic synchronous composition.*

Proof. We present two compatible deterministic structured Mealy automata with a non-deterministic composition.

Consider $P_1 = (\{0,1\}, \{\}, \{x\}, \{y\}, \epsilon, \delta_1)$, where $\delta_1(q) = \{\{y \mapsto q(x)\}\}$, and $P_2 = (\{0,1\}, \{\}, \{y\}, \{x\}, \epsilon, \delta_2)$, where $\delta_2(q) = \{\{x \mapsto q(y)\}\}$. Then the transition function δ of $P_1 \| P_2$ is defined by $\delta(\epsilon) = \{\{x \mapsto u, y \mapsto u\} \mid u \in \mathbb{U}\}$, which has two elements.

Note that by replacing δ_2 in the proof above by $\delta_2(q) = \{\{x \mapsto 1 - q(y)\}\}$, a δ would result which is empty, i.e., the composition of the two automata is inconsistent.

Corollary 9.2.1. *The class of deterministic structured Mealy automata is not closed with respect to synchronous composition.*

This means that we need a more restrictive compatibility criterion in order to ensure that the synchronous composition of deterministic structured Mealy automata is deterministic. In order to define such a criterion, we need the

concept of independence of some output locations from some input locations
in a transition function δ. We will, from now on, focus on Mealy automata:

Definition 9.2.4. *For a deterministic structured Mealy automaton P, we
say that* **location $l^O \in P.\mathbb{L}^O$ depends on location $l^I \in P.\mathbb{L}^I$ in state
$q \in P.\mathfrak{A}$** *if*

$$\exists i, i' \in \mathbb{U}^{P.\mathbb{L}^I} :$$
$$\forall (l \in P.\mathbb{L}^I - \{l^I\}) : i(l) = i'(l)$$
$$\wedge \quad \epsilon(P.\delta(q[i]))(l^O) \neq \epsilon(P.\delta(q[i']))(l^O)$$

*If there exists some state q so that location $l^O \in P.\mathbb{L}^O$ depends on location
$l^I \in P.\mathbb{L}^I$ in state q, we simply say that l^O* **depends on** *l^I.*

The first conjunct ensures that the input value combinations i and i' differ
at most at location l^I, and the second conjunct ensures that the difference
at location l^I between i and i' leads to a difference between the values of l^O
in the two resulting states. Note that the selection function ϵ yields the only
element of $P.\delta(q[i])$ rsp. $P.\delta(q[i'])$, because we only consider deterministic I/O
automata.

Dependency of l^O on l^I in state q means that there are values for the
input locations in which the value of the output location l^O depends on the
input l^I. Independence means that in order to compute the value of l_O, the
value of l_I does not have to be known.

Definition 9.2.5. *Let $P = (\mathbb{U}, \mathbb{L}^Q, \mathbb{L}^I, \mathbb{L}^O, \mathfrak{A}_0, \delta)$ be a deterministic structured Mealy automaton. The dependence relation between input locations and
output locations defines, for each $q \in \mathfrak{A}$, a partial order $\leq_q$ on $\mathbb{L}^I \cup \mathbb{L}^O$, by
defining $l \leq l'$ if l' depends on l in state q or $l' = l$.*

This partial order is called the **state-relative I/O dependency relation** *of P.*

*The union of the $\leq_q$ for all states q is a partial order $\leq$ so that $l^I \leq l^O$
expresses that there exists a state in which l^O depends on l^I.*

This relation is called the **I/O dependency relation** *of P, since it is
not relative to some state.*

If two automata are combined, some output locations of one automaton
are typically identical to some input locations of the other automaton. If the
transitive hull of the union of the partial orders of the single automata is
not a partial order, then there is a dependency cycle between some locations
which might lead to problems. The concept of "causal compatibility" between
deterministic structured Mealy automata encapsulates the idea that if no
dependency cycles are generated by a combination of the two dependency
relations, the resulting automaton is deterministic again.

Definition 9.2.6. *Two deterministic structured Mealy automata are called*
causally compatible *if they are compatible and the transitive hull of the
union of the I/O dependency relations is a partial order.*

Note that in order to exclude dependency cycles in the synchronous composition, it would have been enough to require that for any commonly reachable pair of states $q_1 \in P_1.\mathfrak{A}$ and $q_2 \in P_2.\mathfrak{A}$, the state-relative I/O dependency relations of P_1 and P_2 fit together.

Proposition 9.2.2. *The synchronous composition of two causally compatible deterministic structured Mealy automata is deterministic.*

Proof. Let P be the composition of two causally compatible deterministic structured Mealy automata P_1 and P_2. Assume that $q \in P.\mathfrak{A}$ and $i \in P.\mathbb{L}^I \to P.\mathbb{U}$. We have to prove that $q' \in P.\mathfrak{A}$ and $o \in P.\mathbb{L}^O \to P.\mathbb{U}$ with $q'[o] \in P.\delta(q[i])$ exist and are unambiguously determined. We (1) prove that values of locations in $P.\mathbb{L}^O$ are unambiguously determined, and (2) we deal with values of locations in $P.\mathbb{L}^Q$.

(1) The causal compatibility of P_1 and P_2 implies the existence of a partial order on the interface locations of the component automata, i.e., of $P_1.\mathbb{L}^I \cup P_1.\mathbb{L}^O \cup P_2.\mathbb{L}^I \cup P_2.\mathbb{L}^O$, which is equal to $P.\mathbb{L}^I \cup P.\mathbb{L}^O$, induced by the I/O dependency relations of the components. The idea is to compute the values of the interface locations of the component automata in the order of the partial order. Since the automata are Mealy automata, each location has only a finite number of predecessors. Smaller values in the partial order do not depend on larger ones. This means that also the value of an output location of an automaton can be determined for which there exist input signals with not yet known values.

Consider a location l in the partial order so that the values $q'[o](l')$ of all locations $l' \in P.\mathbb{L}^I \cup P.\mathbb{L}^O$ smaller than l in the partial order have already been determined. Then the value of $q'[o](l)$ does not depend on as yet unknown values: q is given, and the values of predecessors or l are given. By induction, this defines unambiguously the values of all elements of the partial order in $q'[o]$, which is a superset of $P.\mathbb{L}^O$.

(2) Consider a location $l \in P.\mathbb{L}^Q$. By definition of synchronous composition, l is a state location of either P_1 or P_2, and the value of l in $q'[o]$ is equal to some corresponding value in P_1 or P_2. Since both P_1 and P_2 are deterministic, and by (1), also all values of input locations to both P_1 and P_2 are determined unambiguously, also $q'[o](l)$ is determined unambiguously.

Note that the proof just given also hints to possibilities of implementing the synchronous composition of causally compatible Mealy automata, either partly in parallel (by concurrent evaluation of values of locations which do not depend on each other) or sequentially (by using some linearization of the partial order of the composition).

In different formalisms for the description of synchronous systems, a problem can occur which Halbwachs [Hal93] calls a "causality" problem. In the framework just described, non-causal synchronous systems can occur by combining modules which are not causally compatible. In practice, non-causality is sometimes detected by the compiler, but it might also simply lead to the

non-termination of the computation of some step of the Mealy automaton in
the operational model (e.g., in hardware description languages, simulation of
a system with a feedback from the output of an inverter into its input might
lead to an infinite non-stabilizing sequence of steps, each toggling the value
of the inverter).

9.3 Micro-steps of Synchronous Systems as ASMs

Like interleaving systems, also synchronous systems can be described by a
finite set of guarded assignments. In an interleaving-based system, only one
of the enabled rules is selected and executed, which might disable rules which
were enabled before. Thus, a rule which is enabled in some state is not guaranteed to be executed.

The abstraction level of these simple steps is lower than that of Mealy
automata considered earlier. On this lower abstraction level, the execution
policy of the rules of a synchronous system can be described like this: **A rule
is executed once for each moment in which it is enabled.** Intuitively,
this means that each rule R "notices" instantly if its guard is true: if once
enabled, the execution of R can not be preempted by another rule which gets
a chance to be executed earlier and which might disable R by its execution.

This execution policy is logically independent from the synchrony hypothesis. The Mealy machine and the synchrony hypothesis describe how a
synchronous system interacts with its environment, and the execution policy
describes how a synchronous system is implemented by micro-steps.

There are several strategies to implement this idea. We will give a rule
implementing one micro-step for each strategy. In order to describe these
rules we assume that `Rules` is the finite set of rules which define together the
synchronous system. We assume that the state of the synchronous system
is represented by the interpretation of a dynamic unary symbol `mem`, which
maps the locations of the synchronous system (which we characterize by an
effective static unary predicate symbol $\mathbb{L}$) to the universe of the synchronous
system (which we characterize by a static unary predicate symbol $\mathbb{U}$). Typical
strategies for defining the micro-step semantics of synchronous languages are
the following:

– All enabled rules are executed **synchronously in parallel**; an ASM rule
  describing a micro-step of this approach is the following:

$\|_{R \in \texttt{Rules}} R$

The indexed $\|$ abbreviates a synchronous execution of the finite set of
rules from `Rules`. Each rule has the form

```
IF <guard>
THEN mem(l_1):=t_{l_1}||...||mem(l_n):=t_{l_n}
ELSE SKIP
```

The `<guard>` must evaluate to a Boolean, l_i are locations of the synchronous system to be updated by this rule, and t_{l_i} are the terms denoting the values to be assigned to the locations.

This strategy leads to a completely deterministic system, which is typically wanted in the description of synchronous systems. The rule can only be used if the system of rules is conflict free, i.e., any two different rules by which a common location may be updated must have contradictory guards. Some formalisms for synchronous systems require that the semantics of described systems be conflict-free in exactly this sense, but others do not require this and have thus to describe a semantics which can deal with conflicts in concurrently enabled rules. The other two strategies we give describe semantics which can deal with such conflicts.

- The enabled rules are not executed immediately, but they are scheduled for future execution, which is done in an **interleaving** manner. We assume that the ASM provides in its universe a subset of updates, which are constructed by a static 3-ary function `update` taking as arguments (1) a location of the synchronous system, (2) an element of the universe of the synchronous system, and (3) a point in time at which it should be performed. Three static unary accessor functions `location`, `value` and `time` are defined on updates which yield the respective components of the argument update. Finally, we use an effective dynamic unary predicate `ScheduledUpdates` to characterize those updates which have been scheduled and not yet executed. These updates are performed in an interleaving fashion as soon as their time has come. The strategy is described by the ASM rule in Fig. 9.1, in which the scheduler rule, which executes nondeterministically one of the updates scheduled for the current time, is executed in parallel with the rules which schedule some updates for execution at some point in time. As a variant, the THEN branch may contain several update

---

```
|| IF (∃(u:ScheduledUpdates): time(u) <= now) THEN
      CHOOSE(u:ScheduledUpdates): time(u) <= now IN
       || mem(location(u)) := value(u)
       || ScheduledUpdates(u) := false
   ELSE SKIP
|| (||_{R∈Rules} R)
```

Rules R are of the form

```
IF <guard> THEN
  ScheduledUpdates(update(<loc>,<val>,<time>)) := true
ELSE SKIP
```

where `<loc>`, `<val>`, `<time>` are terms evaluating to the location, the value and the time of the update.

Fig. 9.1. A synchronous system scheduler managing a set of scheduled updates in an interleaving fashion.

constructions, to be performed in parallel. Care must be taken that each scheduled update is generated just once during a synchronous execution. Note that the interleaved execution might introduce nondeterminism if conflicting updates are generated for some point in time.

An execution model basically like this is found to underlie the hardware description languages of the family of synchronous formalisms.

– A common variant allowing the production of inconsistent update sets, but executing the updates not just one by one, but a maximal consistent set of updates in each step, i.e., an approach implementing **maximal progress** might be taken. We refine the vocabulary and universe of the ASM described in the previous strategy by the following additional requirements: The universe contains also sets of updates (and the vocabulary the binary static function symbols $\in$ and $\subseteq$ with the expected interpretations, to be used in the definition of the terms of some derived functions; we will not give the definitions here). A derived static binary predicate on sets of updates `maximalConflictFree(s,t)` determines if a set of updates `s` is a maximal conflict free subset of the updates which may be scheduled at time `t`. A derived unary predicate $\mathcal{P}$ is true exactly for the subsets of updates for which `ScheduledUpdates` is true. The ASM description of the maximal progress strategy is given in Fig. 9.2. As for the strategy of Fig. 9.1, inconsistent rules might lead to nondeterminism when the maximal-progress strategy is used.

|| IF($\exists$(u:ScheduledUpdates): time(u) <= now) THEN
    CHOOSE(s:$\mathcal{P}$): maximalConflictFree(s,now) IN
        FORALL(u:s) DO
           || mem(location(u)) := value(u)
           || ScheduledUpdates(u) := false
    ELSE SKIP
|| ($||_{R \in \text{Rules}}$ R)
           The rules R are of the form of the strategy of Fig. 9.1.

Fig. 9.2. A maximal progress scheduler for a synchronous system.

Sometimes, it is convenient to be able to refer to the previous values of a term in the guard of a rule; for example, the hardware description languages can use guards involving changes, or, for Boolean terms, edges of a specific direction. In order to support this in the ASM context, we would use a nullary static symbol previous_l for each location l whose previous we might need, which is interpreted as yet another location, and execute $\text{mem}(\text{previous}_l) \text{:=} \text{mem}(l)$ in parallel to the micro-step rule for all such locations l.

9.4 Environment Interaction and the Synchrony Hypothesis

The synchrony hypothesis is the condition for the synchronous approach to reactive systems to work. It says that the reactive system works very quickly in comparison to the environment, or more precisely: that the reaction time of the reactive system in the computation of the outputs can be ignored.

In order to explore the meaning of this hypothesis, we will describe how the micro-step semantics and the macro-step semantics (i.e., the Mealy automaton semantics) of a reactive system are related. A macro-step of the synchronous system consists of the following phases:

1. The environment waits until the next input has to be processed by the reactive system.
   For the strategies based on timed scheduled updates, the reactive system must also be re-activated when one of the elements of `ScheduledUpdates` might have become enabled because of the flow of time.
2. When the environment decides that a new input has to be processed, the new input to be processed is filled in. We assume that a subset $\mathbb{L}^I$ of the locations of the micro-step ASM is designated as the input locations. New inputs are provided for these locations by putting these values into $\text{mem}(l)$ for $l \in \mathbb{L}^I$. Then, the micro-step ASM is activated.
3. Now, the environment waits for the system to terminate its computation. The synchrony hypothesis is valid if the computation is terminated in negligible time in relation to the reaction time of the environment.
4. After the reactive system has finished its work, the micro-step ASM is deactivated and its outputs are fed back from the synchronous system into the environment. We assume that a subset $\mathbb{L}^O$ of the locations is designated as output locations, and the output of the synchronous system consists of the values of the output locations after the stabilization.

At system start, we can either assume that the environment must wait for the end of an initialization phase before the first inputs may be provided, or we can assume that in the first state, the reactive system already waits for the first set of inputs. We consider this to be just a technical point, and we assume the second.

We will shortly make precise what it means in the ASM context for a rule to be activated or dis-activated, and how the environment can recognize if the computation has finished:

– **Activation of a rule** R is modelled by a dynamic nullary predicate symbol active_R, where the rule is used in a context of the form IF active_R THEN R ELSE SKIP. The rule is active in states in which active_R is true, and it is inactive if active_R is false.
– **Termination** of the computation is signaled to the environment by the synchronous system by the value of a dynamic nullary symbol `terminated`. On activation of the rule, the environment updates this symbol to false, and the system sets it to true when it is ready.

With these conventions, the environment rule, to be executed synchronously with the reactive system, can be described like in Fig. 9.3, where we assume that the environment starts in state `waitingForInput`, and the reactive system is inactive at the start:

```
IF (envstate = waitingForInput) ∧ inputAvailable THEN
   || ProvideInput
   || envstate := waitingForResult
   || active_SyncRule := true
   || terminated := false
ELIF (envstate = waitingForOutput) ∧ terminated THEN
   || envstate := waitingForInput
   || active_SyncRule := false
   || TransferOutput
ELSE SKIP
```

Fig. 9.3. A rule describing the environment of a synchronous system.

`envstate` is the state of the environment, which is one of `waitingForInput` and `waitingForOutput`. `inputAvailable` is a predicate signaling if an input is available for the synchronous system. `ProvideInput` is a rule providing the input to the synchronous system, `SyncRule` is the name of the rule describing the synchronous system, and `TransferOutput` is a rule for processing the outputs from the synchronous system.

In the non-standard approach to real-time systems, we can make the synchrony hypothesis more precise: A system fulfills the synchrony hypothesis if the abstraction is adequate that the computation of any macro-step uses only infinitesimal time, and that the distances between moments at which the environment provides inputs are appreciable. Under this interpretation of the synchrony hypothesis, any limited number of micro-steps may be used to compute a macro-step. An unlimited number of micro-steps would imply unlimited activity of the system.

A consequence of this assumption is that the time stamp of a next scheduled assumption should not be in the non-zero infinitesimal future: it should either be in the appreciable future, or it should be the current moment.

9.5 Synchronous NTASM Models

We propose a very basic model of synchronous concurrent systems by associating a rule with each concurrent agent and executing them synchronously. For this, we have to require that the rules associated with the agents are compatible, i.e., there is no resolution of the nondeterminism so that different synchronously executed rules update the same location:

Definition 9.5.1. *A* **synchronous NTASM model** *of a concurrent system consists of*

– *A set of (sequentially executing)* **agents**, *represented by an effective set. We characterize agents by the unary predicate symbol* Agent. *The agent set may be static or dynamic. The latter case allows us to model that agents are generated or destroyed in the course of a computation.*
– *A finite static set of* **rule identifiers**. *Each rule identifier r is associated with a rule, which we denote by* R_r.
– *A mapping from agents to rule identifiers. We use a unary function* rule *from agents to rule identifiers to represent this mapping. The rules must be compatible in each state, i.e., there must be no resolution of the nondeterminism in the rules so that two rules update the same location in the same state.*

The following rule scheme describes a synchronous scheduler.

Definition 9.5.2. *A* **synchronous NTASM model scheduler** *is a rule of the following form:*

```
|| now := now + dt
|| FORALL (a:Agent) DO
      || IF rule(a)=r₁ THEN R_{r₁} ELSE SKIP
      || ...
      || IF rule(a)=rₙ THEN R_{rₙ} ELSE SKIP
```

The set of system behaviors of a synchronous NTASM model defined thus:

Definition 9.5.3. *An infinite sequence σ of states is a run of a synchronous NTASM model if each step of σ is a step of the same synchronous NTASM model scheduler.*

The list of | |-prefixed rules inside the FORALL rule has one line for each rule identifier r_i and associated Rule R_{r_i}. Note that as in the interleaving NTASM model, each rule R_{r_i} might contain occurrences of the unbound variable a, which it can use to refer to the agent for which it works.

9.6 Summary

This chapter describes a way to model reactive systems based on the synchronous composition of subsystems rather than on interleaving composition. We explain the approach by describing a system as a Mealy automaton and explain why in order to compose systems, more structure is necessary than there is explicit in Mealy automata descriptions. We define the concepts of compatibility and causal compatibility of Mealy automata, which are needed to understand the needs of the composition operation. Finally, we describe three strategies of implementing micro-step semantics of synchronous systems based on ASMs, and we describe how the interaction with the environment might be modelled.

10. Deadlines

A concept which is often used in models of real-time systems is the deadline. A deadline is a point in time associated with an event so that the event must take place in a system run, and it must not take place after the deadline. This section will discuss how deadlines might be modelled in NTASMs.

The deadline concept is related to the concept of urgency of an event. An event is urgent at some point in time when its deadline has come, i.e., when no more time may pass until the event takes place.

In several formalisms, two points in time are associated with an event. In addition to the deadline, there is an enabling time. The enabling time is a point in time so that before that point in time, the event does not take place. Since we model standard systems, it is no restriction to assume that both the enabling time and the deadline are standard. For a fixed event, let us denote by e the enabling time and by d the deadline. In general, each of the times might be understood as strict or as non-strict, i.e., that the intervals (e, d), $(e, d]$, $[e, d)$ or $[e, d]$ might describe the time during which the event must take place. We will restrict our investigation to non-strict enabling times and deadlines. We call the interval during which an event is required to take place the **execution interval** of the event. In order to make the event description non-contradictory, we assume additionally that the execution interval of an event is not empty. If the execution interval is a point interval, this models that there is exactly one moment at which the event might take place. And if $e < d$, there is an interval with strictly positive length during which the event is required to take place.

Deadlines and enabling times are typically used in the assumptions of a system specification: They restrict nondeterminism similarly to fairness restrictions in concurrent systems modelled in an interleaving fashion.

We will model each event by an agent. This concept is used in Definitions 8.4.2 and 9.5.2 for modelling concurrency. Since agents can be created and destroyed, for the execution of an event it is also relevant when the agent associated with the event is created. We simply assume that the enabling time of an event is not earlier than the creation time of the associated agent. By this assumption, we do not have to consider the creation time of the agent when we investigate when an event can take place: only enabling time and deadline matter.

In formalisms in which during a discrete step of the system, no time is assumed to pass, deadlines can be modelled in the following way: as long as at least one event is urgent, only discrete transitions can take place, executing the urgent transitions or disabling them. Otherwise, the system might do a time step whose length is so small that no strict deadline of any event is reached, and no non-strict deadline of any event is transgressed.

There are two reasons why this simple strategy does not work in NTASM systems in general: (1) In each step, also when a discrete step takes place, a non-zero amount of time passes. (2) If the execution interval of some event is a point interval, the use of a constant step width implies that the execution interval does not intersect the time domain if the point is not an integer multiple of the step width.

In this section, we describe several ways to model deadlines in the NTASM context under different conditions. We use the convention that an event is modelled by an agent a. Thus, we will talk about the enabling time of a, the deadline of a or about urgency of a, always transferring the concepts from an event to the agent modelling the event. For an agent a, $\texttt{enablingTime}(a)$ and $\texttt{deadline}(a)$ denote the enabling time and the deadline of a. By $\texttt{performEvent}(a)$, we denote a rule which describes the effect of performing the event associated with agent a. Since agent a models only a single event, it is assumed that one of the effects of the execution of $\texttt{performEvent}(a)$ is the destruction of agent a.

10.1 Synchronous NTASM Systems

We have the most simple case if the system is a synchronous NTASM, the enabling times and deadlines lie at standard rational numbers, and the infinitesimal time step dt divides all standard rational numbers. This case is especially easily dealt with because we can tune the step width to the enabling times and deadlines.

Lemma 10.1.1. *There is a non-zero rational infinitesimal dt such that for any standard rational number q, $\frac{q}{dt}$ is an integer.*

Proof. This follows from the idealization axiom: For any standard finite set $\{\frac{m_1}{n_1}, \dots, \frac{m_k}{n_k}\}$ of rational numbers (the m_i are all integers, the n_i are all non-zero integers), a rational number dividing them all is $\frac{1}{\prod_{1 \le i \le k} n_i}$. A number dt dividing **all** standard rational numbers must necessarily be infinitesimal, since (by contradiction) if it were not, it would be standard, and then it would not divide the standard rational number $dt/2$.

Since NTASMs use a discrete time domain with equidistant points and infinitesimal steps, it is important that we can find a step width which touches each standard rational number:

Corollary 10.1.1. *There is an infinitesimal dt so that $\mathbb{T} = \{n * dt : n \in \mathbb{N}_0\}$ contains each non-negative standard rational number.*

The corollary does not hold for standard real numbers:

Proposition 10.1.1. *There are two standard real numbers a and b so that no number divides both without rest.*

Proof. Just take $a = 1$ and $b = \sqrt{2}$.

Corollary 10.1.2. *No infinitesimal divides all standard real numbers without rest.*

A rule $R(a)$ defining the activity of an agent a with enabling time and deadline might be given as in Fig. 10.1.

```
IF enablingTime(a) ≤ now
THEN IF now+dt ≤ deadline(a)
     THEN OR SKIP
          OR performEvent(a)
     ELSE performEvent(a)
ELSE SKIP
```

Fig. 10.1. Form of a rule in a synchronous NTASM model with enabling times and deadlines.

The outermost IF ensures that before the enabling time has come, the effect of the rule is equivalent to SKIP, i.e., that the rule has no effect, but does not interfere with any synchronously executed rules. The inner IF checks whether execution of the event can wait. This is the case if at the next point in time, i.e., at now+dt, the deadline condition has not yet been violated. In this case, the event might either take place, or it might wait. Otherwise the current moment is the last one at which the event might take place, i.e., a has become urgent, and the ELSE branch of the inner IF ensures that the event in fact takes place.

Since we consider rules of a synchronous NTASM model as presented in Chap. 9.5, it is ensured that the different instances of performEvent(a) in synchronously executed rules are pairwise compatible. Thus, no synchronization is necessary between concurrent agents whose deadlines run out at the same point in time.

Under the conditions described, the rule of Fig. 10.1 will not miss a deadline:

Theorem 10.1.1. *Consider a rule $R(a)$ of the form of Fig. 10.1. Assume that*

(1) rule $R(a)$ is executed by a synchronous NTASM model scheduler,
(2) both enablingTime(a) and deadline(a) are standard numbers,
(3) the constant step width dt divides deadline(a),
(4) the execution interval is non-empty,
(5) the agent a is created before its deadline has run out, and
(6) the agent a is destroyed only by the rule performEvent(a), which only occurs in $R(a)$.

These assumption given, it is ensured that rule `performEvent(a)` *is taken at a time during the execution interval of the event, i.e., at a state with* `enablingTime(a)` $\leq$ `now` $\leq$ `deadline(a)`.

Proof. We proceed in two steps. First we show (A) that if the execution interval (an interval of $\mathbb{R}_0^+$) and the interval I of $\mathbb{T}$ which starts with the first moment at which a exists and which extends to infinity have a non-empty intersection, `performEvent(a)` is ensured to be executed, and then we will prove (B) that the intersection mentioned in the antecedent of (A) is indeed non-empty.

(A) Assumption (1) ensures that $R(a)$ is taken exactly at the moments in $\mathbb{T}$ at which the agent a exists, i.e., exactly for the times in I up to the first moment at which `performEvent(a)` is taken (by assumption (6)). Now assume that the execution interval and I have a non-empty intersection. Call this intersection J. Since the execution interval has standard bounds, it is standard. Since the execution interval is bounded, J has a last element. This is the time at which a is urgent, if it exists by that time.

a exists from the beginning of I to the first (and only) state in which `performEvent(a)` is taken. The outer IF of $R(a)$ (and assumption (6)) ensure that `performEvent(a)` is at most taken after the enabling time of a has come, i.e., there are elements of J where a exists. At any point during J but the last, the THEN branch of the inner IF of $R(a)$ allows `performEvent(a)` to be taken, but does not force this. If `performEvent(a)` is not taken at one of these moments, it will be taken at the last moment in J, because of urgency, by execution of the ELSE branch of the inner IF. In any case, `performEvent(a)` is executed.

(B) Assumptions (2) and (4) together imply that the execution interval is appreciable or a point interval. For appreciable intervals I and an infinitesimal dt, there is an unlimited number of multiples of dt which lie in I, i.e., $I \cap \mathbb{T}$ is non-empty. For a point interval, assumption (3) implies that the only point also lies in $\mathbb{T}$. For both cases, assumption (5) ensures that the smallest element of I does not violate the deadline condition, and since all elements greater than that belong to I and $I \subseteq \mathbb{T}$, it follows that the intersection of I and the execution interval is non-empty.

Let us discuss the practical relevance of the assumptions of Theorem 10.1.1. Many systems are more easily modelled as interleaving systems than as synchronous systems, which means that assumption (1) can be a real restriction. Since we deal with modelling standard systems, assumption (2) will typically be fulfilled. Applications of real-time systems do seldom use the abstraction that time is Dedekind-complete like the real numbers, which means that the restriction to rational enabling times and deadlines is also typically no restriction in practice, which allows fulfillment of assumption (3), by Corollary 10.1.1, quite easily. Non-fulfillment of assumptions (4) or (5) leads to systems in which the deadline has no function, and assumption (6) does not have to be a real restriction if destruction of a by another rule is modelled as setting some flag which leads `performEvent`(a) to do nothing but destroy a.

Altogether, we conclude that in synchronous NTASM models, deadlines can in general be operationalized quite directly, as described by the rule in Fig. 10.1 and made precise by Theorem 10.1.1. Interleaving NTASM models need more consideration.

10.2 Interleaving NTASM Systems

If some processes of a concurrent system update the same locations without using an explicit access protocol, the system is most easily modelled in an interleaving manner, because this implies the existence of an implicit access protocol. Sect. 8.4 presented a simple scheduler for an interleaving system. In the definition of that section, the nondeterminism induced by the choice between SKIP and the enabled rules is only restricted by the fairness requirements. For dealing with deadlines operationally, the interleaving approach presents the main problem that several agents might become urgent at the same time, but only one of them can be taken at that time.

A simple solution to this problem is to deal with deadlines as with fairness: declaratively, by considering only runs in which the formula

$$\forall (a : \texttt{Agent}) : \texttt{deadline}(a) \neq \perp \rightarrow \texttt{now} \leq \texttt{deadline}(a)$$

is invariantly true. This formula assumes that `deadline`$(a) = \perp$ encodes that there is no deadline for agent a.

The problem with declarative requirements is typically to show that they are not contradictory. Thus, we have to find conditions under which there exists a resolution of the nondeterminism of an interleaving NTASM model scheduler as described in Definition 8.4.2 so that each event can take place before its deadline runs out. In the case at hand, sufficient conditions on the enabling times and deadlines of the agents have to be found which ensure that the deadlines can be observed by the system, similar to the synchronous case dealt with above.

The main idea is to ensure that for each time interval of a run of the system, there are at most as many events which have to take place in that interval as there are steps in that interval. In that case, each event to be performed can also be performed.

The main conditions which we use are limited activity and relaxed punctuality:

Theorem 10.2.1. *Consider an interleaving NTASM model. Each agent a might, on its creation, be associated with an enabling time `enablingTime`(a) and a deadline `deadline`(a), which obey the following conditions:*

(1) The agent a is created not later than its enabling time.
(2) Both `enablingTime`(a) and `deadline`(a) are standard numbers.
(3) The execution interval is non-empty and is not a point interval.

The agent fulfills the following conditions:

(4) At each moment during the execution interval of a, the rule $R_{rule(a)}$ is the only rule which, if executed, would execute rule performEvent(a).

(5) The agent a is destroyed only by the rule performEvent(a).

Under these conditions, and if **(6)** *the system admits runs of limited activity, there is a run of the interleaving NTASM model which obeys the deadline conditions, i.e., in which each agent associated with a deadline can do its work before its deadline has expired.*

Proof. Because of condition (1), enabling time and deadline are the bounds of the interval in which the event must take place, i.e., we can ignore the creation time. Conditions (4) and (5) imply that the agent remains in existence until its associated rule $R_{rule(a)}$ is scheduled for execution. Condition (6) and the definition of limited activity imply that there is a run so that in each interval of limited length, only a limited number of non-SKIP transitions take place. Consider such a run, and consider an agent a which is associated with a deadline. Since the bounds of the execution interval are standard (2), the execution interval is of limited time length. By limited activity, this implies that the agents different from a only do a limited number of steps in that interval. By (3) and infinitesimality of the step width, the execution interval contains an unlimited number of steps. Note that strictness or non-strictness of enabling time or deadline make no difference. Thus, there is room enough for a to do its only step in the execution interval, since only a limited number of the unlimited number of steps is used by agents other than a: The scheduler of an interleaving NTASM model can resolve its nondeterminism so that deadlines are obeyed.

Let us discuss the practical relevance also of the precondition in this theorem. Condition (1) has a technical character, and condition (2) is no real restriction if standard systems are modelled. The second conjunct of (3) might be inconvenient: punctuality of a deadline is a convenient abstraction in many cases. We could allow punctual deadlines if we required that at most one event would be allowed to be punctual for a given point in time, and that such a punctual deadline would be placed at a rational point in time and using an infinitesimal step width touching each standard rational, similar to the strategy chosen for expressing deadlines in synchronous NTASM models. But this would induce inconvenient interdependencies in processes to be executed in an interleaving fashion: Their set of potential punctual deadline times would have to be disjoint. Conditions (4) and (5) have merely technical character, and condition (6) is a natural assumption for implementable systems, as already discussed. Thus, the only real inconvenience is the second conjunction of (3), i.e., the requirement of non-punctuality.

10.3 Admitting Infinitesimal Delays

The two sections above investigate sufficient conditions so that in an NTASM system, enabling times and deadlines can be modelled faithfully. As has been demonstrated, one condition might be rather inconvenient. This condition might be weakened if a more liberal interpretation of the runs of NTASM systems is assumed.

The idea can be presented by a distinction between simulation time and real time. As before, the real time at a moment is the value of a dynamic nonstandard symbol `now` which starts as 0 and is incremented by the same infinitesimal `dt` in each step. The simulation time is the value of a dynamic nonstandard symbol `simNow` which also starts as 0, and which is incremented in a similar but different way than `now`. Consider the following idea:

- Deadlines and enabling times of agents are interpreted with respect to simulation time, not with respect to real time.
- The scheduler updates `simNow`, the simulation time, in the following way:
  - In a step in which a discrete transition takes place, `simNow` is not changed. This implies that the simulation time does not change in a step when an agent is urgent.
  - In a step in which no discrete transitions take place, `simNow` is incremented at most by `dt`, in the following way:
    If strictly between `simNow` and `simNow+dt`, there is a deadline t of some agent, set `simNow` to t, otherwise set it to `simNow+dt`.
    This means that `simNow` is incremented by `dt`, or in the next state, there is an urgent transition.

Using this strategy, we do not have to assume very sharp restrictions on enabling times and deadlines. Punctual deadlines will be obeyed no matter what the time step `dt` is, and no matter if the deadline times are rational or not, but only with respect to `simNow`, not with respect to real time. Because of this, the relation between simulation time and real time is important.

Let us look at the runs which are generated by this strategy. The simulation time will always be smaller than or equal to the real time, i.e., `simNow<=now` is an invariant of the system. This implies that an event which obeys its deadline with respect to `simNow` might be too late by the amount of `now-simNow` with respect to the real time.

The main observation is that for runs with limited activity, it is ensured that for moments with limited value of `now`, `now-simNow` is an infinitesimal, i.e., for such systems and moments, the moment at which an event takes place is at most an infinitesimal too late.

Figures 10.2 and 10.3 show an interleaving scheduler for systems with deadlines implementing the idea. We restrict ourselves to non-strict enabling times and deadlines.

Rule `infinitesimalDelayScheduler` is the scheduler: `now` is incremented invariably by `dt`. If an agent is urgent, a discrete step is done; otherwise, if there is an executable agent, the scheduler selects nondeterministically between a discrete step or a time step. If no agent is executable, a time step is done.

An agent is **urgent** in a state if the deadline is currently reached. The **executability** of an agent depends on enabling time and deadline. A **discrete step** is performed by selecting an executable agent, removing it from the set of agents, executing it, and ensuring that the simulation time stays the same. A **time step** is performed by either stepping with simNow to the next deadline, or by stepping to simNow+dt, whichever is earlier. Note that the set of deadlines from which the minimum is determined is, for standard deadlines and infinitesimal dt, a singleton. The nullary dynamic function lastScheduledAgent yields the agent which has been scheduled in the last step, or $\perp$ if the last step was a time step, or if there was no last step, i.e., it is initialized with $\perp$. Since agents are used just for one event, no agent occurs more than once as value of lastScheduledAgent in a run.

Theorem 10.3.1. *Any run of* infinitesimalDelayScheduler *which is started from a situation in which both* now *and* simNow *are zero fulfills the following properties:*

(1) now *is never smaller than* simNow*:*

$$[\text{simNow} \leq \text{now}]$$

(2) If in limited time, only a limited number of discrete steps are performed, the difference between simulated and real time is infinitesimal for limited real times:

$$\square(\text{limited}(dt * \ell) \to \text{limited}(\#(\text{lastScheduledAgent} \neq \perp)))$$
$$\to$$
$$[\text{limited}(\text{now}) \to \text{infinitesimal}(\text{now} - \text{simNow})]$$

(3) The scheduling obeys causal order in the sense that if agent a has a deadline which is smaller than the enabling time of agent b, then b is scheduled before a:

$$\forall(a, b : \text{Agent}) :$$
$$\quad \text{deadline}(a) < \text{enablingTime}(b)$$
$$\quad \to$$
$$\quad \neg\diamondsuit([\text{scheduledAgent} = b]; tt; [\text{scheduledAgent} = a])$$

Proof. (1) Use induction on the number of steps: Each step increments now by dt, and simNow by a value which is between zero and dt.

(2) We proceed in three steps (a), (b) and (c): (a) Consider a run of rule infinitesimalDelayScheduler and any position i of the run at which now is limited. The interval between the start of the run and position i is of limited time length (now is the time length, and is limited), and, thus, by the limited activity assumption, only a limited number of discrete steps have taken place up to position i. Let us call this limited number j. (b) By induction, it is clear that the difference now-simNow at any position k in the run is not larger than

```
infinitesimalDelayScheduler =def
  || now := now + dt
  || IF ∃(a:Agent):urgent(a)
     THEN doDiscreteStep
     ELIF ∃(a:Agent):executable(a)
     THEN OR doDiscreteStep
          OR doTimeStep
     ELSE doTimeStep

urgent(a) ⇔def
  simNow = deadline(a)

executable(a) ⇔def
  ∧ enablingTime(a) ≤ simNow
  ∧ simNow ≤ deadline(a)
```

Fig. 10.2. A scheduler for an interleaving NTASM model admitting infinitesimal delays; see Fig. 10.3 for definitions of the step rules.

```
doDiscreteStep =def
  CHOOSE (a:Agent):executable(a) IN
    || simNow := simNow
    || lastScheduledAgent := a
    || Agent(a) := false
    || OR IF rule(a)=r₁ THEN R_{r₁} ELSE HALT
       OR ...
       OR IF rule(a)=rₙ THEN R_{rₙ} ELSE HALT

doTimeStep =def
  || lastScheduledAgent := ⊥
  || IF (∃(a:Agent):deadline(a)<simNow+dt) THEN
        simNow := min {t | ∃(a:Agent):t=deadline(a)<simNow+dt}
     ELSE
        simNow := simNow+dt
```

Fig. 10.3. The step rules used in the scheduler of Fig. 10.2.

dt times the number of discrete steps which have taken place up to position k. (c) We put (a) and (b) together: For a limited j and an infinitesimal dt, $j * $dt is infinitesimal, which is an upper bound for the value of now-simNow by (b).

(3) Since enabling times and deadlines of events are compared to simNow, and simNow increases in a (weakly) monotone way, agent b will not be enabled before the deadline of agent a has passed.

The fact that there is only an infinitesimal difference between the time when an event takes place and the time when it should take place and the fact that we only consider strict enabling times and deadlines implies that the standard part of the time at which an event takes place fulfills the enabledness conditions:

Corollary 10.3.1. *Consider a run as in the precondition of Theorem 10.3.1. If the discrete step of an event agent takes place at a state with a limited value of* now, *the standard part of* now *is an element of the execution interval.*

Note that the result only holds for the standard part. now itself might be an infinitesimal too large.

10.4 Summary

Deadlines are an important modelling technique in quantitatively timed systems. In this chapter, we discuss two strategies for modelling deadlines in a system description: they can be dealt with **declaratively**, in which case a consistency argument is necessary, or they can be dealt with **operationally**, i.e., it can be built into the scheduler that deadlines have to be obeyed. Synchronous systems and interleaving systems pose different requirements on the way in which deadlines are expressed, where interleaving systems are more difficultly dealt with. One can choose a fairly simple approach if execution intervals are non-punctual. A more complicated approach is necessary if the timed algorithm admits punctual execution intervals; we present a method which is based on an infinitesimal difference between "real time" and "simulation time".

11. Open Systems

An application is modelled as an open system if the environment is not expressed explicitly in the model. Open systems are the paradigmatic case of reactive systems.

11.1 Receptivity Simplified

An important property of open systems is receptivity. In classical real-time formalisms, it is modelled as the possibility that time can become larger than any value, or put otherwise: That Zeno behavior can be avoided, even in adversarial environments.

If we just require a system to be non-Zeno, i.e., to admit that time diverges from any state, it is not ensured that a composition of two such systems is also non-Zeno, since the composition of two non-Zeno systems might be Zeno. The point is that for open systems, it is necessary to distinguish possible nondeterminism in the environment E and in the system S. While the nondeterminism in S is typically understood to be controlled, i.e., it is used to model freedom of behavior, the nondeterminism in E is typically understood to model missing knowledge about the environment, and is not understood to be controllable by the system. These two kinds of nondeterminism might be called "existential" and "universal" nondeterminism: There must **exist** a resolution of the controlled nondeterminism so that **for all** alternatives of the non-controlled nondeterminism, the specification is fulfilled. In order to ensure that S fulfills some specification, it can be assumed that the resolution of its internal nondeterminism can be controlled, while the resolution of the external nondeterminism, i.e., that of E, can only be reacted upon. This means that it is not enough that there exists a possible behavior of the combined system $S\|E$ so that time increases indefinitely; rather, there should **exist** a resolution of the system nondeterminism **for each** resolution of the environment nondeterminism so that time diverges, or possibly not if the environment can be blamed for the Zeno behavior of a resulting run.

A consequence of this is that receptivity of real-time systems can be formalized as a game between a system S and its environment E, in the following way [AH97]: In each step, S and E propose a move to some arbiter A. The arbiter charges the step to the component proposing the shorter move. In case of a tie, S is charged. A discrete move has length 0, a time move can have any non-negative length. If both S and E propose a discrete move, the arbiter performs their moves synchronously; if one proposes a time move and the other a discrete move, the arbiter just performs the discrete move; and if both components propose a time move, the arbiter performs a time move of a length which is the minimum of the lengths of the proposed moves. The goal of S is to let time increase for time 1, or to get charged only for a finite number of steps; the goal of the environment is the opposite. S is receptive if there is a strategy for S to win this game from every reachable state.

Note that this game-theoretical conceptualization expresses exactly the difference between the existential quantification of the non-determinism of the system and the universal quantification of the non-determinism of its environment.

Let us transfer the ideas to the NTASM framework. We assume that the whole system is composed synchronously from two rules R_S and R_E, where R_E includes the effect of the time rule, i.e., the whole system is modelled by a rule $R_S \| R_E$.

The "proposal" of some step in the classical framework is replaced just by the execution of an action, which might be equivalent to SKIP to model the "proposal" of an infinitesimal time step. The proposal of a discrete step is replaced by the execution of a step which is not equivalent to SKIP; and the proposal of a time step of some length is expressed by a sequence of infinitesimal time steps the lengths of which sum up to the proposed length. The number of moves charged to R_S in some interval is then simply the number of non-SKIP steps performed by R_S in the interval.

This approach means that we assume that the "strategy" the existence of which the classical game-theoretical definition requires for receptivity is already assumed to be implemented in the rule. If we want to use non-determinism of the system rule to model freedom of implementation, it should not be restricted by a receptivity requirement. Interpreting nondeterminism in a rule in this way, we have to require that each resolution of the non-determinism of R_S leads to an admissible system behavior.

Using these ideas, and replacing the finiteness requirement of the classical formulation by a limitedness requirement in the NTASM framework, we define:

Definition 11.1.1. *A rule R_S is* **receptive** *if in any limited span of time of any system behavior of some $R_S \| R_E$, where R_E includes the effect of a time rule, R_S is taken only a limited number of times non-vacuously; or as a formula:*

$[\text{takenAlone}(R_S \| R_E)]$

$\rightarrow$

$\Box(\text{limited}(dt * \ell) \rightarrow \text{limited}(\# \text{takenNonvacuously}(R_S)))$

Note that the receptivity definition has become far simpler than in the classical game-theoretical formulation. This can be traced back to one property of the NTASM framework and one interpretational decision:

- The uniform model of time makes it unnecessary to treat discrete steps and time steps of different lengths differently. The arbiter of the classical definition is not necessary any more.
- The decision to interpret the nondeterminism of the system as freedom of implementation which should not be restricted by the receptivity requirements obviates the need to distinguish between existential and universal occurrences of nondeterminism.

The most important consequence of the receptivity definition is that synchronous composition of two receptive rules yields a receptive rule:

Proposition 11.1.1. *Let R_1 and R_2 be compatible receptive rules. Then also $R_1 \| R_2$ is a receptive rule.*

Proof. No matter what the environment of R_1 does: in a limited interval of time, R_1 is taken non-vacuously only a limited number of times. The same is true for R_2. The number of non-vacuous steps of $R_1 \| R_2$ in an interval is bounded from above by the sum of the non-vacuous steps of R_1 and R_2 in the interval. The sum of two limited numbers is limited, and a natural number bounded by a limited number is limited; thus, also $R_1 \| R_2$ performs only a limited number of non-vacuous steps in a limited interval.

11.2 (m,n)-Receptivity

The receptivity concept described in Definition 11.1.1 is a strict requirement on a receptive rule: No matter how wildly the environment acts, a receptive rule must behave orderly. In specifications of open systems which use the assume/guarantee scheme [FP78, AL95], a system may start to behave disorderly if its environment previously started to do so. Thus, the system is not required to behave orderly under all conditions: The exception is if the environment can be blamed for the disorder of the system behavior.

In order for this freedom to be usable, the system must be able to notice if the assumptions are fulfilled by the environment. In the formalism used by Abadi and Lamport [AL95], this can be expressed by looking at the safety part of the assumption: remember that a safety property is defined so that if it is not fulfilled by a system behavior, then there is a first moment at which this can be noticed. The liveness part of the assumption can not be used, since a liveness property is one which can always be fulfilled by some future behavior, no matter what has happened up to now, i.e., the system can not decide, based on the finite prefix of a system behavior known up to some moment, if the environment will fulfill the liveness assumption or not. Because of this, Abadi and Lamport use the safety closure of the assumption as the effective assumption in an assumption/guarantee paradigm.

While each classical property can be defined as conjunction of a safety property and a liveness property, as proved by Alpern and Schneider [AS85], for non-classical "properties" (which are not necessarily properties, in the sense that non-classical predicates on system behaviors do not necessarily define sets of system behaviors) this is not necessarily true; more specifically, the property that a rule shows unlimited activity in a system behavior is not a safety property (there is no first moment at which it is clear that the condition can not be fulfilled: If there was unlimited activity of rule R in a prefix of a system behavior up to position n, then this was already true at position $n - 1$), even though it is equal to its safety closure (if in each finite prefix of a system behavior, rule R shows only limited activity, then this is also true in the whole system behavior).

Thus, we can not use the safety closure of the assumption on the environment to decide when the system is not bound any more to its guarantee, since there is no first moment at which the system can detect that the environment does not hold its promise of limited activity. Thus, in order to use the extra freedom which is allowed by an assumption/guarantee principle, we will construct a (true) safety property which implies limited activity, but which is stronger.

The idea which we use is the following: Instead of assuming limited activity, we use the stronger assumption of bounded activity in unit intervals of time. We define bounded activity in the following way:

Definition 11.2.1. *We say that a rule R shows* **bounded activity with bound** $n \in \mathbb{N}_0$*, as formula:* $\mathrm{ba}(R, n)$*, if and only if:*

$$\Box((dt * \ell \leq 1) \rightarrow (\# \operatorname{takenNonvacuously}(R) \leq n))$$

Bounded activity with a fixed bound is a safety property: in each moment, it can be checked if rule R has already been taken n times, and if this is the case, it can be checked if since the earliest of the last n events, more than one time unit has passed.

Bounded activity might even be a more adequate formalization of a requirement for an implementable system than finite activity: A system which performs n discrete transitions in each time interval from n to $n + 1$ (for $n \in \mathbb{N}_0$) shows finite activity, but since there is no bound for the number of discrete transitions in intervals of length 1, such a system is not implementable. This makes it plausible to use bounded activity with limited bounds rather than just limited activity as a criterion for implementability. Note the similarity of the relation between limited activity and activity with limited bounds for timed systems to the relation between continuity and uniform continuity in analysis. In both relations, the existence quantifier describing admissible changes occurs once behind the universal quantifier describing positions in a system development, allowing the change parameter to depend on the position, and occurs the second time in front of the universal position quantifier, requiring that the same change parameter is valid for all positions considered.

For standard n, bounded activity is a stronger property than limited activity:

Proposition 11.2.1. *For standard n, $ba(R, n)$ implies $la(R)$.*

Proof. In an interval of length l, at most $n * \lceil l \rceil$ non-vacuous R-steps take place, which is a limited number for limited n and l.

Using the concept of bounded activity, we can define (m, n)-receptivity of a rule R like this:

Definition 11.2.2. *A rule R_S is (m, n)-receptive (for some $m, n \in \mathbb{N}_0$) if the following formula holds for all rules R_E compatible with R_S:*

$$\Box\left((\text{takenAlone}(R_S\|R_E) \wedge ba(R_E, m)) \rightarrow ba(R_S, n)\right)$$

The definition implies that an (m, n)-receptive rule may "go wild", i.e., may perform more than n discrete steps per unit of time, as soon as its environment has shown discrete activity which is not bounded by m per unit of time.

A rule which admits more activity from the environment or guarantees a tighter bound for its own activity fulfills also the less strict conditions:

Proposition 11.2.2. *If a rule R is (m, n)-receptive and $m' \leq m$ and $n \leq n'$, then R is also (m', n')-receptive.*

Proof. $m' \leq m$ implies that an (m, n)-receptive rule assumes not more than an (m', n)-receptive rule about the environment, and $n \leq n'$ implies that an (m, n)-receptive rule guarantees not less than an (m, n')-receptive rule. Thus, the concept of (m, n)-receptivity is not weaker than that of (m', n')-receptivity.

We now consider the synchronous composition of two rules R_1 and R_2:

Proposition 11.2.3. *Consider an (m_1, n_1)-receptive rule R_1 and an (m_2, n_2)-receptive rule R_2, with $m_1 \geq n_2$ and $m_2 \geq n_1$. Then $R_1\|R_2$ is $(\min(m_1 - n_2, m_2 - n_1), n1 + n2)$-receptive.*

Proof. In unit time, R_1 will at most perform n_1 discrete transitions, if its environment performs at most m_1 discrete transitions. $m_1 \geq n_2$ implies that as far as R_1 is concerned, the environment of $R_1\|R_2$ might do at most $m_1 - n_2$ discrete steps per unit time before R_1 may start "going wild". For R_2, this number is $m_2 - n_1$. If the environment of $R_1\|R_2$ performs not more discrete transitions in unit time than are given by these two bounds, R_1 and R_2 fulfill their guarantees, which in the worst case means that their discrete steps never fall together, and in this case at most $n_1 + n_2$ steps are performed in unit time. Thus, if the environment of $R_1\|R_2$ is guaranteed to do at most $\min(m_1 - n_2, m_2 - n_1)$ discrete steps in any unit time interval, then $R_1\|R_2$ will do not more than $n_1 + n_2$ steps in a unit time interval, which means that $R_1\|R_2$ is $(\min(m_1 - n_2, m_2 - n_1), n_1 + n_2)$-receptive.

11.3 Summary

Open systems pose special problems to designers of real-time systems. The concept of receptivity has been developed in order to come to grips with one of the most important of these problems: That composition might lead to systems which do not fulfill basic acceptability conditions, even though the components fulfill them. In order to avoid this, acceptability requirements have to be made sharper. Non-Zenoness does not suffice any longer, the stronger concept of receptivity is needed. We demonstrated that in our non-standard context, receptivity can be extremely simply formulated, but the use of the idea in the classical way is not possible, which is why we develop the concept of (m, n)-receptivity.

12. Making Use of Different Magnitudes of Reals

Consider the following scenario: A flip-flop is wired up so that with every rising edge of the clock, it changes its state. Modelling time using the real numbers and voltage levels using the numbers zero and one, we assume that the clock line changes its value from 0 to 1 at every even number, and from 1 to 0 at every odd number, and the specification for the flip flop is that there is an infinitesimal ϵ so that the output of the flip flop changes from x to $1 - x$ from time n to $n + \epsilon$ for $n \in \mathbb{N}$ and stays constant from $n + \epsilon$ to $n + 1$, where the ϵ allows for the reaction time of the flip flop. The implementation for this specification would be a set of interconnected digital gates with their associated timings. The timings would naturally be expressed by infinitesimals, which expresses that we assume that the gates react very quickly in comparison to the clock changes of the flip flop. In this context, it would be convenient to assign different infinitesimals as timings to different gates, or even to be unspecific about the exact timing values, which would express that we do not know the relative speeds of the circuits, but only that they are all far quicker than the global clock.

While at first sight, a constant infinitesimal step width for the time might seem to make such models difficult, this is not the case. It is natural to assume that the timings of all the gates, while infinitesimal, belong to the same magnitude, and that their differences are either exactly zero or again of the same magnitude, because we can use just standard real numbers for expressing the timings, scaled by some freely chosen real number, where the latter is typically an infinitesimal. The only inconvenience using this approach is that the possible non-determinism with respect to the timings of different gates must be made explicit and can not stay implicit as with other strategies in which non-determinism is the default.

Using non-standard means, the concept "x and y belong to the same magnitude" can be formalized as "$\frac{x}{y}$ is defined and is neither infinitesimal nor unlimited", or (equivalently) as "there are standard $m, n \in \mathbb{N}$ such that $m * |x| > |y|$ and $n * |y| > |x|$".

In this case, we take as infinitesimal step width an infinitesimal which is smaller in magnitude than the timings of the gates; the error introduced by this discretization is smaller in magnitude than the timings.

This idea is described in some detail in this section. As a first illustrating example, we use a hierarchical model of a counter.

12.1 The Magnitude Concept

Definition 12.1.1. *Two real numbers x and y belong to the same* **magnitude,** *which we abbreviate as $x \sim y$, if $\frac{x}{y}$ is defined and appreciable.*

The definition implies that neither x nor y may be zero. Understood as a relation on non-zero numbers, magnitude is obviously symmetric, transitive and reflexive, which means that is an equivalence relation. For simplicity, we also call the induced equivalence classes magnitudes. Note that zero does not belong to a magnitude by this definition (which is a technical decision), and note that they are not sets – the use of the "standard" predicate in their definition is essential. For example, the magnitude to which the number 1 belongs are just the appreciable numbers.

We make some simple consequences from the definition explicit:

Scaling a number by a non-zero standard number does not change its magnitude, and after both of a pair of numbers of the same magnitudes are scaled by the same non-zero number, the results are again of the same magnitude:

Proposition 12.1.1. *For $y \in \mathbb{R}$ and standard non-zero $x \in \mathbb{R}$, we have $y \sim x * y$.*

For $x, y, z \in \mathbb{R}$ with $y \sim z$, $x \neq 0$, we have $x * y \sim x * z$.

The following proposition is important for the case that a system is designed using a standard number of standard timing constants and is, as a whole, scaled to some other magnitude. In some cases, derived timing behavior can be described by values computed by via linear combination of design timing with standard factors; the following proposition is applicable.

Proposition 12.1.2. *Let C' denote a class containing only standard non-zero real numbers, and let C be defined by $x \in C \leftrightarrow \exists (x' \in C') : x = x' * a$ for some fixed non-zero $a \in \mathbb{R}$, i.e., all elements of C are scaled by the same (not necessarily standard) a. Then for any y which can be constructed as a linear combination from elements of C with standard factors and with a standard number of summands, we have $y = 0 \vee \forall (z \in C) : y \sim z$.*

The proposition tells us that under some plausible assumptions on design constants of a system, a linear combination of such values will either be equal to zero or belong to the same magnitude as the timing constants.

Proof. All standard values but zero belong to the same magnitude. This implies that also the scaled elements in C all belong to the same magnitude. Considering the multiplications in the linear combination, note that multiplying a number by a standard number does not change its magnitude, or it yields zero. In our case, the product can also be expressed as the scaling factor a times a standard number. The sum of a standard number of such elements can be expressed, by factoring out a, as the product of a and the sum of a standard number of standard numbers, which means that it can be written as the product of a and a standard number. If the latter number is not zero, the product is of the same magnitude as the originally scaled numbers, since it is a standard number scaled by the same a as used for scaling the original elements.

We define an order $<$ between magnitudes (understood as equivalence classes) via the normal order $<$ of absolute values of their representatives.

Proposition 12.1.3. *With respect to the magnitude order $<$, the collection of magnitudes is dense and unbounded.*

Proof. **Denseness:** Take two positive Representatives of two different magnitudes, and call the smaller one x and the larger one y. Consider $z = \sqrt{x * y}$. It is a standard result that z is located between x and y. We will prove that both $\frac{z}{x}$ and $\frac{y}{z}$ are unlimited, which implies that the magnitude to which z belongs lies between those of x and y.

Since x and y belong to different magnitudes, $\frac{y}{x}$ is unlimited; this implies (use contradiction) that also $\sqrt{\frac{y}{x}}$ is unlimited.

Since $\frac{z}{x} = \frac{\sqrt{x*y}}{x} = \frac{\sqrt{y}}{\sqrt{x}}$, where the latter is unlimited, z belongs to a strictly larger magnitude than x. And since $\frac{y}{z} = \frac{y}{\sqrt{x*y}} = \frac{\sqrt{y}}{\sqrt{x}}$, y belongs to a strictly larger magnitude than z.

Unboundedness: For any unlimited number u and for nonzero x, $u * x$ obviously belongs to a strictly larger magnitude than x, and $\frac{x}{u}$ obviously belongs to a strictly smaller magnitude than x.

Proposition 12.1.3 has convenient consequences for our ability to choose different time scales for describing phenomena of timed systems, since given any system in the description of which a standard finite number of time scales is used, if a time scale is needed which is larger or smaller than all already employed, or which lies between any two already used, we are assured that such a time scale exists.

The following proposition encapsulates the insight that the truth of a strict relation between two numbers does not depend on errors which are smaller than the magnitude of the difference of the numbers:

Proposition 12.1.4. *Consider two numbers x and y with $x > y$. Then, adding any number smaller in magnitude than $x - y$ to either x or y does not change the relation.*

This is a trivial corollary of the fact that in order to change the truth value of $x > y$ by addition of a number z to one summand, the absolute value of z must be at least $x - y$.

12.2 Rule Schemes and the Ripple Counter Example

For the description of systems with a repetitive structure, it is convenient to allow rule schemes. They allow multiple invocations of similar rules working just with different locations. Rule schemes are rules with formal parameters for values and locations. Such a rule scheme sometimes can make good use of non-parameter locations which should be local to itself. We use the keyword "LOCAL" to introduce function symbols which are understood to be interpreted as different functions for different instantiations of the rule scheme. Additionally, we will use function schemes, i.e., symbols which get terms, not values as their arguments and can build other terms out of them.

```
Counter  =def
  IF falling_clock_edge
  THEN value := (value + 1) mod 16
  ELSE SKIP
```

Fig. 12.1. Rule describing a 4-bit counter.

As an example, consider a model of a 4-bit counter which performs one step when the clock has a falling edge. On a high abstraction level, we can express such a counter with the rule in Fig. 12.1.

```
JKFF(J, K, T, Q)  =def
  LOCAL risingT_J, risingT_K
  IF rising_edge(T)
  THEN || risingT_J := J
       || risingT_K := K
  ELIF falling_edge(T)
  THEN IF risingT_J = 1 AND risingT_K = 1
       THEN Q := 1-Q
       ELIF risingT_J != risingT_K
       THEN Q := risingT_J
       ELSE SKIP
  ELSE SKIP
```

Fig. 12.2. A rule modelling a JK-master-slave flipflop.

We construct such a counter as a four bit ripple counter consisting of four JK master slave flip flops. Let us first describe the function of such a circuit. If the data inputs J and K of such a flip flop are both set to 1 during a rising edge of the clock, the circuit changes its output Q on the following falling edge of the clock input T. If the data inputs are both zero, the flip flop does not change its state; and if the data inputs differ, the output assumes the values of input J on the falling edge of the clock. A high level model of such a circuit is the rule scheme given in Fig. 12.2. The expressions with the symbols rising_edge and falling_edge are assumed to yield "true" if the respective signal change has been detected for the argument symbol. Thus, the symbols can not just represent functions (since not only the current value of T is relevant for the value of the expression, and the current value would be the only value available to a proper ASM function); we assume that they represent function schemes and we assume that such function schemes can be defined so that they yield the expected results for their arguments.

The local symbols `risingT_J` and `risingT_K` are used to record the values of the input during rising edges of the clock which have to be known on the next falling edge of clock. T, Q, J and K are formal parameters for the clock, the output and the two data inputs of the circuit.

Using the JK flip flop rule scheme, we can put together a ripple counter scheme and instantiate it in the manner described in Fig. 12.3. The scheme describes how the output of one flip flop is wired up with the clock input of the other, as is characteristic of a ripple counter, and that the data inputs are set to one; the last line is an instantiation of the scheme which uses nullary symbols whose values represent the current clock and the current values of the four flip flops.

```
RippleCounter(T, Q0, Q1, Q2, Q3) =def
   || JKFF(1, 1, T, Q0)
   || JKFF(1, 1, Q0, Q1)
   || JKFF(1, 1, Q1, Q2)
   || JKFF(1, 1, Q2, Q3)

RippleCounter(clock,q0,q1,q2,q3)
```

Fig. 12.3. A model of a ripple counter.

In which sense can the ripple counter scheme be considered an implementation of the high level counter scheme? We have to deal with several problems, disregarding initialization: (1) We have to relate values of the low level `falling_edge(clock)` predicate and the high level `falling_clock_edge` predicate. (2) The `value` of the high level counter has to be mapped somehow to the four q-parameters of the ripple counter instantiation. (3) We have to allow for the fact that one incrementation step of the high-level counter might be expressed by several steps of the ripple counter: from a situation in which all q-values are 1 and a falling edge is detected, it takes not just one but four dt-steps until the highest bit has switched to 0.

Problem (1) is solved by just assuming that the low-level predicate and the high level predicate are true exactly when a falling edge of the clock edge is detected.

The first step to the solution of problem (2) is an abstraction function which computes the `value` of the high-level rule as 8*q3+4*q2+2*q1+q0, to be interpreted in corresponding states of the low-level rule. This abstraction function is only a first step, since during "ripples", i.e., when a carry occurs for some bit(s) of the counter, the low level ASM goes through extra values (as described in problem (3)): where the high-level run has a transition from value 15 to value 0, the latter value being stable up to the next falling clock edge, the low level run has (using the order q3,q2,q1,q0 for the bits) 1111->1110->1100->1000->0000 (but only if no other falling clock edge is detected), where the last value is also stable up to the next falling clock edge. If one or more other falling clock edges intervene, such a sequence might also look like 1111->1110->1101->1001->0001 (and there are many other possibilities, depending on the moments of further falling edges of clock).

We might deal with this problem by assuming that changes of the clock are separated by time intervals of a larger magnitude than the reaction time of the flip flop; this is a natural abstraction as long as the reaction time of the circuits driven by a clock is negligible in comparison to the clock cycle, which exactly means that we can disregard the working times of some circuit. In this case, no other falling clock edge can happen during the ripple phase of the counter (as long as it has standard finite length). Thus, the only possible value sequence is 1111->1110->1100->1000->0000.

But also if no falling clock edge intervenes during a ripple phase of the counter, we have the problem that the ripple counter goes through the values 14, 12 and 8 before it reaches the zero during a ripple phase of maximal length (and through a shorter sequence of intermediate values in some other cases). A circuit using the output of the counter as input might malfunction because of this; but when? Here again, time scale considerations can help. We associate a reaction time with the inputs of a circuit: Single changes on an input line are only noticed by the circuit after the line has stabilized for some time; this is a plausible abstraction, as long as the input does not change its value often during such a reaction time phase. If the reaction time of the circuit which uses the output of the counter as input is of a larger scale than the flip flop reaction time, the ripple phase would not hurt, since this phase would, because of its short duration (a standard finite multiple of the flip flop reaction time), not be noticed. And if the reaction time plus the working time of the circuit reading the output of the ripple counter is, at the same time, of a smaller scale than the clock cycle, this ensures that it has enough time to compute its result before the counter value changes again.

12.3 Making Delays Explicit

A problem of the ripple counter implementation of the high level counter is its dependence on the step width dt. If another step width is chosen, the timing does not only change because of the different discretization of some timing constants. This results from the fact that the timing of the flip flop is not modelled explicitly – the flip flop model assumes that after a falling edge on the clock input, it takes just time dt until the output is updated.

The timing might be modelled explicitly in different ways. One strategy which is common in hardware languages is to split the behavior of a circuit into a logical and a timing part. E.g., a NAND which changes its output only after some delay after an input has changed is modelled by the serial connection of an instantaneously working NAND and a circuit only representing the delay.

Hardware description languages commonly allow the expression of several forms of delay mechanisms. Two common ones are inertial delay and transport delay. The specific semantics differ for different formalizations, but the basic idea is that a change at the input of an inertial delay circuit cancels a change event for the output which has been scheduled but not yet performed, while for transport delay, no such cancellation takes place.

To be specific, we describe the two forms of delay by two rule schemes with formal parameters for the input signal, the delay time and the output signal, both with two local symbols: one for detecting changes of the input signal, and one for recording information for one (InertialDelay) or several (TransportDelay) scheduled changes. Fig. 12.4 gives rules implementing these forms of delay.

```
InertialDelay(In, Delay, Out) =def
  LOCAL old_In, next_change_time
  || old_In := In
  || IF old_In ≠ In
     THEN next_change_time := now+Delay
     ELIF now ≥ next_change_time
     THEN next_change_time := ∞
     ELSE SKIP
  || IF now ≥ next_change_time
     THEN Out := old_In
     ELSE SKIP

TransportDelay(In, Delay, Out) =def
  LOCAL old_In, change
  || old_In := In
  || IF old_In ≠ In
     THEN change(In, now+Delay) := true
     ELSE SKIP
  || IF ∃(s,t : change(s,t) AND t ≤now)
     THEN CHOOSE s,t : change(s,t) AND t ≤now IN
             Out := s
             change(s,t) := false
     ELSE SKIP
```

Fig. 12.4. Rule schemes expressing two forms of delay.

Let us first consider rule scheme InertialDelay. It has three synchronous branches: The first just records the current value of the input so that in the next cycle, an input signal change can be detected. The second updates the internal information about scheduled changes; and the third performs an update if its time has come. Rule scheme TransportDelay is similar, but here, the update of the internal data structure representing scheduled updates is performed in the third branch for those changes which have just been performed. Note that in the third synchronous branch of `TransportDelay`, if there exists a pair of values s and t as in the condition, there is just one such pair, which is then chosen and processed in the `THEN` branch.

The important point about an inertial delay is that at its output, pulses are never shorter than the delay time:

Proposition 12.3.1. *Consider a location l which is written at most by an instantiation of rule scheme `InertialDelay`. Then, between value changes of l, at least the delay time of the instantiation passes.*

Proof. Consider a system with an instantiation of `InertialDelay` so that the output location l of that instantiation is not written by any other rule. Consider any run q of this system and a position $i \in \mathbb{N}, i > 0$ with a value change at l, i.e., a position which fulfills $q(i)(l) \neq q(i-1)(l)$.

We use an induction to prove an invariant for the value of `next_change_time`:

Claimed invariant. From position i on, the value of the symbol `next_change_time` local to the rule scheme instantiation considered will never be smaller than $t = q(i-1)(\text{now+Delay}) = (i-1) * dt + Delay$.

Induction start. For position i, inspection of the rule scheme shows that the occurrence of an update of location l at position i in the run implies that at that position, the value of the symbol `next_change_time` local to the rule scheme instantiation considered must either be ∞ (if no input change has just been detected at position $i-1$ in the run) or t (as defined above, if an input change has been detected at position $i-1$). It can not be smaller.

Induction step. For a position $j > i$, either the value of `next_change_time` did not change in the last step (which implies the claim because of the induction assumption), or it has just been set to $(j-1) * dt + Delay$ because of a detection of an input change, which is larger than t because of $j > i$.

The first moment at which the value of the output location might change is dt after the first moment when $\text{now} \geq t$ holds. Let us call the position at which that condition is fulfilled $j - 1$, so that j is the position of the first possible change after that at position i. We see that the condition $\text{now} \geq t$ at that moment means $(j-1) * dt \geq (i-1) * dt + \text{Delay}$; adding dt on both sides, we see that $j * dt$, which is the moment of the first possible change after that of $i * dt$, comes at least by `Delay` later than $i * dt$.

As long as the time interval between changes of the inputs is always longer than the delay time, both delay rules are equivalent. They only differ if during the propagation time for one signal change, the input signal changes anew. For `InertialDelay`, the propagation of the earlier signal change is canceled;

for `TransportDelay`, each signal change of the input is replayed after the delay (plus a discretization error) on the output.

Let us assume that the delay behavior of a JK flip flop with timing constant D (for the delay from the falling edge of the clock input to the update of the output) is well expressed as an inertial delay. Then we can describe a JK flip flop with explicit timing as in Fig. 12.5

```
JKFF_D(J,K,T,D,Q)  =def
  LOCAL internal_Q
  || JKFF(J, K, T, internal_Q)
  || InertialDelay(internal_Q, D, Q)
```

Fig. 12.5. A JK-master-slave flipflop with explicit delay.

If a ripple counter is implemented with instances of the rule scheme JKFF_D, the appropriateness of the implementation of the high level counter depends on the relative timing of distances of falling edges of the global clock and the delay time of the flip flop. The common assumption that the delay time of the flip flop is negligible with respect to the clock cycle can be expressed formally by the assumption that the delay time is of a smaller magnitude than the clock cycle; and since we can assume that the step width dt of the underlying non-standard time model is of a smaller scale than the delay time, we ensure that discretization errors are very small in comparison to the delay time.

12.4 Analyzing a Logical Circuit for Hazards

Another timing-related problem of digital circuits are hazards. Hazards are short-term changes of an output of a circuit after changes of the inputs resulting from gate delays. As a simple example, consider a circuit computing the logical function q := (x AND y) OR (z AND NOT y) from the inputs x, y and z. Such a circuit can be implemented from two AND gates, a NOT gate and an OR gate as given in Fig. 12.6.

Assuming that all gates react with the same inertial delay of τ (for simplicity assumed to be a multiple of dt) on input changes, we can express this circuit by the instantiation of the rule scheme `HazardCircuit` given at the end of the set of ASM definitions in Fig. 12.7.

The definition and use of rule scheme `UpdateIfChanged` expresses the modelling decision that the logical gates are not assumed to perform any work if the next value they compute is equal to the current value of the output wire. Otherwise, the system would show unlimited activity in these components, since in each step, an update would be generated. Another approach dealing with this problem would have been to ignore the locations updated by the gates when it is determined if the system shows finite or infinite activity.

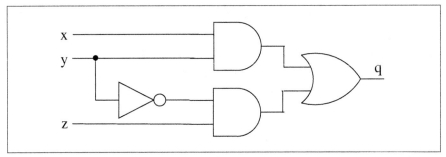

Fig. 12.6. A circuit leading to a hazard in some situations.

We will now analyze the system and detect a possible hazard. Let us consider the following situation: The inputs x, y, z are all set to 1, and we wait until the system has stabilized (there is no feedback and there are no active components, so it will stabilize in finite time). The output of the first AND gate is 1; the outputs of the NOT gate and of the second AND gate are 0; and the output of the OR gate is 1.

In a run starting from this situation, the system stays stable as long as none of the inputs change, which implies that the output stays at 1. Now consider that input y changes from 1 to 0 and let the first moment with the new value of y be at time t. The logic formula for our system shows that the output should not change in this case. But in fact, a negative pulse of width τ, a hazard, will occur at the output; let us first look at this in a rough manner, disregarding the infinitesimal step widths which might lead to infinitesimal errors:

1. At time t, the change of y leads to changes of the outputs of the first AND and of the NOT being scheduled for time $t + \tau + dt$.
2. Around time $t + \tau$, the change of y has propagated through the first AND (making its output 0) and through the NOT, but not yet through the second AND or the OR gate; but in this moment, both inputs of the OR gate are zero, and, thus, a change of the output of the circuit from 1 to 0 is scheduled; and both inputs of the second AND gate are 0, so a change of its output from 0 to 1 is scheduled.
3. Around time $t + 2*\tau$, both scheduled changes become effective: q becomes 0, and the second input of the OR gate becomes 1 again, leading to another change of the output being scheduled.
4. Around time $t + 3 * \tau$, the scheduled change of q is performed, and the system becomes stable again.

This analysis is not exact because it disregards the following facts about our model:

– When a change of the input of a gate with explicit timing takes place, first the untimed ("instantaneous") version of the gate computes its output, which needs time dt.

```
UpdateIfChanged(loc, newVal) =def
  IF loc ≠ newVal
  THEN loc := newVal
  ELSE SKIP
AND(X,Y,Q) =def
  UpdateIfChanged(Q, min(X,Y))
OR(X,Y,Q) =def
  UpdateIfChanged(Q, max(X,Y))
NOT(X,Q) =def
  UpdateIfChanged(Q, 1-X)

AND_D(X,Y,D,Q) =def
  LOCAL internal_Q
  || AND(X, Y, internal_Q)
  || InertialDelay(internal_Q, D, Q)
OR_D(X,Y,D,Q) =def
  LOCAL internal_Q
  || OR(X, Y, internal_Q)
  || InertialDelay(internal_Q, D, Q)
NOT_D(X,D,Q) =def
  LOCAL internal_Q
  || NOT(X, internal_Q)
  || InertialDelay(internal_Q, D, Q)

HazardCircuit(X,Y,Z,Q) =def
  LOCAL neg_Y, O1, O2
  || NOT_D(Y, τ, neg_Y)
  || AND_D(X, Y, τ, O1)
  || AND_D(neg_Y, Z, τ, O2)
  || OR_D(O1, O2, τ, Q)

HazardCircuit(x,y,z,q)
```

Fig. 12.7. Model of a circuit illustrating a hazard.

– When a change of the output of the untimed gate is detected at its input by the delay rule, its output only changes after $\lceil \frac{\tau}{dt} \rceil * dt$ time units.

Altogether, a change at an input of a timed circuit can only lead to a change at its output (if at all) after time $\tau + dt$. Since we assume that the time delay τ is of a larger magnitude than dt, this difference can be ignored in most cases. In our specific case, this might just lead to the hazard being an infinitesimal of magnitude dt being shifted or longer than expected.

The following section discusses conditions under which such tedious cycle-counting as just performed is not necessary.

12.5 Modelling Missing Knowledge Explicitly

Let us consider another variant of the timing problem for digital circuits. Mandrioli[1] points out that the assumption of a constant infinitesimal step width for the work of system components yields a high degree of synchronicity which might be inappropriate in some cases. He specifically mentions models of electronic circuits in which gate delays and other signal propagation times can depend on many factors not modelled explicitly.

As an example for such a case, we consider a situation in which under synchronous execution, no hazards can occur, while under more realistic assumptions about our knowledge about relative signal propagation times of system components, the occurrence of hazards can not be excluded.

Consider again the circuit of Fig. 12.6, but consider now a stable situation resulting from the inputs x=1, y=0 and z=1 and a change of y to 1. Under a synchronous interpretation (or under an interpretation in which all gate delays are identical), no hazard occurs since the output of the first AND gate becomes 1 in this case before the output of the second AND turns to 0; thus, there is always at least one input of the OR gate equal to 1, which means that the output of the OR stays 1 all the time.

But now consider the case in which the first AND takes longer to compute its result than the NOT and the second AND combined. In this case, the output of the first AND turns to 1 only after the output of the second AND has turned to 0, which means that there is some time in which both inputs of the OR gate are zero. If this time is longer than the inertial delay modelling the gate delay of the OR gate, a hazard will occur at its output.

This discrepancy can be resolved by making explicit in our model that knowledge is missing about the relative gate delays of the gates. Firstly, this means that we have to use gate models with explicit timing; and secondly, we have to express that the delays might be different for the different gates. For this case, an NTASM model of the circuit might look like in Fig. 12.8.

```
IndependentDelaysHazardCircuit(X,Y,Z,Q,T1,T2,T3,T4)  =def
  LOCAL neg_Y, O1, O2
  || NOT_D(Y, T1, neg_Y)
  || AND_D(X, Y, T2, O1)
  || AND_D(neg_Y, Z, T3, O2)
  || OR_D(O1, O2, T4, Q)

IndependentDelaysHazardCircuit(x,y,z,q,$\tau_1$,$\tau_2$,$\tau_3$,$\tau_4$)
```

Fig. 12.8. A circuit illustrating a hazard, where speeds of components are independent from each other.

---

[1] Personal communication.

Here, we make explicit that the delay times of the gates might be different; further declarative restrictions on the different τ_i might be used to express knowledge about relative timings of the gates which we might possibly have.

Note that this description might seem unnecessarily wordy in comparison to models using formalisms in which nondeterminism can be implicit; this is just the price we have to pay for explicit nondeterminism.

Let us analyze in more detail a condition under which hazards can not occur in the system above if only a single input bit changes. This will illustrate an example of the case where we do not have to count each cycle in order to avoid errors.

Proposition 12.5.1. *Consider   the   instantiated   rule   scheme* `IndependentDelaysHazardCircuit`$(x,y,z,q,\tau_1,\tau_2,\tau_3,\tau_4)$, *where the τ_i result from standard real numbers scaled by some arbitrary non-zero real number, and the step width dt is assumed to be of a smaller magnitude than the τ_i.*

If τ_4 is larger than the absolute value of $\tau_1 + \tau_3 - \tau_2$, hazards resulting from single input bit changes of that circuit can not occur.

Proof. From the inputs to the output of the circuit, four different paths are possible, one from the x, two from the y and one from the z. We only look for hazards occurring from changes of a single input bit when the system is in a stable state. If the x or the z input changes, the change will propagate along its only path until it either stops being propagated at some gate or it reaches the output q; this depends on the rest of the system, but is not relevant for hazard generation. Thus, only with changes of y, from where two paths lead to the output, hazards can happen.

If some of the single-path inputs x and z are zero during the change of y, propagation of the y-signal change along the paths which are common with the zero-inputs is blocked at the AND gates, i.e., in this case, at most one, and possibly none, of the inputs of the OR gate changes because of the signal change. In these cases, no hazard can occur. Thus, we only have to deal with the case that x and z are both one, since only in this case, two changes can in general occur at inputs of the OR gate.

Note that in both steady states which are left to be considered, one input of the OR gate is zero and the other is one. The accumulated signal propagation times from y to the inputs of the OR gate are τ_2 for the upper path and $\tau_1 + \tau_3$ for the lower path. If the absolute value of the difference between them is smaller than τ_4, there is no problem, because the inertial delay of the OR gate will buffer possible effects of the first signal change away.

This almost closes the argument; it only rests to be shown why it does not invalidate our argument that we disregarded the infinitesimal errors induced by our discretization of time. For this, we apply Proposition 12.1.2 to the τ_i, which fulfill the requirements of the proposition. The proposition implies that $\tau_4 - |\tau_1 + \tau_3 - \tau_2|$ is either zero or of the same magnitude as the τ_i. Under the condition that it is positive (which is the condition considered in the proposition), this means that the difference is of a larger magnitude than *dt*. Applying Proposition 12.1.4, we see that additive errors of magnitude *dt* during the computation of the propagation times will not invalidate the argument.

Arguments like the above about the possibility of ignoring errors of sufficiently small magnitude are only valid if (1) we use strict comparisons of quantities, (2) errors are additive, and (3) we know that the absolute value of the difference of the quantities compared is larger in magnitude than the error; or in short, if the conditions of Proposition 12.1.4 are fulfilled.

12.6 Hazards Resulting
from the Infinitesimal Discretization

Consider the circuit of Fig. 12.6 again and an NTASM model for it using untimed gates instead of the timed gates used earlier, as in Fig. 12.9. Considering the initial configuration corresponding to that of the case considered earlier and a change of y from 1 to 0, we see that after time *dt*, the output of the first AND changes from 1 to 0 and that of the NOT from 0 to 1. After time $2 * dt$ the second AND has changed from 0 to 1 and the OR from 1 to 0, resulting in the start of the hazard. After time $3 * dt$ the output of the OR changes again, finishing the hazard and leading to the new stable state. Thus, similar to the case considered before, we have a hazard at q, but this time it is only of length *dt*.

Can infinitesimal hazards like this also happen in circuits in which timing is handled explicitly? This would be an inconvenient counter-intuitive consequence of our model of time which would make it difficult to express refinement of a more complex untimed circuit (e.g., one computing the function q := (x AND y) OR (z AND NOT y) directly) into components.

Note that also semantical approaches for gates not using discretized time but "real" zero-time steps have analoguos problems, in which the output waveform resulting from a simulation might depend on the order of schedulings chosen for the gate activities, possibly resulting in zero-time hazards – so, this problem is not specific to our model of time. In hardware simulation languages based on a classical model of time, this problem is sometimes dealt with by not propagating any output signal changes until the system stabilizes.

```
UntimedHazardCircuit(X,Y,Z,Q)  =def
  LOCAL neg_Y, O1, O2
  || NOT(Y, neg_Y)
  || AND(X, Y, O1)
  || AND(neg_Y, Z, O2)
  || OR(O1, O2, Q)

UntimedHazardCircuit(x,y,z,q)
```

Fig. 12.9. An untimed hazard circuit.

An example is VHDL [LMS86].

We can identify a modelling strategy under which the problem disappears in our framework, and which is based on the same idea as just described for classical approaches, in the following way: We ensure that on every data path from some wire where hazards might occur to any wire of the system where hazards must not occur, an inertial delay must be passed which has a timing constant larger than the maximal length of the hazard. In this case, the first signal change resulting from a possible hazard will be cancelled by the second signal changed before the first has been propagated to the output. With the strategy used above for modelling timing, i.e., by appending inertial delays of a larger magnitude than the step width dt to the outputs of the untimed circuits, this condition is fulfilled automatically: At the outputs of circuits with explicitly given timing, no hazards resulting from infinitesimal discretization can occur.

12.7 Summary

It is illustrated how different magnitudes of infinitesimals can be used to make explicit that a system might be considered at different time scales, or at different levels of dynamical abstraction.

There are infinitely many magnitudes, and they form a dense collection which has neither a lower nor an upper bound, i.e., between any two magnitudes, there is always another, and for any magnitude, there is always a larger and always a smaller one. Because of this denseness and unboundedness of magnitudes, we are able to very flexibly choose time scales for different levels of abstraction.

Often, the abstraction that the propagation time of circuits is negligible with respect to the global clock cycle is not appropriate. In this case, magnitudes can be use to separate functional and timing related concerns, by first dealing with functional and logical issues and ignoring timing issues (made explicit by assuming that the relevant timing constants are of different magnitudes), and by afterwards taking timing issues into account, by using estimations of the timing constants which fulfill more realistic conditions.

If it is appropriate to assume that the timing of the gates and the time step width dt are of different magnitudes, reasoning about the system can become quite simple because one does not have to count each single step of width dt as long as the number of ignored steps is standard.

Part III

Applications

13. A Case Study: Fischer's Protocol

As another example for the NTASM approach, let us describe and analyze Fischer's real-time based synchronization protocol [Lam87]. It is meant to ensure mutual exclusion of access to commonly used resources via real-time properties of a shared variable. The idea is to use just one shared variable (which we call v) for coordinating the access to the critical section. The variable can contain a process id or some neutral value (which we call noProc). When a process wants to enter its critical section, it first has to wait until v=noProc; then it sets v to its process id, waits some time, and then reads v again. If v has kept the old value, i.e., the id of the process considered, the process may enter its critical section; on leaving the critical section, v is set to noProc again. If v has not kept its old value, the attempt has failed and the process must go back and wait again till v=noProc.

Two time distances are relevant for the correctness of the protocol: the time from ensuring that v=noProc holds up to the moment at which v is set to the process id; this span is required to be smaller than or equal to a value called d1. The other time span is that from setting v to the process id to checking it again. This is assumed to be greater than or equal to a value called d2. Mutual exclusion is ensured for d2>d1.

What distinguishes our approach from classical ones is that the formalization and proof is based on an infinitesimal discretization of time.

13.1 A Hybrid Abstract State Machine Describing Fischer's Protocol

In the NTASM for Fischer's protocol, we will model processes as being in one of five different states. For a process p, s(p) denotes the current state. The states are the following:

- s(p)=nc, "non-critical": this state represents situations in which the process does not attempt to enter its critical section.
- s(p)=rv, "read v": the process attempts to enter its critical section and reads the shared variable.
- s(p)=w1, "wait at most d1": after checking v, the process waits at most time d1 before v is set to the process id.

– s(p)=w2, "wait at least d2": after setting v to its process id, the process waits at least time d2 before v is checked again.

– s(p)=cr, "critical section": the process is in its critical section.

In order to express the waiting times, we will use two dynamic functions tr(p) and tw(p) mapping processes to points in time. tr(p) will be equal to the time when process p has read v as being noProc for the last time, and tw(p) will be equal to the time when process p has written the process id the last time to v.

Proc is the finite set of process ids.

The initial conditions of the system are the following:

FischerInitial ⇔$_{\text{def}}$
    now=0 ∧ v=noProc ∧ ∀(p ∈ Proc) : s(p)=nc

This means that at the start, time is zero, the coordination variable signifies that no process attempts to enter its critical section or is there, and that all processes are non-critical.

The system transitions are described by the following rule. In each step, one of seven alternatives is chosen. The first alternative is that only time flows, i.e., no process attempts to move from one state to another. The other alternatives describe that some process attempts to move from one state to another. As will be seen when the rules are defined, each rule increments the time and chooses some process nondeterministically from the processes in some state, and possibly under some additional conditions. The six alternatives for possible moves of the process are given by named rules which are defined and discussed in sequence.

FischerRule =$_{\text{def}}$
    OR incremTime
    OR enterrv
    OR enterw1
    OR enterw2
    OR resign
    OR entercr
    OR exitcr

Rule incremTime describes the steady flow of time:

incremTime =$_{\text{def}}$
    now := now + dt

Rule enterrv describes that a process in the non-critical state might decide to attempt to use its critical section. It does this by moving on to the state where the shared variable is checked.

enterrv =$_{\text{def}}$
    || incremTime
    || CHOOSE(p:Proc):s(p)=nc IN
        s(p):=rv

Rule `enterw1` describes that from rv, w1 can be entered if v=noProc. The time when the variable is read is recorded in `tr(p)`.

```
enterw1 =def
  || incremTime
  || CHOOSE(p:Proc):s(p)=rv ∧ v=noProc IN
       || s(p):=w1
       || tr(p):=now
```

Rule `enterw2` describes that a process in w1 might move on to w2. v is set to p, which is used as the process id, and the time of this write access to v is recorded in `tw(p)`. The assumption that the move from w1 to w2 happens in time d1 after reading v as noProc will be encoded by a global assumption which will be discussed later.

```
enterw2 =def
  || incremTime
  || CHOOSE(p:Proc):s(p)=w1 IN
       || s(p):=w2
       || v:=p
       || tw(p):=now+dt
```

Rule `resign` describes that a process in w2 might move back to rv if at least time d2 has passed since v has been written and if the value in v has changed since process p set it to its id.

```
resign =def
  || incremTime
  || CHOOSE(p:Proc):s(p)=w2 ∧ now>=tw(p)+d2 ∧ v!=p IN
       s(p):=rv
```

Rule `entercr` is very similar to rule `resign`; the difference is that it checks that v has not changed since process p wrote to it, and that the target state is then cr.

```
entercr =def
  || incremTime
  || CHOOSE(p:Proc):s(p)=w2 ∧ now>=tw(p)+d2 ∧ v=p IN
       s(p):=cr
```

The last rule `exitcr` describes that process p leaves the critical state for the noncritical and resets v to noProc.

```
exitcr =def
  || incremTime
  || CHOOSE(p:Proc):s(p)=cr IN
       || s(p):=nc
       || v:=noProc
```

Our ASM does not express the assumption that between checking that v=noProc and setting v to p not more than time d1 passes. We might operationalize this assumption, but it is more convenient to express this assumption declaratively by restricting our attention to system behaviors of the ASM which fulfill the following formula invariantly:

FischerAssumption $=_{\text{def}}$
   $\forall$(p $\in$ Proc): s(p)=w1 $\rightarrow$ now+dt$\leq$tr(p)+d1

If we are in a configuration in which process p in state w1 is selected to move on to w2, v has the new value p at the next moment, i.e., at time now+dt. Formula FischerAssumption ensures that all processes in state w1 leave for w2 before it is too late, i.e., before time d1 has passed since v=noProc has been checked; otherwise, the mutex property might be invalidated.

13.2 Specification and Proof of the Mutex Property

Formally, we will use the assumption by showing that for all system behaviors of the ASM for which FischerAssumption is valid, the mutual exclusion property holds, which we describe by the following formula:

FischerMutex $=_{\text{def}}$ $\forall$(p, q $\in$ Proc): s(p)=s(q)=cr $\rightarrow$ p=q

Now we are ready to formulate the main theorem:

Theorem 13.2.1. *All ASM-runs starting in the state fulfilling* FischerInitial*, allowed by* FischerRule *with* d1<d2 *and fulfilling invariantly* FischerAssumption *fulfill invariantly* FischerMutex.

We prove the theorem with completely discrete means, by finding an inductive invariant of the system which implies FischerMutex. The hard part, as is typical in proving invariants of discrete systems, is in finding an adequate inductive invariant, i.e., a state property which is fulfilled by the initial condition, which is preserved by each transition of the system, and which implies the property to be shown to be invariant [MP95]. We use the following idea for constructing an inductive invariant: We see the development of the whole system as proceeding cyclically through four phases:

– The system is passive. We describe this phase by the following formula:

PhPassive $=_{\text{def}}$
   $\wedge$ $\forall$(p $\in$ Proc): s(p) $\in$ {nc,rv,w2}
   $\wedge$ v=noProc

Processes are non-critical (nc), just reading the variable (rv), or waiting to be allowed to re-check the variable (w2). v=noProc implies that processes in state w2 will have to pass through rv again before they get a new chance to access their critical sections.

− Processes have started pouring into state `w1`:

`PhFillingW1` $=_{\mathrm{def}}$
   $\wedge$ $\forall$(p ∈ Proc) : s(p) ∈ {nc,rv,w1,w2}
   $\wedge$ v=noProc
   $\wedge$ $\exists$(p ∈ Proc) : s(p)=w1
   $\wedge$ $\forall$(p ∈ Proc) : s(p)=w1 $\rightarrow$ tr(p)$\leq$now

Now, the only forbidden state is `cr`, and there is at least one process in
state `w1`. `v=noProc` means that in this cycle, none of the processes which
have entered `w1` have left that state. The last conjunct expresses that the
time recorded in `tr(p)` for `w1`-processes is smaller than or equal to the
current time. We will need that conjunct in the proof of the fact that when
a process enters state `cr`, no process is in `w1`.

− Processes are leaving state `w1`:

`PhEmptyingW1` $=_{\mathrm{def}}$
   $\wedge$ $\forall$(p ∈ Proc) : s(p) ∈ {nc,rv,w1,w2}
   $\wedge$ v$\neq$noProc
   $\wedge$ $\forall$(p ∈ Proc) : s(p)=w1 $\rightarrow$ tr(p)$\leq$now
   $\wedge$ $\forall$(p ∈ Proc) : s(p)=w1 $\rightarrow$ tr(p)<tw(v)

This phase is entered as soon as the first process leaves `w1` in `PhFillingW1`,
and it extends until the first process enters `cr`. In this phase, `v` is equal to
the id of the last process which has entered `w2`. The last conjunct expresses
that since the last process has entered `w2` (and written its id to `v`, i.e.,
since time `tw(v)`), no process has entered `w1`, i.e., the read-times for all
`w1`-processes are smaller than the write-time of process `v`. This property
will also be used for proving that no process is in `w1` when some process
enters `cr`.

This phase is left as soon as some process leaves `w2` for `cr`.

− Some process is in its critical section:

`PhUsingResource` $=_{\mathrm{def}}$
   $\wedge$ $\forall$(p ∈ Proc) : s(p) ∈ {nc,rv,w2,cr}
   $\wedge$ v$\neq$noProc
   $\wedge$ s(v)=cr
   $\wedge$ $\forall$(p ∈ Proc) : s(p)=cr $\rightarrow$ p=v

The last process having entered `w2` from `w1` will be granted the right to
enter its critical section. Because of the real-time properties of the protocol,
it will be ensured that `w1` is empty when a process enters `cr`. Thus, in this
phase, no process is in state `w1`. The only process in `cr` is the one with id `v`.

In order to make our idea precise, we show that the following formula is
indeed inductive under the assumption `FischerAssumption`:

FischerInductive $=_{\mathrm{def}}$
   ∨ PhPassive
   ∨ PhFillingW1
   ∨ PhEmptyingW1
   ∨ PhUsingResource

Several lemmata will be used to establish the validity of the following formulas. Let us denote by rule[c] the set of configurations reachable from configuration c by one application of rule rule, and let us denote by ⟦formula⟧ the set of all configurations in which formula holds.

LemInitial $=_{\mathrm{def}}$
   FischerInitial → FischerInductive
LemOnlyTime $=_{\mathrm{def}}$
   ∀(c ∈ ⟦FischerInductive ∧ FischerAssumption ∧ d1 < d2⟧) :
      incremTime[c] ⊆ ⟦FischerInductive⟧
LemEnterrv $=_{\mathrm{def}}$
   ∀(c ∈ ⟦FischerInductive ∧ FischerAssumption ∧ d1 < d2⟧) :
      enterrv[c] ⊆ ⟦FischerInductive⟧
LemEnterw1 $=_{\mathrm{def}}$
   ∀(c ∈ ⟦FischerInductive ∧ FischerAssumption ∧ d1 < d2⟧) :
      enterw1[c] ⊆ ⟦FischerInductive⟧
LemEnterw2 $=_{\mathrm{def}}$
   ∀(c ∈ ⟦FischerInductive ∧ FischerAssumption ∧ d1 < d2⟧) :
      enterw2[c] ⊆ ⟦FischerInductive⟧
LemResign $=_{\mathrm{def}}$
   ∀(c ∈ ⟦FischerInductive ∧ FischerAssumption ∧ d1 < d2⟧) :
      resign[c] ⊆ ⟦FischerInductive⟧
LemEntercr $=_{\mathrm{def}}$
   ∀(c ∈ ⟦FischerInductive ∧ FischerAssumption ∧ d1 < d2⟧) :
      entercr[c] ⊆ ⟦FischerInductive⟧
LemExitcr $=_{\mathrm{def}}$
   ∀(c ∈ ⟦FischerInductive ∧ FischerAssumption ∧ d1 < d2⟧) :
      exitcr[c] ⊆ ⟦FischerInductive⟧

LemMutexImplied $=_{\mathrm{def}}$
   FischerInductive → FischerMutex

LemInital claims that FischerInductive holds in the start configurations. LemMutexImplied claims that the inductive property implies the mutex-property, and the other lemma-formulas claim for each possible transition of the system that from an inductive configuration which fulfills the assumption, an inductive configuration is reached. We now proceed to prove the lemmata given above.

Proof (Proof of `LemInitial`*).* `LemInitial` claims that initial configurations fulfill the inductive property. This follows from the fact that all initial configurations fulfill `PhPassive`, a disjunct of the inductive property.

The proofs of the following lemmata will typically be done by considering each disjunct of `FischerInductive` as a possible phase to be left by the transitions separately and show that a transition leaving the phase described by some disjunct enters a phase described by some other disjunct.

Proof (Proof of `LemOnlyTime`*).* Incrementation of `now` can not change any conjunct in any disjunct of `FischerInductive` from true to false. Thus, no phase will be left just because the flow of time which is expressed by rule `incremTime`.

The incrementation of time is a component of all other transitions to be considered now, and it is as harmless in combination with other changes as it is when it happens without other changes. We will not mention the incrementation of time in the other proofs. Implicitly, the incrementation of time might make it necessary for a process in state `w1` to leave that state for `w2`, but this is dealt with by the assumption `FischerAssumption`.

Proof (Proof of `LemEnterrv`*).* The move of a process from `nc` to `rv` can not change any conjunct of any disjunct from true to false. Thus, rule `enterrv` is as harmless as `incremTime` in this respect.

Proof (Proof of `LemEnterw1`*).* Rule `enterw1` might leave `PhPassive` by moving a process into state `w1`, and if this is the case, all four conjuncts of `Ph-FillingW1` are true after the transition.

Also `PhFillingW1` contains states in which `enterW1` might move some process from one state to another, but this can not leave the phase.

When the system is in one of the two other phases, rule `enterw1` is equivalent to `incremTime` because `v!=noProc`.

Proof (Proof of `LemEnterw2`*).* Rule `enterw2` is equivalent to `incremTime` in phases `PhPassive` and `PhUsingResource` because no process is in state `w1` in these two phases.

If executed in `PhFillingW1`, this phase is left for `PhEmptyingW1`: `v` is set to a value different from `noProc`, and the time of writing an id to `v`, i.e., `now+dt` in the configuration left, which is equal to `now` in the configuration reached, as recorded in `tw(v)`, is larger than the read-times for all processes in `w1`.

If executed in `PhEmptyingW1`, this phase is not left. Again, the property `tr(p)<=now` for `w1`-processes in the start configuration of the transition is used to establish `tr(p)<tw(v)` for `w1`-processes in the target configuration.

Proof (Proof of `LemResign`*).* The rule `resign` does not change the truth value of any conjunct in any disjunct of `FischerInductive`.

Proof (Proof of `LemEntercr`*)*. The only phase in which rule `entercr` is not equivalent to `incremTime` is `PhEmptyingW1`. In order to move process `p` to state `cr`, enough time must have been spent: the formula `now>tw(p)+d2` must be true; `p=v` must also hold. We will demonstrate that this implies that no process is in `w1` under these conditions, the only problematical consequence from `PhUsingResource` under these conditions.

`now>tw(p)+d2` and `v=p` implies `now>tw(v)+d2`. Since `d2` is larger than `d1` and `tw(v)` is larger than `tr(p)` for processes `p` in `w1`, this means that `now>tr(p)+d1` for processes in `w1`. Together with `FischerAssumption`, this implies that there is no process in `w1` when a process leaves `w2` for `cr`.

Proof (Proof of `LemExitcr`*)*. Rule `exitcr` can only be non-equivalent to rule `incremTime` in phase `PhUsingResource`, and it moves the system obviously into phase `PhPassive`

Proof (Proof of `LemMutexImplied`*)*. `LemMutexImplied` claims that inductive configurations fulfill the mutex property. Only phase `PhUsingResource`, has to be considered, since only in this phase there can be a process in state `cr`. Since any process in state `cr` must have id `v`, this implies that in `PhUsingResource`, exactly one process is in state `cr` – the mutex-property.

Now, we can prove the main theorem:

Proof (Proof of main theorem). The formula `FischerInductive` is inductive for initial condition `FischerInitial` and rule `FischerRule`, under the assumptions `d1<d2` and `FischerAssumption`, by the lemmata `LemInitial`, `LemOnlyTime`, `LemEnterrv`, `LemEnterw1`, `LemEnterw2`, `LemResign`, `LemEntercr` and `LemExitcr`, and `FischerInductive` implies `FischerMutex` by lemma `LemMutexImplied`. Thus, `FischerMutex` is an invariant of the system.

13.3 Infinitesimality of Step-Width and Plausibility of Assumptions

Perhaps it might seem strange that the infinitesimality of `dt` does not enter the proof. The fact that `dt` can be chosen infinitesimally is only relevant in two regards: for the plausibility that the ASM given describes the Fischer protocol faithfully, and, more specifically, for the plausibility that the assumption that processes having read `v` as `noProc` write `v` before time `d1` has been passed is properly formalized as `FischerAssumption`. More exactly, we have to assume that no matter how many processes there are, there are enough time steps in phase `PhFillingW1` for as many of them to enter `w1`, and there are enough time steps so that each of them can leave state `w1` before its timer runs out. This can be made formal by requiring that the specification, i.e., the program together with `FischerAssumption`, is not contradictory, since the latter would mean that the main theorem holds only vacuously.

The assumption of non-contradictivity is only adequate for numbers of processes smaller than $d1/dt$; thus, when $d1$ and dt are fixed, we have to admit that the proof is only meaningful for some maximal number of processes, but it would be quite messy and involve some additional assumptions to determine this number exactly. For the original protocol description, this would be unnatural. By assuming that the number of processes is standard, that $d1$ is standard, and that dt is infinitesimal, we can conclude that there are enough discrete moments to approximate each continuous behavior with infinitesimal exactness.

13.4 Summary

This chapter applies the framework developed in the previous chapters to a well-known real-time mutual-exclusion protocol. It is shown that a purely discrete approach suffices to prove the correctness of the protocol, and that the infinitesimality of the step width is only relevant in order make plausible the abstractions used in the algorithm.

14. An ASM Meta-model
for Petri Nets with Timing

14.1 ASM Models of Discrete Nets

This section will present several NTASM interpretations of timing enhanced Petri nets. Petri nets without timing [Pet62, Rei86] are a widely used model for discrete nondeterministic distributed systems.

Petri nets are used in several variants, also for discrete systems. We will build on the quantitatively timed variants on place-transition nets without capacity restrictions in the places, and call them shortly just nets. The static structure of a net is defined by two finite disjoint sets P and T, the **places** and the **transitions** of the net, and a function $E : P \times T \cup T \times P \to \mathbb{N}_0$ describing the number of edges from a place to a transition, or from a transition to a place. A configuration of a net is called a **marking**, which is a function $m : P \to \mathbb{N}_0$, expressing how many tokens are currently associated with a place $p \in P$. An initial marking $m_0 : P \to \mathbb{N}_0$ defines the start configuration of the net. A discrete step of the net consists in a change of the marking. Possible changes are defined by transitions $t \in T$ so that in the current marking, each $p \in P$ carries at least as many tokens as there are edges from p to t; such a transition is called "enabled" or "firable". The effect of firing such a transition is to take away from each place p the number of tokens which equals the number of edges from p to t, and then to add to each place p the number of tokens which equals the number of edges from t to p.

For each transition t, a place p so that $E(p,t) \neq 0$ is called a **pre-place** of t and a place p so that $E(t,p) \neq 0$ is called a **post-place** of t. Thus, firing of a transition t means taking away the number of tokens given by E from the pre-places of t, and adding the number of tokens given by E to the post-places of t.

In a place-transition net, places can be considered to model stores of identical elements of the modelled system, and transitions can naturally be considered to model processes which take some inputs away from the stores represented by the pre-places of the transition, process them, and provide outputs to the post-places of the transition.

Different strategies are possible for determining how global system steps are computed based on such local steps: (a) Just one of the enabled transitions might be selected and fired in a global step (this is the "interleaving dynamics"); or (b) an arbitrary subset of enabled transitions is fired for which there exist enough tokens in the current marking so that they all can be fired synchronously; or (c) a maximal such set of transitions might be fired. The latter dynamics is the "maximal progress dynamics". The dynamics in (a) is adequate if it is assumed that firing a transition takes very short time and it is not relevant if the processes modelled by some transitions perform their work (partially) overlapping. (b) expresses synchronous execution of any set of transitions so that enough tokens exist in the pre-places of all the transitions in the set, and (c) is a variant of (b) in which each transition is taken as early as possible, where we must deal with the case that a transition t might be in (dynamic) conflict with a set of transitions st, i.e., while st might be fired and t might be fired alone, it might be the case that $st \cup \{t\}$ can not be fired because there are not enough tokens for all these transitions at once. In general, the use of variant (c) reduces the nondeterminism of variant (b) quite considerably, at least in states which admit a large number of non-conflicting transitions to be taken.

To model a net as an ASM, we assume that the vocabulary contains the static unary predicates P and T characterizing finite effective sets, a static binary function $E : P \times T \cup T \times P \to \mathbb{N}_0$; the dynamic state component is modelled by a dynamic marking function $m : P \to \mathbb{N}_0$, which is initialized as the initial marking. The interleaving dynamics is described by the rule in Fig. 14.1. enabled(t) expresses if a transition t can be taken. If no transition can be taken, the CHOOSE rule is equivalent to a HALT rule, and if some transition can be taken, one of the enabled transitions is chosen and the new values of all places are computed.

```
InterleavingNetDynamics =def
  CHOOSE(t:T):enabled(t) IN
    FORALL(p:P) DO
      m(p) := m(p) - E(p,t) + E(t,p)

enabled(t) ⇔def ∀(p:P):m(p)≥E(p,t)
```

Fig. 14.1. A rule capturing the interleaving dynamics of a discrete place-transition net.

The maximal progress dynamics is described by rule MaximalProgress-NetDynamics in Fig. 14.2. $\mathcal{P}$ determines the power set of its argument predicate, understood as a set; setEnabled(st), for a set of transitions st, is a derived function which determines if there are transitions in st and if they can be fired synchronously in the current state; and the $\sum$-terms are short-hand notations for derived functions with a place parameter p and a transition set parameter st which determine the number of edges from p into transitions in st or vice versa.

```
MaximalProgressNetDynamics  =def
  CHOOSE(st ∈ P(T)):maximalSetEnabled(st) IN
    FORALL(p:P) DO
      m(p) := m(p) - ∑_{t∈st}E(p,t) + ∑_{t∈st} E(t,p)

setEnabled(st)  ⇔def
  st ≠ {} ∧ ∀(p:P):m(p)≥ ∑_{t∈st} E(p,t)

maximalSetEnabled(st)  ⇔def
  ∧ setEnabled(st)
  ∧ ¬∃(st1 ∈ P(T)):
        ∧ setEnabled(st1)
        ∧ st⊆st1
        ∧ st1≠st
```

Fig. 14.2. A rule capturing the maximal progress dynamics of a discrete place-transition net.

14.2 Quantitatively Timed Nets

Several approaches exist for extending discrete nets with the possibility of modelling properties of systems which involve quantitative time. Two well-known examples are the timed Petri nets of Ramchandani [Ram74] and the time Petri nets of Merlin and Farber [MF76]. We will investigate these two models in some depth. In both approaches, quantitative times are associated with the transitions of a place-transition net.

In the model of Ramchandani, time is assumed to pass between the moment in which the tokens are taken away from the pre-places and the moment in which they are added to the post-places. The net variant is called "timed Petri nets". In this approach a transition models nicely a process which, when started, synchronously takes away its inputs from their respective stores, then needs some time for computing the results, and finally provides synchronously its outputs to their respective stores. Normally, it is assumed that the time needed by the process is given by a single number, which models that it is fairly exactly known what time the modelled process needs. Popova-Zeugmann and Heiner [HPZ97] present a variant in which a non-empty interval of the non-negative rational numbers is used instead; this models explicitly that knowledge is missing about the precise time the process might take after its start, but that there is a minimal time and a maximal time so that it is known that the processes need a time between these two times.

The model of Merlin and Farber is based on another basic idea. Some processes can be assumed to perform their work (almost) instantaneously, but they need time before they notice that they may work. An example is used in the original paper [MF76]: Merlin and Farber use their model to express a watch-dog mechanism in a communication protocol. Formally, each transition is associated with an interval of the non-negative real numbers.

When a Merlin-Farber transition starts to be enabled, a timer associated with it starts running, but the tokens in the pre-places stay untouched. As soon as the timer value is in the interval, the transition **may** fire; and as soon as the timer value is equal to the upper bound of the interval, the transition **must** fire. Variants allow ∞ as upper value of the interval, or restrict the interval boundaries to rational numbers. This approach to adding quantitative time to Petri nets is normally called "time Petri nets". Analysis techniques for this kind of nets are described in [Pop91], [BD91] and [DS94].

Felder et al. [FMM94, p. 132f] distinguish several semantical variants for the time interval which might be associated with a transition in a Merlin-Farber net. The original paper of Merlin and Farber is not entirely clear, and Felder et al.'s method is to use an axiomatization in the temporal logic TRIO to make explicit their interpretational decisions. We cite some of the possibilities here:

- Felder et al. distinguish a *strong time semantics* and a *weak time semantics*. They differ with respect to interpretation of the upper time bound. Strong time semantics is as described above: If the upper time bound is reached for a transition, the transition must fire; weak time semantics means: If the transition fires, the waiting time is between the lower and the upper time bound; but it is not required to fire. In the present work, we use a strong time semantics.
- The number of waiting processes associated with an enabled transition might be restricted to one, or it might be allowed that several such processes are running at once if there are enough tokens in the pre-places so that a transition is enabled multiple times. In the latter case, each token in a pre-place of a transition is associated with at most one process of the transition. In the present work, we use a single-process semantics.
- One might allow simultaneous firings of several transitions or not; and when it is allowed, it might also happen that the same transition fires simultaneously several times (because several of its processes might fire at the same moment). If zero-time transitions are allowed, there might be several firings at the same point in real time, some of which might depend causally on earliers, i.e., they happen at the same point in real time, but in some fixed order. In the present work, we will describe both an interleaving semantics without simultaneous firings, and a maximal progress semantics with simultaneous firings.
- As upper time bound, typically ∞ belongs to the allowed values. Two interpretations for this are discussed by Felder et al.: One might be that the transition might wait as long as it wants before it fires, but that it must fire at some point in time. The other interpretation is that the transition might not fire at all. In the present work, we use the second interpretation.

Time Petri nets can be used to model timed Petri nets, by modelling the start and the end of each transition of the timed net by firing distinct transitions of the time net, where the first is associated with an interval of the form $[0,0]$ and the second by a point interval expressing the duration of the work of the modelled process. Two new further places for each timed transition to be simulated are used to model the state of the transition, i.e., if it is currently working or not, and the function E is defined for these new places so that the start transition can only be fired if the transition is currently passive. Note that in this simulation, one process of the original application is modelled by several transitions and additional places of the time net.

14.3 STASM Models of Doubly Timed Nets

We propose to model both time Petri nets and timed Petri nets in common ASM models. We start with an STASM model. We do not use the encoding of timed Petri nets by time Petri nets described above, but we express directly both the reaction time (from time Petri nets) and the working time (from timed Petri nets) in one model. This will allow us to model one process by one transition and express explicitly in the model which times are to be understood as reaction times and which are to be understood as working times of the process; thus, as is consistent with the main *raison d'être* of ASMs, we avoid complex encodings of the real-world entities which we want to model. We will call the net type "doubly timed nets".

In order to be able to describe the additional static structure of a doubly timed net, we extend the static vocabulary of the ASM model of discrete nets described above with four functions from transitions to the reals: two functions for the lower bound and the upper bound for the reaction time of the transition (reactionTimeLB and reactionTimeUB), and two functions for the lower bound and the upper bound for the working time of the transition (workingTimeLB and workingTimeUB), where we assume that for each transition, the upper bound is not smaller than the corresponding lower bound. In addition to the reals, we allow a value ∞ as upper bound, which is assumed to be larger than any real.

The dynamic state of discrete nets is represented by the marking alone. This does not suffice any longer, since we have to represent the reaction time or the working time which has passed so far. We use two dynamic functions enabledSince and workingSince from T to $\mathbb{R}_0^+ \cup \{\perp\}$. A value of $\perp$ means that the transition is not currently in the respective state, i.e., it is not currently waiting for the reaction time to finish or it is not currently working. In each moment and for all transitions, at most one of these two functions has a value unequal from $\perp$. In the start state, enabledSince(t) is 0 for transitions t which are initially enabled, and is $\perp$ for other transitions, and workingSince(t) starts with a value of $\perp$ for all transitions.

14.3.1 An Interleaving Dynamics for Doubly Timed Nets

The STASM rule InterleavingTimeNetDynamics in Figures 14.3 and 14.4 expresses an interleaving dynamics of doubly timed nets. If there is an urgent

```
InterleavingTimeNetDynamics =def
  IF (∃(t:T):mustStartWork(t) ∨ mustStopWork(t))
  THEN DoDiscreteStep
  ELIF (∃(t:T):canStartWork(t) ∨ canStopWork(t))
  THEN OR DoDiscreteStep
       OR SKIP
  ELSE SKIP

canStartWork(t) ⇔def
  ∧ now - enabledSince(t) ≥ reactionTimeLB(t)
  ∧ now - enabledSince(t) ≤ reactionTimeUB(t)

mustStartWork(t) ⇔def
  now - enabledSince(t) = reactionTimeUB(t)

canStopWork(t) ⇔def
  ∧ now - workingSince(t) ≥ workingTimeLB(t)
  ∧ now - workingSince(t) ≤ workingTimeUB(t)

mustStopWork(t) ⇔def
  now - workingSince(t) = workingTimeUB(t)
```

Fig. 14.3. An STASM rule capturing the interleaving dynamics of a doubly timed net (part 1).

transition (i.e., a transition which must start or stop work immediately), a discrete transition is taken. Otherwise, if some transition can be taken, it is decided nondeterministically if a discrete step is performed or time is allowed to pass; and finally, if no transition can be taken, time passes.

In the definition of the predicates which describe if a transition can or must start or stop work, we use the convention that the predicates $\geq$ and $\leq$ yield false if at least one argument is $\bot$, and the subtraction function yields $\bot$ if at least one argument is $\bot$; thus, we do not have to deal with the case of an undefined enabling- or working-time with a special sub-term.

Figure 14.4 contains the definition of the rule DoDiscreteStep which describes what happens in a discrete step. It is only called if there is a transition which can start or stop to work. This means that the initial CHOOSE statement will find a binding for t. The IF statement distinguishes the two cases: start resp. stop of work.

If transition t starts a working phase, its enabledSince time is reset to undefined, workingSince is set to the current time, the marking is updated for all places, and for all transitions t1 different from t, it is checked if it is disabled by the transition t being taken. This is only the case if currently, t1 is not disabled, but with the new marking, there is a pre-place p of t1 which does not carry enough tokens.

If transition t stops a working phase, its workingSince time is reset and the marking is updated. Then, for all transitions t1, including t itself, it is

```
DoDiscreteStep =def
  CHOOSE(t:T):canStartWork(t) ∨ canStopWork(t) IN
    IF canStartWork(t)
    THEN
      || enabledSince(t) := ⊥
      || workingSince(t) := now
      || FORALL(p:P) DO m(p) := m(p)-E(p,t)
      || FORALL(t1:T):t1≠t DO
           IF ∧ enabledSince(t1)≠⊥
              ∧ (∃(p:P):m(p)-E(p,t)<E(p,t1))
           THEN enabledSince(t1) := ⊥
           ELSE SKIP
    ELSE
      || workingSince(t) := ⊥
      || FORALL(p:P) DO m(p) := m(p)+E(p,t)
      || FORALL(t1:T) DO
           IF ∧ enabledSince(t1)=⊥
              ∧ (∀(p:P):m(p)+E(p,t)≥E(p,t1))
           THEN enabledSince(t1) := now
           ELSE SKIP
```

Fig. 14.4. An STASM rule capturing the interleaving dynamics of a doubly timed net (part 2).

checked if with the new tokens produced by t finishing its work, t1 switches from disabled to enabled. This is the case if currently, enabledSince(t1) is undefined, but with the marking in the next state, all pre-places of t1 have enough tokens for t1 to be taken. In this case, the enabledSince time of t1 is set to the current time, which is equal to that of the next state since a discrete step is done.

14.3.2 A Maximal Progress Dynamics for Doubly Timed Nets

The dynamics described in Figures 14.3 and 14.4 is based on interleaving. A maximal progress rule can also be given, again assuming that we have sets of transitions in the universe, together with the relevant operations on sets. Figures 14.5 and 14.6 present a rule which describes a maximal progress strategy. In each step, a set of transitions which can start work is selected which is maximal relative to the transitions which must start work; this means that a transition which must start work is only omitted from this set if the union would not be synchronously firable. Additionally and in the same step, a set of transitions is selected which can stop their work, and which contains all transitions which must stop their work. This rule does not select maximal sets of transitions of those which can start or finish their work, since this would imply that a transition becomes urgent as soon as it becomes enabled, which contradicts the idea behind the lower bounds on reaction time and working time. Rather, maximality is enforced only with respect to urgent transitions.

```
MaxTimeNetDynamics =def
  CHOOSE(st1:P(T)):maxStartWork(st1) IN
    CHOOSE(st2:P(T)):maxStopWork(st2) IN
      IF st1 ∪ st2 = {} THEN SKIP
      ELSE
          || FORALL(p:P) DO
                m(p) := nextMarking(p,st1,st2)
          || FORALL(t:T) DO
                IF t ∈ st1 THEN workingSince(t) := now
                ELIF t ∈ st2 THEN workingSince(t) := ⊥
                ELSE SKIP
          || FORALL(t:T) DO
                IF t ∈ st1 THEN enabledSince(t) := ⊥
                ELIF ∧ enabledSince(t)=⊥
                     ∧ nextMarkingEnabled(t,st1,st2)
                THEN enabledSince(t) := now
                ELIF ∧ enabledSince(t) ≠ ⊥
                     ∧ NOT halfNextMarkingEnabled(t,st1)
                THEN IF nextMarkingEnabled(t,st1,st2)
                       THEN enabledSince(t) := now
                       ELSE enabledSince(t) := ⊥
                ELSE SKIP
```

Fig. 14.5. An STASM rule capturing the maximal progress dynamics of a doubly timed net (without derived functions).

If the union of the transitions for which some discrete step is to be performed is empty, just a SKIP is performed, which means that time may flow. Otherwise, three statements are performed in parallel. The first updates the marking of the places; the second updates the workingSince-values for the transitions which start or stop working. The third is responsible for computing necessary changes of the enabledSince-times for all transitions. For transitions which start work, the time is reset to the undefined value; for transitions which are currently not enabled but are after the current step, this value is set to the current time; and for transitions which are currently enabled, but are disabled by the next half-step (where we assume that first, the tokens of started transitions are taken away, and then, the tokens of stopped transitions are added; other alternatives exist, and no alternative is the obviously best choice, so our decision might be called arbitrary), it is checked if they are enabled after the next full step: If they are, the value is set to the current time; otherwise, it is undefined.

The derived functions in Fig. 14.6 describe important conditions and functions. maxStartWork defines, for a set of transitions, if they can start working together in a maximal progress dynamics. canStartWorkTogether defines, for a set of transitions, if there are enough tokens in the places so that all transitions can be fired synchronously. maxStopWork is the analogue of maxStartWork for stopping work. nextMarkingEnabled checks, for a transition

```
maxStartWork(st) ⇔def
  ∧ st ⊆ T
  ∧ canStartWorkTogether(st)
  ∧ ∀(t:T):
        mustStartWork(t)
    →
        (t ∈ st ∨ ¬ canStartWorkTogether(st ∪ {t})

canStartWorkTogether(st) ⇔def
  ∧ ∀(t:st):canStartWork(t)
  ∧ ∀(p:P):∑_{t:st} E(p,t) ≤ m(p)

maxStopWork(st) ⇔def
  ∧ st ⊆ T
  ∧ ∀(t:st):canStopWork(t)
  ∧ ∀(t:T): mustStopWork(t) → (t ∈ st)

nextMarkingEnabled(t1,st1,st2) ⇔def
  ∀(p:P):m(p) - ∑_{t∈st1} E(p,t) + ∑_{t∈st2} E(t,p) ≥ E(p,t1)

halfNextMarkingEnabled(t1,st1) ⇔def
  ∀(p:P):m(p) - ∑_{t∈st1} E(p,t) ≥ E(p,t1)
```

Fig. 14.6. Derived functions of the STASM rule capturing a maximal progress dynamics of a time net.

t1, a set st1 of transitions which start work and a set st2 of transitions which stop work, if t1 will be enabled after the transition. halfNextMarkingEnabled determines, for a transition t1 and a set st1 of transitions, if after taking away the tokens needed by the transitions in st1 from the current marking, t1 is enabled or not.

14.3.3 Discussion of the STASM Models of Doubly Timed Nets

Note that the semantics of Ramchandani nets can be recovered by requiring that both the lower and upper bound for the reaction times of all transitions is zero, and that the lower and upper bound of the working time are equal for all transitions. The semantics of Merlin-Farber nets can be recovered by requiring that the lower and upper bounds of the working time for all transitions are zero.

Both variants of dynamics of doubly timed nets assume that at any one time at most one instance of a transition is working (or is computing its reaction time). A variant would be to instantiate several reaction time processes, as many as are allowed by the current marking, and to allow several instantiations of the working process.

One might ask if the two dynamics are essentially equivalent, in the sense that whatever can happen in a run of one dynamics can be simulated by a run of the other dynamics. A possible understanding of 'simulation' might be

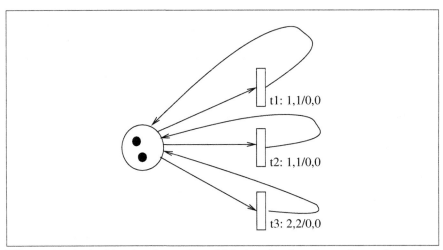

Fig. 14.7. A doubly timed net for which interleaving dynamics and maximal progress dynamics are essentially different.

to allow that what happens in one run in a maximal sub-sequence of discrete steps happens in the other run in a maximal sub-sequence of discrete steps. In this case, the runs would just differ with respect to the refinement of the discrete steps. But in our case, the two dynamics can differ in an essential way: There are nets and initial configurations so that the interleaving dynamics allows some transition to be taken at some time for some resolution of the nondeterminism, while the maximal progress dynamics does not admit the same transition to be taken at any time. We look at an example.

Consider the net and marking described in Fig. 14.7. The notation is partly the customary one for Petri nets: The circle represents a place, which carries two tokens in the situation represented; transitions are represented by rectangles; and edges are represented by arrows, where a non-existing arrow means that the weight is 0, an unlabeled arrow represents an edge with weight 1, and an arrow labeled with a natural number represents an edge with the given weight. We label the transitions with a name and the four times which are associated with them; first, lower and upper bound for the reaction time are given, and then, lower and upper bound for the working time are given. In the example, transitions t1 and t2 have identical behavior: they have a punctual reaction time of 1 and a working time of 0. Transition t3 has a punctual reaction time of 2 and also a working time of 0.

Configurations of the system are concisely represented as 8-tuples; we use semicola for making them more readable. Configuration $(x_0, x_1; x_2, x_3, x_4; x_5, x_6, x_7)$ means that the current timed is x_0, the only place carries x_1 tokens, the enabledSince-times of t1, t2 and t3 are x_2, x_3 and x_4, respectively, and their workingSince-times are x_5, x_6 and x_7.

The start configuration of the net given in the figure is $(0, 2; 0, 0, 0; \perp, \perp, \perp)$. For this net, the maximal progress dynamics can be considered as deterministic if we ignore differences between runs which only arise from

$$(0, 2; 0, 0, 0; \perp, \perp, \perp)$$
$$\downarrow 1$$
$$(1, 2; 0, 0, 0; \perp, \perp, \perp)$$
$$\downarrow (\{t1, t2\}, \{\})$$
$$(1, 0; \perp, \perp, \perp; 1, 1, \perp)$$
$$\downarrow (\{\}, \{t1, t2\})$$
$$(1, 2; 1, 1, 1; \perp, \perp, \perp)$$
$$\downarrow 1$$
$$(2, 2; 1, 1, 1; \perp, \perp, \perp)$$
$$\vdots$$

Fig. 14.8. Start of the configuration sequence of the net in Fig. 14.7 with a maximal progress dynamics.

splitting a time step into several time steps, or by unifying neighbouring time steps. The configuration sequence in Fig. 14.8 is the only possible, where steps labeled with reals represent time steps of the given length, and steps labeled with pairs of transition sets represent discrete actions in which the transitions in the first set start working, and transitions in the second set stop working. The behavior repeats after the first three steps, which means that transition t3 is never fired: it is always preempted by the common firing of transitions t1 and t2.

Figure 14.9 is the start of a configuration sequence admitted by the interleaving dynamics. This system is not deterministic, and while there are sequences of transitions which together mimic the effect of the maximal progress

$$(0, 2; 0, 0, 0; \perp, \perp, \perp)$$
$$\downarrow 1$$
$$(1, 2; 0, 0, 0; \perp, \perp, \perp)$$
$$\downarrow (\{t1\}, \{\})$$
$$(1, 1; \perp, 0, 0; 1, \perp, \perp)$$
$$\downarrow (\{\}, \{t1\})$$
$$(1, 2; 1, 0, 0; \perp, \perp, \perp)$$
$$\downarrow (\{t2\}, \{\})$$
$$(1, 1; 1, \perp, 0; \perp, 1, \perp)$$
$$\downarrow (\{\}, \{t2\})$$
$$(1, 2; 1, 1, 0; \perp, \perp, \perp)$$
$$\downarrow 1$$
$$(2, 2; 1, 1, 0; \perp, \perp, \perp)$$
$$\downarrow (\{t3\}, \{\})$$
$$(2, 1; 1, 1, \perp; \perp, \perp, 2)$$
$$\downarrow (\{\}, \{t3\})$$
$$(2, 2; 1, 1, 2; \perp, \perp, \perp)$$

Fig. 14.9. Start of a configuration sequence of the net in Fig. 14.7 with an interleaving dynamics.

dynamics (if we allow action refinement, i.e., what happens in one discrete step in the maximal progress dynamics is allowed to happen in a finite sequence of discrete steps in the interleaving dynamics), there are also runs for which no similar run of the maximal progress dynamics exist, e.g., runs in which t3 is fired. This is possible because t1 and t2, which do their work earlier than t3, might take turns, in which case there are always enough tokens in the place so that t3 does not become disabled, and, thus, after 2 time units, t3 can be fired.

This illustrates that if semantics for timed Petri nets are investigated, details like that when exactly an enabling time is reset can be very important; this has not been defined unambiguously in the original definition of timed Petri nets by Merlin and Farber.

14.4 Comparison of STASM and NTASM Semantics

The rules given as descriptions of the dynamics of doubly timed Petri nets are in general not well-behaved. For example, punctual reaction times and punctual working times can in general not be simulated by the NTASM system based on the same rules. We will now investigate this phenomenon.

14.4.1 Well-Behavedness of the Interleaving Dynamics Rule for Doubly Timed Petri Nets

While the interleaving dynamics rule for doubly timed Petri nets seems intuitively adequate, there is a drawback for implementability: It does not admit infinitesimal discretization:

Proposition 14.4.1. *Let R be the rule of Figures 14.3 and 14.4. Rule R is not well-behaved for the start state of all doubly timed Petri nets.*

Proof. The main problem are punctual reaction times or working times. Consider once again the net from Fig. 14.7. Transitions t1 and t2 must both be started taken exactly at time 1, but in the infinitesimal discretization, this is only possible for at most one of the transitions, and if the infinitesimal step width divides 1.

The fact stated in the last proposition hints to a way to classify doubly timed Petri nets as well-behaved or not, by looking at the interpreting ASM rule and the start state defined by the doubly timed Petri net under consideration. Obviously, punctuality requirements of the doubly timed Petri net lead to non-well-behaved systems. Let us consider systems in which all reaction time intervals and all working time intervals are non-punctual. Does this suffice to ensure that the resulting system is well-behaved? It does not:

Proposition 14.4.2. *Let R be the rule of Figures 14.3 and 14.4. Rule R is not necessarily well-behaved for the start state of a standard doubly timed Petri net in which the intervals defining possible reaction times and working times are all non-punctual.*

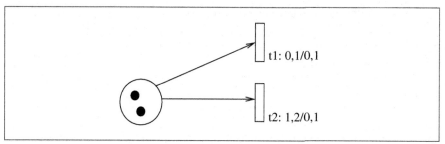

Fig. 14.10. A non-punctual doubly timed Petri net which is not well-behaved.

Proof. Consider the doubly timed Petri net of Fig. 14.10. An STASM run of this net can start with a time step of one time unit length, followed by transition t2 starting to work, and this followed by transition t1 starting to work. Now consider an NTASM with a step with dt which does not divide 1. The earliest time at which t2 can start work is $\mathtt{dt} * \lceil \frac{1}{\mathtt{dt}} \rceil$, which, by the condition on dt, is strictly larger than 1. But this is too late for t1 to start work. Thus, the described standard run can not be mimicked by an NTASM run independently from the choice of the infinitesimal step width.

The counter-example to well-behavedness given in the last proof can be traced back to the phenomenon that a state is reachable by a standard run – in this case, it is the initial state – in which the two future "event windows" overlap, but in just one point. This leads us to a sufficient condition on well-behavedness for doubly timed Petri nets.

We will use the following strategy: Consider a standard STASM run with finite activity. We will construct a simulating run of the corresponding NTASM from this, and discover in doing so a sufficient condition for this to be possible.

(1) We can associate, with each state q of the run, a set of next possible discrete events $E(q)$, i.e., transitions starting or stopping to work. For each transition currently enabled, there is an interval of time when it can start its work, and for each transition currently working, there is an interval of time when it can stop work. These intervals are called the "execution windows" $I(e)$ of the associated events $e \in E(q)$. Note that an enabled transition might be disabled before it starts work, i.e., for these events, it is not really ensured that they are taken in this run.

(2) We restrict our attention to standard states reachable by standard STASM runs in which no event is urgent, i.e., in which time may be spent. Let us fix such a state q. If there are no events associated with this state, the system can only let time pass. Otherwise, we can single out an event e_q with a minimal upper bound of the associated execution window $I(e_q)$.

(3) We now require from the system, and this is the sufficient condition for well-behavedness, that the intersection of e_q's window with the window of any other event e' waiting currently for execution is no point interval (i.e., is

either empty, which implies that the window of e' starts later than when the window of e ends, or the intersection is an interval of strictly positive length). We now investigate why this condition suffices for well-behavedness.

(4) Since there are only finitely many transitions in a doubly timed Petri net, there are only finitely many events and associated windows, and the intersection of the window of e with the windows of all events with which the intersection is not empty is again no point interval. Let us call this non-empty result of the intersection I_q.

(5) Consider a standard, finite activity STASM run of a doubly timed Petri net. As any STASM run, it consists of a sequence of clusters consisting of contiguous discrete events, and these clusters are separated by time transitions. From this run, we construct a simulating run of the associated NTASM system.

(6) The first step in this construction consists in replacing each time step of real length l in the run by a sequence of $\lceil \frac{l}{dt} \rceil$ time steps of length dt, and by changing each discrete step by incrementing `now` by dt in it instead of keeping `now` constant. If there exists a last infinite time step in the run, it is replaced by an infinite sequence of dt-length time steps. This translation yields a run in which `now` is incremented in each step by dt, but since the discrete steps necessarily and the time step sequences possibly use more time than they used in the STASM run, some events might occur too late in this translation. This has yet to be detected and corrected.

(7) The second step in the construction of a simulating run consists of this correction. Note that since the original STASM run was assumed to be standard and have finite activity, the n'th cluster for all standard n only contains a standard natural number of discrete transitions, and it is preceded by a standard number of time transitions. Altogether, this implies that each event takes place at most an infinitesimal later in the translated run than in the original run. We now correct the position of each nth cluster (for all standard n), if necessary. We can classify the events in a cluster into two sets:

(7.i) One set consists of events which became possible because some previous event in the cluster has taken place; these can be transitions starting to work with a lower bound for reaction time of zero, and transitions stopping to work with a working time of zero. For these transitions, the infinitesimal delay can be no problem, since each positive infinitesimal lies in the execution window of the event, which is assumed to have strictly positive length.

(7.ii) The other set consists of events with a preparation time which was already running since the start of the time transition preceding the cluster. This set might contain events which now are delayed unduly. If it does not, we are ready with this cluster; if there are unduly delayed events, we move so many dt-step time transitions from the sequence of time transitions in front of the cluster to the sequence of time transitions behind the cluster that no event is unduly delayed after this change. This operation moves the current cluster a bit into the direction of the beginning of the run, an infinitesimal which is just enough so that all events in the cluster take place not later than in the corresponding STASM run. A consequence might be that by this operation, events in later clusters might have become unduly delayed by another infinitesimal; but this will be taken care of when we deal with the later cluster.

(8) We only have to show that by the operation last described, the cluster can not move so much that afterward, some events in it take place *too early*. This can not happen because the intersection of execution windows has standard non-zero length, which is larger than any infinitesimal, and because the expanded cluster has also only infinitesimal length. Moving the expanded cluster of discrete transitions in the direction of the beginning by an infinitesimal can not move it out of the intersection of execution windows at the left end if before the move, the cluster touched the right end. But the latter is ensured because the right end must be touched if there was an event in the cluster which took place too late, which is the precondition for the cluster being moved.

We conclude:

Proposition 14.4.3. *Let R be the rule of Figures 14.3 and 14.4, and fix a doubly timed Petri net which is encoded by the initial state. This defines an STASM. Let $\mathfrak{A}_t$ be the set of states which is reachable by a standard finite run of the STASM. If, for all $q \in \mathfrak{A}_t$, the intersection of the execution window of an event with a minimal upper bound with any other execution window associated with q does not form a point interval, R is well-behaved for the start state defined by the doubly timed Petri net under consideration.*

14.4.2 A Well-Behaved Rule for Interleaving Dynamics of Doubly Timed Petri Nets

As before, we will restrict ourselves to the investigation of the interleaving rule; the arising phenomena would be similar for the maximal progress rule. We investigate a variant of the rule given in Figures 14.3 and 14.4 which differs from the original rule with respect to the definition of the derived predicates which specify when a transition can or must start or stop work. We use the definitions in Fig. 14.11.

The difference between the original definitions and the currently investigated ones are the following: (a) The can-functions only consider the lower bound, i.e., a transition can start or stop work if it has it has waited or worked long enough, and it does not matter any longer if he maximal waiting or working time has already come. (b) The must-functions do not check for equality of the time passed since waiting or working started; it is also acceptable if more time has passed.

The idea behind these changes is the following: Infinitesimal discretization of time means that in general, the rule can not fulfill punctual requirements; thus, we have to admit some error. We use the strategy to admit that in the

```
canStartWork(t) ⇔_def
  now - enabledSince(t) ≥ reactionTimeLB(t)

mustStartWork(t) ⇔_def
  now - enabledSince(t) ≥ reactionTimeUB(t)

canStopWork(t) ⇔_def
  now - workingSince(t) ≥ workingTimeLB(t)

mustStopWork(t) ⇔_def
  now - workingSince(t) ≥ workingTimeUB(t)
```

Fig. 14.11. Definitions of derived predicates of a well-behaved rule capturing an interleaving dynamics of a doubly timed net.

NTASM system, the steps happen an infinitesimal later than the corresponding steps in the STASM dynamics. Note that the STASM interpretations of the original rule and of the variant define the same runs:

Proposition 14.4.4. *Let R be the rule of Figures 14.3 and 14.4, and let R' be the variant rule with the definitions of Fig. 14.11. For definitions of static symbols and of initial conditions for doubly timed Petri nets, the runs of $[\![R]\!]^h$ and $[\![R']\!]^h$ are the same.*

Proof. (I) Consider a run of $[\![R]\!]^h$ from the start state. (a) The discrete steps consist of some transition t starting or stopping to work. If in some state, $[\![R]\!]^h$ allows t to start or stop work, also $[\![R']\!]^h$ allows this (since the can-conditions are weaker in R' than in R). (b) And if, in some state, the STASM semantics of R admits a time transition of some length, i.e., no transitions becomes urgent during that time, the same is true for the STASM semantics of R from that state, since the states in which a transition is urgent with respect to R' but not with respect to R can not be reached by a discrete transition, and by a time transition from a reachable state it could only be reached from another state in which the transition was already urgent, which can not happen because of the urgency, which means that these states are not reachable in a run of $[\![R']\!]^h$. (c) Thus, each R-run is also an R'-run.

(II) Conversely, consider a run of $[\![R']\!]^h$ from the start state. (a) Here, too, the discrete steps consist of some transition t starting or stopping to work; but there are states in which R' admits a discrete step in which R does not admit it, namely: if the upper bound of the time for the transition to take place has passed. But since these states are not reachable (such a state can not be reached by a discrete step, and before such a state could be reached by a time step, the transition would become urgent), this is irrelevant. (b) If, in some state, the STASM semantics of R' admits a time step of some length, i.e., no transition becomes urgent for this time, the same is true for the STASM semantics of R, since the states in which a transition is urgent for R is a subset of the states in which a transition is urgent for R'; just compare the definition of the must-predicates. (c) Thus, each R'-run is also an R-run.

Thus, if considered as defining STASM systems, the original rule R and the variant R' define the same system, since states in which the values of $[\![R]\!]^h$ and $[\![R']\!]^h$ differ are not reachable by either system. The nice thing about rule R' is that it admits infinitesimal discretization, or more exactly:

Proposition 14.4.5. *Rule R' as defined in Proposition 14.4.4 is well-behaved for the start state of a doubly timed Petri net.*

Proof. We have to show that for a standard run of $[\![R']\!]^h$ from the start state, there is a simulating run of $[\![R'\|\text{now:=now+dt}]\!]$ from the start state. This proof is a bit lengthy and technical, so we provide it with further structure. Part (A) presents the main idea, to show the existence of a specific predicate on state pairs, part (B) shows why this existence suffices, and part (C) presents a predicate as needed.

(A) We consider a predicate $q \rhd r$ on states q and r with the following properties:

– For standard states q, $q \rhd q$.
– For states q, r with $q \rhd r$, q standard, each standard step of $[\![R']\!]^h$ from q to a (necessarily standard) q' can be mimicked by a (possibly empty) sequence of steps of $[\![R'\|\text{now:=now+dt}]\!]$ from r, leading to r', with $q' \rhd r'$.

(B) If a predicate $\rhd$ as in (A) exists, then R' is well-behaved.

We show this by a standard induction on the number of actions in the standard run, in two steps, (B.i) and (B.ii)

(B.i) We show: For each standard $n \in \mathbb{N}_0$, if there is a standard run of $[\![R']\!]^h$ with n actions from the (standard) start state (which we call q_0) leading to a state q, there is a simulating run of $[\![R'\|\text{now:=now+dt}]\!]$ from q_0 leading to a state r with $q \rhd r$. **Case** $n = 0$: $q_0 \rhd q_0$ holds obviously. **Case** $n > 0$, n **standard:** Assume that q (resp. r) is the final state of any $(n-1)$-action run of the STASM system (resp, the final state of a simulating run of the NTASM system), fulfilling $q \rhd r$. This exists by the induction assumption. For each standard STASM step from q to a state q', there exists, by definition of $\rhd$, a mimicking sequence of NTASM steps from r to a state r' so that $q' \rhd r'$.

(B.ii) If each finite standard STASM run can be mimicked by an NTASM run, this is also true for infinite standard runs for the steps with standard numbers. Indeed, if there was an infinite standard run in which some step with a standard position can not be simulated, there would be a first such position $n \in \mathbb{N}$, which can not be the case because of the induction of (B.i).

(C) Consider $\rhd$ as defined by

$q \triangleright r \Leftrightarrow_{\mathrm{def}}$
    $\wedge \; q$ standard
    $\wedge \; d(q,r) \simeq 0$
    $\wedge \; q$ reachable by $[\![R']\!]^h$ from the start state
    $\wedge \; \forall(p \in P) : q(m(p)) = r(m(p))$
    $\wedge \; \forall(t \in T) : q(\mathtt{enabledSince}(t)) \neq \bot$
                $\longrightarrow$
                        $\wedge \; r(\mathtt{enabledSince}(t)) \neq \bot$
                        $\wedge \; q(\mathtt{now} - \mathtt{enabledSince}(t)) \leq r(\mathtt{now} - \mathtt{enabledSince}(t))$
    $\wedge \; \forall(t \in T) : q(\mathtt{workingSince}(t)) \neq \bot$
                $\longrightarrow$
                        $\wedge \; r(\mathtt{workingSince}(t)) \neq \bot$
                        $\wedge \; q(\mathtt{now} - \mathtt{workingSince}(t)) \leq r(\mathtt{now} - \mathtt{workingSince}(t))$

The most interesting consequence probably is that the time which has passed since a transition started its reaction time or its work might be an infinitesimal longer in r than in q. This is because we have to allow that the infinitesimal discretization might come an infinitesimal too late.

We claim: This predicate fulfills the conditions of (A). Together with (B), this implies that R' is well-behaved.

(C.i) Assume that the STASM system admits a standard discrete step a from q. a represents a transition t starting or stopping to work. Let us consider the first case and the second case in that order. (C.i.a) If t can *start* work in q by an STASM step, t can also start work in a state r with $q \triangleright r$. This start is represented by an action a' so that $d(a, a') \simeq 0$ and for the reached states q' and r', $q' \triangleright r'$ holds:

- If q and a are standard, then $q' = q[a]$ is standard.
- $d(q,r) \simeq 0$ and $d(a, a') \simeq 0$ implies $d(q[a], r[a']) = d(q', r') \simeq 0$.
- If q is reachable in the STASM system, also $q[a]$ is reachable.
- The (initially identical) markings of q and r are changed in an identical way.
- Starting t can at most disable some $t' \in T$, i.e., the condition on $\mathtt{enabledSince}$ is not falsified.
- In the transitions, $\mathtt{workingSince}$ changes only for t, and in the follower states we have
  $q'(\mathtt{now} - \mathtt{workingSince}(t)) = 0$ and $r'(\mathtt{now} - \mathtt{workingSince}(t)) = \mathtt{dt}$.

This completes the proof for the case that a represents a start of work of a transition.

(C.i.b) If t can *stop* work in state q, the reasoning is similar to the previous case, only for newly enabled $t' \in T$, $q'(\mathtt{now} - \mathtt{enabledSince}(t')) = 0$ and $r'(\mathtt{now} - \mathtt{enabledSince}(t')) = \mathtt{dt}$, and $\mathtt{workingSince}$ is only changed, for t, to undefined. This completes the proof for the case that a represents a stop of work of a transition.

(C.ii) Assume that the STASM system admits a standard time step of length l from q, i.e., for all l' with $0 \leq l' < l$, $v \in [\![R']\!](q[\texttt{now:=now+}l'])$, or: for no $t \in T$, t *must* start or stop work in these states. We call such a transition "urgent". Let us consider the start case; the stop case is similar.

(C.ii.a) If, after time l waiting from state q, no transition is urgent, the same is true for time $l+\delta$ for an infinitesimal $\delta \geq 0$. Thus, $[\![R'\|\texttt{now:=now+dt}]\!]$ can do $\lceil \frac{l}{dt} \rceil$ time steps from r, the two behaviors leading to states q' and r' with $q' \rhd r'$.

(C.ii.b) If after time l, some non-empty set T' of transitions become urgent, the NTASM can do $n = \lceil \frac{\max_{t \in T'}(r(x(t))-q(x(t)))}{dt} \rceil$ time steps from r, where $x(t)$ is the term $\texttt{now-enabledSince}(t)$ for transitions t which must start work, and $x(t)$ is the term $\texttt{now-workingSince}(t)$ for transitions t which must stop work after time l has passed starting in state q. Obviously, $n*dt \simeq l$, i.e., the sequence of n NTASM steps simulates the STASM time step, and for the reached states q' and r', $q' \rhd r'$ holds.

14.5 Summary

In this chapter, we present an NTASM-based meta-model for two kinds of timing-enhanced Petri net formalisms. Our approach helps to work out the details of semantics which partly stayed implicit or ambiguous in the original papers, and it allows us to combine the ideas quite easily into **one** formalism, making the difference between the concepts explicit. Finally, it is shown that the definition well-behavedness can be lifted from our base formalism via our operational semantics to timing-enhanced Petri nets; this means that we can classify timing-enhanced Petri nets with respect to their being suited to the discretization necessary for practical implementation.

15. An ASM Meta-model
for Timed and Hybrid Automata

Timed and hybrid automata are formalisms for the description of real-time systems which are designed primarily to make algorithmic analysis possible [ACD93, AD94, ACH⁺95]. Both formalisms are based on the following ideas:

- Each system component which can change both discretely and continuously is modelled by a real-valued variable.
- The different control states of the system are modelled by a finite set. Each of the states in this finite set is associated with an invariance predicate over the continuous variables, and with a predicate restricting possible changes of these variables with respect to time. The time change predicates define in which way a variable may change during the time when the system is in a control state, and the invariance defines how long the system may stay in a control state: The state must be left before or as soon as the invariance becomes false.
- A transition between two states is labeled with a guard predicate on the continuous variables, and with a discrete-change predicate involving primed and non-primed versions of the continuous variables. A transition from one state to the other may only be taken if the guard is true, and if it is taken, the continuous variables may change as described by the discrete change predicate.
- Several such automata can be combined by using CSP-like labels at the transitions: One transition with a label can only be taken if each parallel automaton which has the label in its alphabet also performs a transition with the same label.

In hybrid automata, as predicates for the definition of invariants, derivations, guards and discrete changes, conjunctions of strict and non-strict inequalities of linear functions of the continuous variables are allowed. The coefficients used in the definition of the linear functions of the continuous variables are required to be integers. Inequalities of linear expressions involving rational numbers can be converted to an equivalent form with integer coefficients in the obvious way.

The tool HyTech [HHWT95] allows reachability checks for systems described with this formalism. A variant formalism allowing the description of modules, instantiation and hierarchy has been developed by the author and a colleague [BR98, BR99, BR00b, BR00a, BR01].

Timed automata are simpler. In a typical variant, invariants and guards are conjunctions of strict and non-strict inequalities, where each inequality compares a variable to a rational number. Derivations of all variables in all states are always equal to one, i.e., all variables can be considered to be always controlled by the same clock. The changes implied by a discrete step consist, for each variable, either in being reset to zero, or in not being changed. Tools supporting analysis of systems described with this formalism are Kronos [DOTY96], UppAal [BLL+96] and Rabbit [Bey01].

Since it is the more general concept, we will use the term "hybrid automaton" also for timed automata.

15.1 An STASM Model of Hybrid Automata

We first model a hybrid automaton at a higher abstraction level than it is done in the original formalism.

Figure 15.1 lists and explains the sub-universes which are used in the STASM model of hybrid automata. On the abstraction level used here, we do not define what formulas look like, or how value assignments are represented. This is in order to give a description abstract enough so that it fits both timed automata and hybrid automata.

Figure 15.2 lists the dynamic functions of the model, i.e., the state components. "active" characterizes the states which are active in a configuration; this will be exactly one state of each automaton. "va" is the value assignment which was chosen after the last discrete step, "vad" is an assignment of derivations to variables chosen after the last discrete step, and

---

AUTOMATON: the partial automata out of which the whole system is composed
FORMULA: formulas involving variables, for describing invariants, guards and admissible derivations
FORMULA2: formulas involving primed and unprimed variables, for describing admissible discrete changes
TRANS: transitions between states
$\mathcal{P}$(TRANS): sets of transitions between states
STATE: the disjoint union of states of all automata
SYNC: synchronization labels
VA: value assignments to variables

Fig. 15.1. Sub-universes of the STASM expressing the semantics of hybrid automata.

---

active: STATE → BOOLEAN
va, vad: VA
last_discrete_step_at: REAL

Fig. 15.2. Dynamic functions.

```
from: TRANS → STATE
to: TRANS → STATE
α: AUTOMATON × SYNC → BOOLEAN
automaton_of: TRANS → AUTOMATON
sync: TRANS → SYNC ∪ {⊥}
inv: STATE → FORMULA
der: STATE → FORMULA
guard: TRANS → FORMULA
discrete_step: TRANS → FORMULA2

fulfills: VA × FORMULA → BOOLEAN
fulfills2: VA × VA × FORMULA2 → BOOLEAN
*: REAL × VA → VA
+: VA × VA → VA
```

Fig. 15.3. Static functions.

```
cur_va =def
  va+(now-last_discrete_step_at)*vad
transition_possible(t,s) ⇔def
  ∧ sync(t)=s
  ∧ active(from(t))
  ∧ fulfills(cur_va, guard(t))
next_va_possible(v,t) ⇔def
  ∧ fulfills2(cur_va, v, disc_step(t))
  ∧ fulfills(v, inv(to(t)))
```

Fig. 15.4. Derived functions.

"last_discrete_step_at" represents the moment of the last discrete step. Together with "now", the last three dynamic function allow us to determine the current value assignment.

Figure 15.3 lists the static functions different from sub-universes. The first group defines the static structure of the hybrid automaton. "from" and "to" express the start and end states of transitions. α characterizes for each automaton if a given synchronization symbol belongs to its alphabet. "automaton_of" determines to which automaton a transition belongs. "sync" defines which synchronization symbol a transition carries, or if it does not carry one (which is expressed by the value $\perp$). "inv" describes the invariant associated with a state and "der" the admissible derivations; "guard" describes the guard of a transition and "discrete_step" describes the possible changes to variables during a discrete step. The next group of static functions allow us to work with formulas and value assignments. "fulfills" is a predicate which describes if a value assignment fulfills a formula. "fulfills2" describes if two value assignments fulfill a formula with both primed and unprimed occurrences of variables, where the second value assignment argument is used for the interpretation of primed occurrences of variables in the formula. "*" is used for time intervals and value assignments interpreted as derivations: if the VA argument expresses the changes to variables in one time unit, then the result expresses the changes after the number of time units as given by the REAL argument. "+", if applied to value assignments, adds the values component-wise.

In Fig. 15.4, the derived function "cur_va" is defined which represents the current value assignment. This is the only place where the static functions "*" and "+" on value assignments are used. The predicate "transition_possible(t,s)" expresses if transition t can be taken and synchronizes with s, and "next_va_possible(v,t)" defines if v is a possible next value assignment if transition t is taken.

```
mainRule:
  OR timeRule
  OR discreteStepRule

timeRule:
  IF ∀(s ∈ STATE) : active(s) → fulfills(cur_va, inv(s))
  THEN SKIP
  ELSE HALT

discreteStepRule:
  || last_discrete_step_at := now
  || OR unsyncedDiscreteStepRule
     OR syncedDiscreteStepRule
```

Fig. 15.5. The top-level rules defining the dynamics of hybrid automata.

The dynamics of hybrid automata is defined by the rule "mainRule", which is defined in Fig. 15.5 and further refined in Fig. 15.6. "mainRule" expresses that time may flow or a discrete step may be taken, whatever of the alternatives is possible. "timeRule" defines under which conditions time may flow: SKIP is possible if the invariants of all active states are fulfilled by the current value assignment. As defined by the STASM semantics of a rule, time may flow as long as the rule can do a SKIP. If some invariant is not fulfilled by the current value assignment, the time rule is equivalent to HALT, which means that the time rule provides no alternative for the possible actions in the current configuration, or: that a discrete step must be taken, or if that is not possible, that the system has reached a time deadlock. "discreteStepRule" describes what might happen as a discrete step. The time of the discrete step is recorded in "last_discrete_step_at", and either an unsynchronized or a synchronized discrete step is done. Note that if neither an unsynchronized nor a synchronized discrete step is possible, the effect of the whole rule is equivalent to HALT, by the semantics of synchronous composition in ASMs.

Figure 15.6 describes the details of the alternatives for discrete steps. The simpler case is dealt with in "unsyncedDiscreteStepRule". A possible

```
unsyncedDiscreteStepRule:
  CHOOSE(t : TRANS) : transition_possible(t, ⊥) IN
    CHOOSE(v : VA) : next_va_possible(v, t) IN
      CHOOSE(d : VA) : fulfills(d, der(to(t))) IN
        || va := v
        || vad := d
        || moveRule(t)

syncedDiscreteStepRule:
  CHOOSE(T : P(TRANS)) IN
    ∧ T ≠ {}
    ∧ ∀(t, t' ∈ T) : automaton_of(t) = automaton_of(t') → t = t'
    ∧ ∃(s ∈ SYNC) :
        ∧ ∀(t ∈ T) : transition_possible(t, s)
        ∧ ∀(a ∈ AUTOMATON) : α(a, s) → ∃(t ∈ T) : a = automaton_of(t)
  IN
    CHOOSE(v : VA) : (∀(t ∈ T) : next_va_possible(v, t)) IN
      CHOOSE(d : VA) : (∀(t ∈ T) : fulfills(d, der(to(t)))) IN
        || va := v
        || vad := d
        || FORALL(t ∈ T) DO moveRule(t)

moveRule(t):
  IF from(t) ≠ to(t)
  THEN || active(from(t)) := FALSE
       || active(to(t))   := TRUE
  ELSE SKIP
```

Fig. 15.6. Rules defining the details of the dynamics of hybrid automata.

transition t is chosen which does not carry a synchronization label, a value assignment v for the values of variables at the start of the phase after the current discrete step is chosen, and another value assignment is chosen for the time derivatives. Finally, the state components "va" and "vad" are updated as necessary, and activity moves from the source state of the transition taken to the target state, which is expressed by rule "moveRule".

"syncedDiscreteStepRule" expresses what happens in a synchronized discrete step. This involves in general not a single transition but several of them. The first CHOOSE construct selects such a set of transitions; it must be non-empty and contain at most one transition from each automaton, and they must all be labeled by the same synchronization label, it must be possible to take all the transitions, and all automata must participate which have the synchronization label in their alphabet. Next value assignments for variables and derivatives are chosen which are admitted by all transitions in the selected set. After this selection, these values are assigned to va and vad, and the activity changes associated with all transitions are performed.

"moveRule" expresses what happens to the dynamic predicate "active" when a transition is taken: If the transition does not lead back to its source state, the activity moves from the source state to the target state.

15.2 Comments on the Modelling Choices

Time deadlocks. Time deadlocks deserve some comment. If "`mainRule`" is equivalent to `HALT` in some reachable configuration, this means that a time deadlock is reached. If such a situation is reachable in a model, this is typically used as a modelling error. In the STASM semantics, we also have a time deadlock in a configuration c in which the main rule is equivalent to `SKIP`, but there is a real numbered $\epsilon > 0$ so that for all δ with $0 < \delta \leq \epsilon$, the main rule is equivalent to `HALT` at configuration $c[\text{now} \mapsto c(\text{now}) + \delta]$, since this means that no time can flow from configuration c. A helpful analysis would be to determine if a time deadlock configuration can be reached from an initial configuration of a hybrid automaton.

Discrete transitions. Note that a discrete step of a hybrid automaton is only admitted by the given dynamics if the chosen value assignment for the state reached by the step fulfills the invariants reached. This is encoded by the conjunct `fulfills(`v`,inv(to(`t`)))` of predicate "`next_va_possible`". An alternative would have been not to use this conjunct. In this case, configurations might be reached in which the conjunction of invariants is not necessarily fulfilled; in such configurations, time could not be spent, but it is possible to leave such configurations by an immediately following discrete step. This would allow us to model urgency of a transition by ensuring that the guard of such a transition implies the negation of the invariant of the source state of such a transition.

15.3 Timed Automata and Their Well-Behavedness

In order to investigate the question of well-behavedness, we have to provide more detail than given before, since the question is easier dealt with for timed automata than for hybrid automata. The form of invariants, guards, derivations and discrete step predicates has already been hinted at in the introduction to this chapter. Now, we will be more precise.

Definition 15.3.1. *A **timed automaton** is a hybrid automaton with the following restrictions:*

- *A further sub-universe "Vars" represents the variables.*
- *All states are associated with the same derivation formula. The derivation formula of a timed automaton is a conjunction of formulas of the form $x = 1$, where for each variable x in the system, there is a conjunct in the derivation formula.*
  This means that during time transitions each variable changes its value just like the time, and different values of variables can only occur by changes during the discrete transitions.
- *A formula describing the change during a discrete step is a conjunction of the formulas of the form $x' = 0$ or $x' = x$, where for each variable x, one such formula occurs in the conjunction.*

This means that in a discrete transitions, each variable is either reset to zero (if $x' = 0$ occurs in the formula), or it rests unchanged (if $x' = x$ occurs in the formula).

- *A formula describing an invariant of a control state or a guard of a transition is a conjunction of formulas of the form $x \leq c$, $x < c$, $c \leq x$ or $c < x$, where x is a variable and c is a rational number.*

Note that the restriction on derivations implies that $\mathrm{vad}(x)$ is identical to 1 for all variables x in all reached configurations.

Not all timed automata as defined by these restrictions on formulas and the ASM defined previously admit infinitesimal discretization. For example, consider the timed automaton of Fig. 15.7. States are represented by circles and transitions by arrows. The initial state is marked by an arrow without a source state. Derivation formulas are not given, since they are implied. Guards are given as labels of transitions, decorated with a question mark. A formula without a question mark labeling a transition represents the discrete change. An invariant is given as a label of a state. If a guard or an invariant is identically true, it is not given explicitly, which means for the automaton of Fig. 15.7 that in the second state, the invariant does not ever force control to move on.

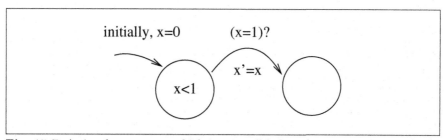

Fig. 15.7. A timed automaton which is not well behaved.

The timed automaton of Fig. 15.7 is not well behaved: In an STASM interpretation, there is a run which starts in the first state with $x = 0$, waits one time unit, then moves on to the second state in a discrete step, not changing x during that step, and stays indefinitely in the second state.

Consider an infinitesimal discretization in which the step width does not divide 1. In this case, the first state can not be left by the discretized run before $\lceil \frac{1}{dt} \rceil$ steps of the system, but then, it is too late for the transition to be taken, because under the condition considered, $dt * \lceil \frac{1}{dt} \rceil$ is larger than 1. Thus, the STASM run can not be mimicked by the NTASM run for the value of dt considered:

Proposition 15.3.1. *The rule of Figures 15.5 and 15.6 is not well-behaved for all timed automata encoded in the initial condition.*

We investigate sufficient conditions for well-behavedness of timed automata. The idea is to find restrictions on guards and invariants so that the following strategy is possible: each discrete step of the STASM system is mimicked by a discrete step of the NTASM system resetting exactly the same variables, and each time step of the STASM system of length l is mimicked by $\lceil \frac{l}{dt} \rceil$ steps of the NTASM system. Using this strategy, we have to deal with the problem that after a sequence of steps mimicking a time step might take an infinitesimal longer, and in a discrete step, the variables not reset also become by an infinitesimal larger in the NTASM system, while in the STASM system, they stay the same.

Under which condition does it not matter if in the NTASM behavior, variables have infinitesimally larger values that in the STASM behavior? We propose to require the following:

Definition 15.3.2. *A* **right-open timed automaton** *is a timed automaton with the following restriction:*

Let ϕ range over the guards and invariants of a timed automaton, and let x range over its variables. If for all such ϕ and x, the conjuncts for x in ϕ describe a standard right-open interval, then the timed automaton is called **right-open***.*

This restriction will allow us to prove:

Proposition 15.3.2. *The rule R as defined by Figures 15.5 and 15.6 is well-behaved for right-open timed automata.*

Proof. We will use the same idea as in the proof of Proposition 14.4.5: We define a predicate $q \triangleright q'$ on state pairs so that each standard step of $[\![R]\!]^h$ from standard q to r can be mimicked by a (possibly empty) sequence of steps of $[\![R||\texttt{now:=now+dt}]\!]$ from q' to some state r' with $r \triangleright r'$.

(A) Define $\triangleright$ by:

$q \triangleright q' \Leftrightarrow_{\text{def}}$
$\quad \wedge \; d(q, q') \simeq 0$
$\quad \wedge \; \forall_{x \in \texttt{Vars}} q(\texttt{cur\_va}(x)) \leq q'(\texttt{cur\_va}(x))$

(B) Consider q and q' with $q \triangleright q'$, q standard. We will prove: (B.i) If $[\![R]\!]^h$ admits a time step of standard length l from q to r, then $[\![R||\texttt{now:=now+dt}]\!]$ admits a sequence of $\lceil \frac{l}{dt} \rceil$ time steps of length dt from q' to r' with $r \triangleright r'$. (B.ii) If $[\![R]\!]^h$ admits a discrete step represented by update set u from q to r, then $[\![R||\texttt{now:=now+dt}]\!]$ admits a discrete step represented by u' simulating u from q' to a state r' with $r \triangleright r'$.

(B.i) Assume that $[\![R]\!]^h$ admits a time step of standard length l from q to r. This means, by the definition of time steps of STASMs, that the change from q to r can be accounted for only by continuous increase of $\texttt{now}$, i.e., by the flow of time, and in all configurations reached on this way (possibly excluding r), $[\![R]\!]$ admits a SKIP step. This is only possible if in all these configurations, all invariants of active states are fulfilled for the values of $\texttt{cur\_va}$ reached during the time step (except possibly the last). Right-openness of the timed automaton implies for the invariants that for standard values of $\texttt{cur\_va}$

which fulfill all active invariants, it does not hurt if the values of some (or all) variables are incremented by an infinitesimal: Also the value assignment computed by such an operation fulfills all active invariants. Thus, if $\llbracket R \rrbracket^h$ admits a time transition of standard length l from q, then $\llbracket R \| \texttt{now:=now+dt} \rrbracket$ admits a sequence of $\lceil \frac{l}{dt} \rceil$ time-only steps from q'; and since this sequence of steps takes at most an infinitesimal longer than l, and also in q', the cur_va-value of all variables is at most an infinitesimal larger than in q, the same is true for the reached state r' in comparison to r, so that $r \rhd r'$ holds.

(B.ii) Assume that $\llbracket R \rrbracket^h$ admits a standard discrete step with update set u from q, leading to r. We have to show that this step can be mimicked by $\llbracket R \| \texttt{now:=now+dt} \rrbracket$ from q' for any q' with $q \rhd q'$. u consists of some discrete transitions being taken. The same transitions can be taken from q', (a) because the same states are active in q and q' (because of $d(q, q') \simeq 0$), and (b) because of the right-openness of the guards of the transitions being taken, so that it does not matter if the cur_va-values of some variables are an infinitesimal larger in q' than in q. The resulting set of updates u' is similar to u. It remains to be shown that the two states reached are in $\rhd$-relation. In the reached states r and r', cur_va-values of variables which have been reset are both zero, and values of non-reset variables are in r', where time has been incremented by dt in the discrete step, have increased by not more than another infinitesimal from q', so that also for the reached states r and r', we have $r \rhd r'$.

(C) A standard induction on the length of STASM-runs yields the result.

15.4 Well-Behavedness of Hybrid Automata

The formalism of hybrid automata is more general than that of timed automata. Guards, invariants and derivation formulas are conjunctions of strict or non-strict inequalities of terms which are linear expressions of the variables of the system, where standard rational coefficients are allowed. Discrete step formulas are similar, the difference is that both non-primed and primed occurrences of the variables are allowed, where primed occurrences represent values of variables after the discrete step.

As for timed automata, we investigate well-behavedness for hybrid automata. Since timed automata are a special case of hybrid automata, the example given above of a timed automaton for which the rule R of Figures 15.5 and 15.6 is not well-behaved is also an example of a hybrid automaton for which the rule is not well-behaved.

We use the same strategy as for timed automata for describing restrictions on hybrid automata so that the rule R is well-behaved for them: We simulate an STASM time step of standard length l by a sequence of $\lceil \frac{l}{dt} \rceil$ NTASM timed steps of length dt, and we simulate a discrete STASM step by a single NTASM step. We also get the same problem: In the simulation, the cur_va-values of variables will be a bit different from the values in the original run because timed step sequences might take a bit longer in the simulation, and discrete steps do take some infinitesimal time (instead of no time) in the simulation. This implies that variables with a positive derivation might have increased a bit more in the simulation, and variables with a negative derivation might have decreased a bit more.

We will first use the restriction that the variables of the hybrid automaton can be divided into three classes, which we will call positive, neutral and negative. If the values of a variable in corresponding states of the original run and of the simulating run are compared, we will allow that positive variables have infinitesimally larger values in the simulation than in the original, negative variables may have infinitesimal smaller values in the simulation than in the original, and neutral variables must have the same values in corresponding states.

In order to simplify the case distinctions, we assume that formulas are given in normal form: (i) The rational factor of a variable in an inequality is always positive, and (ii) each inequality in a discrete-step formula references at least one primed variable. If a formula does not fulfill (i), this can be repaired by moving the variable and its factor to the other side of the inequality, changing the sign of the factor in the operation. If in an inequality of the discrete-step formula, no primed variables occurs, this inequality can be moved from the conjuncts describing the discrete step of a transition to the conjuncts describing the guard of the transition.

Strict inequalities present no problem for the simulation: If in the original run, a standard time step or discrete step is possible, the infinitesimal differences of cur_va-values in the simulation can not turn strict inequalities from fulfilled to not fulfilled: the value of either side of the inequality can only change by an infinitesimal (all factors are standard, and the variable values in the original run are standard); and for two standard values x and y which fulfill $x < y$, changing either or both by an infinitesimal will not change the truth value of $x < y$. This means that only formula conjuncts which are non-strict inequalities may be a problem for the infinitesimally discretized simulation.

Another non-problem are occurrences of variables on the "right" sides. If a positive variable occurs on the "greater" side of an inequality, or a negative variable occurs on the "smaller" side, this is no problem for the simulation: since all factors are positive, an increase of a variable on the "greater" side will not turn a formula from fulfilled to not-fulfilled, and neither does a decrease of a variable of a variable on the "smaller" side. Since neutral variables have identical values in corresponding states of the original run and the simulation, they will never be a problem for a simulating step being taken.

A state q in the original run might correspond to a state q' in the simulating run if all of the following conditions hold:

- q is standard
- $d(q, q') \simeq 0$
- For positive variables x, $q(\texttt{cur\_val}(x)) \leq q'(\texttt{cur\_val}(x))$

- For negative variables x, $q(\texttt{cur\_val}(x)) \geq q'(\texttt{cur\_val}(x))$
- For neutral variables x, $q(\texttt{cur\_val}(x)) = q'(\texttt{cur\_val}(x))$
- For all variables x, $q(\texttt{vad}(x)) = q'(\texttt{vad}(x))$
- $q(\text{last\_discrete\_step\_at}) \leq q'(\text{last\_discrete\_step\_at})$

The first restriction for well-behavedness is that in non-strict invariance or guard inequalities, positive variables occur at most on the "greater" side, and negative variables occur at most on the "smaller" side.

The restriction on invariance inequalities implies that standard length timed steps of the STASM system can be simulated by a sequence of dt-length time steps as described above. The infinitesimal deviations in the start state in the simulation will present no problem, and the possibly infinitesimally longer time of the simulation will also be allowed. The sequence of dt-length steps will end in a state which is in the proper relation to the state reached by the simulated time steps.

The restriction on guard inequalities admit the simulation of discrete steps in the original system, as far as the next values to be chosen are not relevant.

The second restriction is on derivation formulas. They must only allow non-negative values for positive variable, non-positive values for negative variables, and the value zero for neutral variables.

This restriction implies that during the sequence of time steps in the simulation, which can be an infinitesimal longer than the simulated time step, the additional length changes the values of variables into the proper direction.

It is more difficult to find a plausible restriction for discrete-step formulas, since the next values to be chosen may depend on the current values of variables, which might be infinitesimally different in the original run and its simulation. Consider singleton set with a discrete transition without a synchronization label, or a set of discrete hybrid-automaton transitions which belong to different automata and which carry the same synchronization label. A priori, i.e., without consideration of guards, discrete-step formulas or reachability questions, this describes possible discrete steps of the automaton. Such a set of discrete hybrid automaton transitions defines a set of inequalities: those inequalities which occur in the discrete-step formulas of the set considered which are non-strict and in which a non-primed variable occurs on the wrong side. We call this set of inequalities Φ. Only formulas in Φ might be a problem for the simulation, i.e., might require different new values for variables to be chosen in the simulated discrete step than in the original. This is because of the following: In a strict inequality, the standard values chosen for primed variables in the original discrete step are also a possible choice if unprimed variables have slightly deviating values; and if unprimed variables occur only on the right side, the values chosen for primed variables in the original fulfill also the condition in the simulation.

If at least one non-strict inequality occurs in the discrete step formula considered in which at least one unprimed variable occurs on the wrong side, there can be a problem with choosing values for the primed variables. Note that is not necessarily a problem if the values chosen in the step to be simulated do not fulfill the inequalities with the slightly changed values for unprimed variables, since it is possible to choose these value also slightly changed (an infinitesimal larger for positive variables, and an infinitesimal smaller for negative variables). Only neutral variables must be chosen as in the original step.

Unfortunately, just knowing that unprimed variables might be a bit larger or smaller in the original is not enough. Satisfiability of Φ might depend on more specific properties of the unprimed variables. For example, let X be a neutral variable, Y and Z positive variables, which have equal values in the step to be simulated. Consider the discrete-step equation $X' = Z - Y$ (more precisely, assume that $X' + Y \geq Z$ and $X' + Y \leq Z$ are elements of Φ for the discrete step considered). This can be simulated if also in the simulation, before the step $Y = Z$ holds, but we can not guarantee this, since we only know that Y and Z are at most by an infinitesimal larger than zero in the simulation before the step, not that they are equal. This means that investigations of satisfiability of discrete-step formulas would need more specific restrictions of the hybrid automata considered.

We just point out two special cases of hybrid automata which admit infinitesimal discretization. One are right-open timed automata, for which the rule is well-behaved; the other are hybrid automata in which for each discrete transition, the set of potentially problematic formulas Φ is empty.

15.5 Summary

This chapter presents an NTASM semantics for timed and hybrid automata, which is another approach to modelling timed and hybrid systems. It is demonstrated that the concept of well-behavedness can be transferred to this context as well. For timed automata, it is fairly simple to find a plausible condition to ensure well-behavedness. For hybrid automata, this is a bit more complicated, because the values of continuously changing variables might become infinitesimally smaller or infinitesimally larger in the NTASM variant because of the infinitesimally imprecise simulation. This means that more cases have to be distinguished, and in our approach to simulation, more restrictions are necessary. Again it is shown that concepts from the formalism used for expressing the semantics are helpful in defining important properties of models of the defined formalism.

16. A Production Cell with Timing

16.1 Introduction

Lewerentz and Lindner [LL95] designed a case study inspired from an industrial application. This case study was often used for illustration of features of different modelling formalisms for reactive systems.

We will use a case study similar to this, which also seems to be inspired by industrial examples, in order to illustrate features of our approach in such a more practical context.

In the case study by Lewerentz and Lindner, no timing properties were specified; in a similar case study, defined by Lötzbeyer and Mühlfeld [LM96], this changes. Interesting features of this second case study are the following:

- Variants of the system have to be taken into account by implementors; Lötzbeyer and Mühlfeld do not define just one production cell but an abstract scheme for a production cell which can be realized in different ways. Specifically:
  - The realized variants might have different global structure. There might be one or two cranes for transporting blanks being worked an, and there might be two or four processing machines which can be used for working the plates.
  - Each processing machine can be of one of two different types. (a) Oven-type machines work on a blank as long as it is located in the machine; working time can only be controlled by choosing the time interval between putting a blank into a machine and taking it out. The machines do not have to be switched on or off, they are on all the time. (b) A drill-or-press-type machine has to be switched on when a blank has to be processed, and it is switched off automatically when the fixed processing time has ended.
- Blanks have to be processed according to different programs, i.e., the sequence of processing steps is not fixed, but can be different for any blank entering the system.
- Timing is relevant: Each blank may be associated with an upper bound for the time of its being in the system, and for the oven-type processing units, with a time interval defining upper and lower processing time.

The task consists in defining a control program for a flexible production cell and proving some properties of the whole system consisting of the production cell hardware and the control program. We now proceed to describe the main features of the case study task description.

16.2 Task Description

One version of this second production cell case study scheme is depicted in Fig. 16.1. New plates arrive in the system via the feed belt, whose motion is to be controlled by the controller to be designed. At the end of the belt, a light barrier is located which can be used to detect if a new blank has arrived, and a code reader can identify the processing program for the blank.

After the plate has been processed by the system, the blank is supposed to be put on the deposit belt. A sensor tells if it is occupied. The deposit belt is not controlled by the control program to be developed. We assume that the environment will never change the state of the deposit belt from unoccupied to occupied[1].

The program read by the code reader specifies which processing units must be used, possibly also specifying the order, and for processing steps in oven-type processing units, it possibly specifies time constraints. Additionally, the program might specify a maximal time for the interval between taking a blank off the feed belt and putting it on the deposit belt.

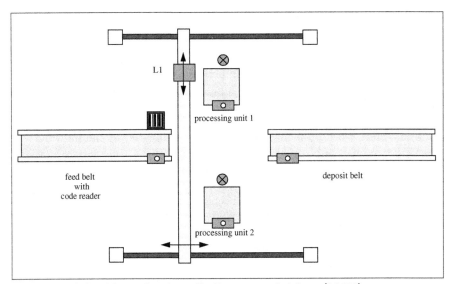

Fig. 16.1. A flexible production cell, diagram copied from [LM96].

---

[1] This assumption is not justified by the original task description, but it is plausible.

In the figure, two processing units are depicted. Each has a sensor which tells if it is working, and each has an actuator with which it might be switched on or off; but oven-type machines are not supposed to be switched on or off by the control program, and drill-or-press-type machines are only switched on; they switch themselves off by themselves. Note that it is not fixed which processing unit is of which type. The specification has to take this into account.

"L1" in the figure is the crane used for moving plates; it can be moved in three directions. The x-direction is that from the feed belt to the deposit belt, the y-direction is that from one processing unit to the other, and the z-direction is the vertical direction, i.e., the crane can move up or down. Two vertical positions are defined explicitly, a "lower" and an "upper" position. In the lower position, the magnet gripper of the crane can pick up or drop blanks; in the upper position, the crane can travel horizontally without that collisions with belts or processing units can occur.

The variant with a different global structure just consists of two cranes which are located in parallel, and of four processing units. See Fig. 16.2 of a view from above.

The actuators to be driven by the control program are the following:

- Switch on/off the feed belt movement.
- Activate the code reader of the feed belt. After activation, the code reader needs some (unspecified) time until the result is presented.
- Switch on processing unit i ($i \in \{1, 2\}$ or $i \in \{1, 2, 3, 4\}$) for processing units of drill-or-press type.

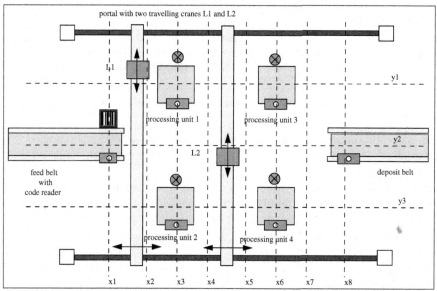

Fig. 16.2. Larger version of a flexible production cell and special crane positions, mostly copied from [LM96].

– Move crane i horizontally into position x_k ($i = 1$ or $i \in \{1,2\}$, $k \in \{1,\dots,8\}$).
  We assume that during a crane movement, a crane will just ignore another movement command. Only after it has reached its target, it will listen again to this actuator[2].
– Move crane i horizontally into position y_k ($i = 1$ or $i \in \{1,2\}$, $k \in \{1,2,3\}$).
– Move gripper of crane i into upper/lower position ($i = 1$ or $i \in \{1,2\}$).
– Switch the magnet of crane i on/off ($i = 1$ or $i \in \{1,2\}$).

A crane can move in both horizontal directions at the same time and stops automatically when its target position is reached.

The following sensors inform the control program about states of the production cell:

– Is there a blank at the end of the feed belt?
– Is there a blank at the beginning of the deposit belt?
– Is processing unit i loaded with a blank ($i \in \{1,2\}$ or $i \in \{1,2,3,4\}$)?
– Is processing unit i currently processing a blank ($i \in \{1,2\}$ or $i \in \{1,2,3,4\}$)?
– Is position x_k occupied by some crane ($k \in \{1,\dots,8\}$)?
– Is the crane i in position y_k ($i = 1$ or $i \in \{1,2\}$, $k \in \{1,2,3\}$)?
– Is the gripper of crane i in the upper position ($i = 1$ or $i \in \{1,2\}$)?
– Is the gripper of crane i in the lower position ($i = 1$ or $i \in \{1,2\}$)?
– What is the output of the code reader?

The dashed lines in Fig. 16.2 show the meanings of the crane positions x_k and y_k. If the smaller version of the scheme is used, we just assume that processing units three and four are missing.

The output of the code reader will either be zero (if the code reader has not yet been activated since the last arrival of a blank at the end of the feed belt, or there is no blank at the end of the feed belt, or the time the code reader needs for determining the program for a blank has not yet passed), or it is the description of a processing program to be executed for the blank by the control program. This program is a quadrupel consisting of the following components:

– The first component is a natural number n ($n \leq 2$ or $n \leq 4$, depending on the number of processing units in the system). It describes the length of the program.
– The second component is a list of length n, where each list element is a triple consisting of the number s of a processing unit ($s \in \{1,2\}$ or $s \in \{1,2,3,4\}$) to use for the step and of two number min and max where min denotes the minimal processing time and max denotes the maximal

---

[2] The original task description does not specify if during the movement of the crane, another movement command is accepted, possibly changing the direction of a movement before the target of the first movement command is reached, or if this is not possible.

processing time for the processing unit s, where ∞ can be used as value for an unbound maximal processing time[3]. For drill-or-press-type processing units, it may be assumed that the numbers for min and max are 0 and ∞, respectively, and for oven-type machines, the max value can be assumed to never be ∞.

We assume that the list ist not empty and each processing unit occurs at most once in it[4].

- The third component is a Boolean value if the order of processing steps is fixed by the list, or of any order can be chosen for the execution of the steps.
- The fourth component is an element of $\mathbb{N} \cup \{\infty\}$ again. It denotes the maximal time in seconds which the blank may spend in the system, i.e., from the moment the gripper takes it from the feed belt to the moment the gripper puts it on the deposit belt.

The initial state of the system is defined by the feed belt movement switch being off, the cranes are not moving, magnets are off and no blanks are carried, and drill-and-press-type processing units are not operating[5]. There may be blanks in the system, which are just moved to the deposit belt[6]. Since in our approach, it is an invariant that at most one blank is in the system-cum-deposit belt, the deposit belt can be assumed to be empty.

Several timing constants are used to describe the production cell.

- vx_i, vy_i and vz_i describe, in meters per second, how quickly the crane i or the gripper moves in the different directions. Positive and negative acceleration times are neglected, i.e., it is assumed that these speeds are instantly reached after a movement is initiated, and that the movement instantly stops after a target position has been reached.
- px_i for $i \in \{1, \ldots, 8\}$ and py_i for $i \in \{1, 2, 3\}$ describe positions in meters. Their differences can be used to compute, together with the speeds, traveling times from one position to another.
- $height$, in meters, is the distance between the lower and upper position of the crane grippers; it is the same for all cranes.
- $t\_station_i$ is the processing time in seconds for processing unit i, which is of the drill-and-press type.

We use several assumptions which are not allowed explicitly by the original task descriptions, but which seem sensible:

---

[3] This interpretation is different from the original task specification, which is presumably false. In the original task specification, the minimal and maximal times of the i-th list entry are presrcibed to be used for processing unit i, not for the processing unit number s.

[4] This assumption is not mentioned explicitly by the original task description.

[5] The original task description says that no processing units are operating, but this is in conflict with the fact that oven-type processing units are switched on all the time.

[6] The original task description does not define what to do with blanks which are in the system in the initial configuration.

- We assume that the restriction regarding the maximal processing time given for a blank in its program is always possible to respect physically, i.e., crane movement times and processing times for blanks in the processing units add up, for an optimal schedule allowed by the program, to at most the time allowed for in the blank's program[7].

  Note that this very weak assumption can lead to quite involved scheduling requirements. We discuss this in some detail later.
- We assume that the production cell works as specified by the timing constants, i.e., we do not deal with malfunctions which might be detected if after the computed time for some movement or processing step has passed, the target is not reached or the processing unit is not ready. Perhaps it would be more realistic that the speeds and times above are lower bounds for the real system constants.
- We assume that during processing of a blank in a processing unit, the gripper is allowed to stay in the lower position above the processing unit[8].
- We assume that we know at the start of the program which processing units are of which type. This information could also be determined from the programs read from the code reader, but it seems natural that the control program has this kind of data from the start off.
- For the variant with two cranes, the crane used for the transport of a plate must be changed at least once. If a program is empty, this change can not be performed without the blank being put into some processing unit where no processing is to be done. But this is excluded by the requirement that a blank only visit processing units given in its program. We assume that programs for blanks may not be empty in the larger variant.

16.3 Requirements to Be Fulfilled by the Control Program

The following requirements are to be fulfilled by the system:

- No two cranes may be at the same x position, and a crane may only move if its gripper is in the upper position.

  Note that this requirement does not specify a minimal distance between x-positions of cranes. This seems to be an omission, which we repair by requiring at least a strictly positive distance min_x_dist between the x-positions of cranes. We assume that between the specially designated positions px_i, the distance is more than min_x_dist.
- A blank may only be put into a processing unit if it is not occupied by some other blank, and it may only be put onto the deposit belt if the sensor does not report that the start of the belt is occupied.

---

[7] The original task description does not specify if this can be assumed, or what has to be done if this is not fulfilled.

[8] The original task description is silent about this.

- The feed belt must be switched off when a blank arrives at its end, and a gripper magnet may only be switched off if the gripper is in the lower position above a processing unit or a belt.
- Every blank taken from the feed belt will eventually be put on the deposit belt.
- Blanks go through the processing units given in their programs; if the program specifies that the order of the program list has to be respected, this is the order used for the blank.
- Between the moment when a blank is picked up from the feed belt and the moment it is put on the deposit belt, no more than the maximal allowed system processing time as specified in its program may be spent.
- The minimal and maximal processing times in oven-type processing units must be respected.

16.4 Direct Consequences from the Task Description

The task description does not show some features which might perhaps have been expected in a description inspired by a real application:

- Efficiency does not belong to the requirements, i.e., it is not required blanks are processed as quickly as possible.
  Thus, the specification allows that at any one moment, at most one blank is resident in the system, even if one could without problem process several; but this makes the second crane of the larger configuration mainly superfluous, and it would make identical processing units in the system superfluous. This second crane only leads to the complication that an optimal scheduling for some blank might be more difficult to compute, as the cranes might move with different speeds and are in different positions.
- The requirement to be able to compute an optimal schedule for a blank comes from the weakness of the assumption regarding the total residence time of a blank in the system for the larger global configuration. This assumption seems to lead to most complications for the design.
  It is not clear if this is an intentional consequence from the original task specification, since fullfilment of the other requirements does not seem too be algorithmically too involved, and this consequence results from an assumption on our part about the interpretation of the upper residence time of a blank in the system.
  Perhaps, stronger assumptions about the maximal residence times of blanks are admissible.

The only obvious way in which the optimal scheduling requirement might be weakened is by ignoring the maximal processing times altogether. Less obvious assumptions are the following:

- It might be assumed that both cranes have the same speeds in all directions, or that the maximal residence time is large enough so that even the

slower times suffice. Then, a repeated crane switching for movements is not necessary; it only has to be ensured that the single crane switch necessary can be done quickly enough.
- It might be assumed that each of the speeds of one crane is larger than or equal to the corresponding speed of the other crane. Only crane one can serve the feed belt and only crane two can serve the deposit belt.

We will not use any of these simplifications.

16.5 An Abstract Control Program

We present a first variant of a system description, on an abstract level, just consisting of (a) the feed belt with its light barrier and the code reader; (b) a transport-and-processing system fetching blanks from the end of the feed belt, executing the program, and putting the processed blank on the deposit belt; and (c) the deposit belt. This system description would be true for all variants allowed in the task description and fix our interpretation of some of the common parts, which should be refined when more details are expressed.

We use the following modes of the control program for the transport-and-processing system:

- cleaningUp: Move a blank possibly residing in the system at startup to the deposit belt; when ready, enter mode waitForNextBlank.
- waitingForNextBlank: Move crane one to the feed belt, wait until another blank arrives, and activate the code reader when it does; then move to mode waitingForNextProgramAndDepositBelt.
- waitingForNextProgramAndDepositBelt: Wait for the next program to become available, and for the deposit belt to become free. As soon as both conditions are fulfilled, compute and activate a new schedule for the program, and move on to mode executingSchedule.
- executingSchedule: Execute the schedule up to its end; when it has come, move back to mode waitingForNextBlank.

In Fig. 16.3 we present a rule for operating the feed belt. It is responsible for switching the feed belt off as soon as a blank arrives at its end, and for switching it on as soon as the light barrier says that a blank has left. feed-BeltIsOn is a flag location which is updated when the feed belt is switched on or off; feedBeltSignalsBlank, SwitchFeedBeltOff and SwitchFeedBeltOn directly correspond to sensors and actuators of the system.

The rule OperateFeedBelt is to be used in parallel to the other rule of the system, which describes the behavior of the transport-and-processing system, which is given in Fig. 16.4. The latter starts in mode cleaningUp and determines if there is a blank in the system. If it is not, it waits for the next blank, otherwise, it moves the only blank in the system to the deposit belt, and then waits for the next blank. Waiting for the next blank means moving crane one to the feed belt, waiting until the deposit belt is empty, waiting

```
OperateFeedBelt =def
  IF AND feedBeltIsOn
     AND feedBeltSignalsBlank
  THEN || SwitchFeedBeltOff
       || feedBeltIsOn := FALSE
  ELIF AND NOT feedBeltIsOn
       AND NOT feedBeltSignalsBlank
  THEN || SwitchFeedBeltOn
       || feedBeltIsOn := TRUE
  ELSE SKIP
```

Fig. 16.3. A rule for operating the feed belt of the system.

```
TPSystem =def
  IF modeTP = cleaningUp
  THEN IF blankInSystem
       THEN CleanUp
       ELSE modeTP := waitingForNextBlank
  ELIF modeTP = waitingForNextBlank
  THEN || MoveCraneOneToFeedBelt
       || IF AND craneOneAtFeedBelt
             AND feedBeltSignalsBlank
          THEN || ActivateCodeReader
               || modeTP := waitingForNextProgramAndDepositBelt
          ELSE SKIP
  ELIF AND modeTP = waitingForNextProgramAndDepositBelt
       AND nextProgramAvailable
       AND NOT depositBeltSignalsBlank
  THEN || ComputeSchedule
       || modeTP := executingSchedule
  ELIF modeTP = executingSchedule
  THEN || ExecuteSchedule
       || IF scheduleHasFinished
          THEN modeTP := waitingForNextBlank
          ELSE SKIP
  ELSE SKIP
```

Fig. 16.4. A rule describing the control program for the transport-and-processing subsystem in an abstract fashion.

for the feed belt to become empty, and waiting for a new blank program to become available. If all this is true, a scheduling for the blank program is determined and its execution starts. As soon as the scheduling has been executed to its end, the system starts waiting for the next blank again. The derived symbol blankInSystem signals if there is a blank in some processing unit or connected to some gripper. Rule CleanUp is supposed to remove a blank from the system if on start, the system is not empty; it moves the blank just to the deposit belt. Rule `MoveCraneToFeedBelt` moves crane one to the end of the feed belt, where the gripper is to stay in the upper position. The derived symbol `craneOneAtFeedBelt` signals if the crane has arrived at the feed belt. Rule `ActivateCodeReader` corresponds directly to an actuator of the system. The derived symbol `nextProgramAvailable` signals if the code reader has computed the next program to use. Rule `ComputeSchedule` computes a new schedule for the transport-and-processing system.

A schedule is a finite list, the elements of which are executed in the order given in the list; each element is either (a) an actuator to be activated when that list element is reached, or (b) a condition on the sensors, meaning that on reaching that list element, the control program waits until the condition becomes true, or (c) a real number, meaning that when the list element is reached, the system waits for the time given by the number before it proceeds to the next element.

The schedule to be computed by `ComputeSchedule` will have to fulfill the correctness and safety requirements for the system. As we assume that such a schedule always exists, the task of `ComputeSchedule` is a possible one.

Rule `ExecuteSchedule` executes the current schedule, as described above for the possible entries. When a schedule entry has been processed, it is removed from the list. The derived symbol `scheduleHasFinished` signals if the currently active schedule has been computed up to its end, by checking if the list representing it is empty.

Only rule `ComputeSchedule` needs more discussion and refinement for the different alternatives of the system. We consider an abstract version of this rule. Figure 16.5 presents this abstract version; it describes which conditions a schedule for a program has to fulfill. Symbol `currentProgram` designates the program for which a schedule is to be computed. `currentSchedule` is to contain the schedule which is being computed. `processingTime`(s) denotes, for a schedule s, the time from the moment when the blank is taken from the feed belt up to the time when it is put at the deposit belt. `maxTimeToUse`(p)

```
ComputeSchedule_Abstract =def
  CHOOSE s:isScheduleForProgram(s,currentProgram) IN
    currentSchedule := s

isScheduleForProgram(s,p) =
  AND processingTime(s)≤maxTimeToUse(p)
  AND setOfPUs(s) = setOfPUs(p)
  AND FORALL (u:setOfPUs(s)):
        AND minProcessingTime(u,p)≤processingTime(u,s)
        AND processingTime(u,s)≤maxProcessingTime(u,p)
  AND followOrder(p)→(listOfPUs(s) = listOfPUs(p))
```

Fig. 16.5. An abstract rule specifying the schedule for the current program.

denotes the maximal time to use for the program p. setOfPUs yields the set of processing units mentioned in a schedule or a program. minProcessing-Time and maxProcessingTime yield, for a processing unit and a program, the minimal and maximal admissible processing times, and processingTime yields, for a processing unit and a schedule, how long the processing unit operates on the blank for the schedule. followOrder extracts the information from a program if the processing machines have to be used in the order given, and listOfPUs yields the list of processing units in the order in which they are mentioned in a schedule or in a program, where for a schedule, several mentionings of the same processing unit are collapsed into one.

Any implementation of ComputeSchedule will have to replace the non-constructive CHOOSE statement with a constructive variant so that the schedule put into currentSchedule fulfills the same conditions as listed in the abstract specification.

16.6 Schedules for Variable-Order Programs

The case for variable order of processing units can, for both the case with one crane and the case with two cranes, be dealt with using the (yet to be determined) solutions for the cases with fixed order of processing units, by just computing the schedules for all permutations of the sequence of processing units and choosing one with a minimal processing time. Since the maximal number of processing units is four, this means that at most $4! = 24$ schedules must be computed, which we assume to be an acceptable number of alternatives to check (the original task description does not limit the resources for computing schedules, which might be an omission).

Figure 16.6 presents this idea as an ASM rule. PUPermutations is assumed to yield, for a program given as argument, the set of (maximally 24) programs resulting from permuting the order of the processing units in the argument. The variable S of the LET expression consists of the schedules for these programs when they are considered to be executed in the order given, and the Hilberts choice function ϵ is used to select an element from this set of schedules with a minimal processing time.

What remains to be defined is a function mkScheduleForFixedOrder which computes a schedule for a fixed order program. The case with two cranes is far more complicated than the one with one crane. We first deal with the simpler version.

16.7 One Crane, Order of Processing Units Fixed

When a schedule is to be computed for a newly determined program, we know that the (only, in this case) crane is waiting above the blank at the end of the feed belt. Thus, the first thing to do is to pick up the blank to be processed: the gripper is moved down, the magnet is turned on, and the gripper is moved

```
ComputeSchedule_Concrete  =def
  currentSchedule :=
    IF followOrder(currentProgram)
    THEN mkScheduleForFixedOrder(currentProgram)
    ELSE mkScheduleForVariableOrder(currentProgram)

mkScheduleForVariableOrder(p)  =def
  LET  S = {s|∃(q : PUPermutations(p)) :
           s = mkScheduleForFixedOrder(q)
         }
  IN  ϵ({s ∈ S : ¬∃(t ∈ S) : processingTime(t) < processingTime(s)})

mkScheduleForFixedOrder(q)  =def
  IF systemHasOneCrane
  THEN mkScheduleForFixedOrder_oneCrane(q)
  ELSE mkScheduleForFixedOrder_twoCranes(q)
```

Fig. 16.6. Rule describing how a schedule for a program with a flexible ordering of processing units is computed.

up again. Then, for each processing unit in the program, the same happens: The crane is moved to the position of the processing unit; the gripper is moved down; the magnet is switched off; for oven-type processing units, the system waits for the minimal processing time as given in the program, while for drill-or-press-type processing units, the processing unit is switched on and it is waited until it has finished its work; remember that we assume that the gripper may stay in the lower position during processing of a blank, which is neither explicitly allowed nor explicitly forbidden by the original task description. Then, the magnet is turned on again, and the gripper moves up again. When there is no more processing unit to be worked with, the crane moves to the deposit belt, lowers the gripper, switches the magnet off, and moves the gripper up gain. The movement back to the feed belt is controlled by the general control program described by rule TPSystem in Fig. 16.4.

Using the dot as denoting list concatenation (again using a prefix syntax as for other associative operators), we can express the computation of the schedule for a one-crane system as given in Fig. 16.7, where the correspondence of list elements with actuators and sensors should be clear. Function list creates a list from its argument(s). isOvenType(q) tells, for an element of the list component of a blank program, if the processing unit to be used is of the oven type; minTime fetches the minimal processing time given for such an element, switchOnPU switches on the processing unit mentioned in the list element, and isProcessing determines if the processing unit is currently processing some blank. isEmpty tells, for a list, if it is empty, and emptySchedule is an empty schedule list. first and rest yield, for a nonempty list, the first element and the list consisting of all elements but the first one.

```
mkInitSchedule =def
  list(moveGripperDown(1), isGripperDown(1),
       switchMagnetOn(1),
       moveGripperUp(1), isGripperUp(1))

mkExitSchedule =def
  list(moveCrane(1,x8), moveCrane(1,y2),
       isCraneAt(1,x8) ∧ isCraneAt(1,y2),
       moveGripperDown(1), isGripperDown(1),
       switchMagnetOff(1),
       moveGripperUp(1), isGripperUp(1))

mkPUSchedule(q) =def
  . list(moveCrane(1,xpos(q)), moveCrane(1,ypos(q)),
         isCraneAt(1, xpos(q)) ∧ isCraneAt(1, ypos(q)),
         moveGripperDown(1), isGripperDown(1),
         switchMagnetOff(1))
  . IF isOvenType(q)
    THEN list(minTime(q))
    ELSE list(switchOnPU(q), ¬ isProcessing(q))
  . list(switchMagnetOn(1),
         moveGripperUp(1), isGripperUp(1))

mkProgramSchedule(p) =def
  IF isEmpty(p)
  THEN emptySchedule
  ELSE mkPUSchedule(first(p)) . mkProgramSchedule(rest(p))

mkScheduleForFixedOrder_oneCrane(p) =def
  . mkInitSchedule
  . mkProgramSchedule(PUList(p))
  . mkExitSchedule
```

Fig. 16.7. Computing the schedule for a program with a one-crane system.

We have yet to discuss if the schedule constructed here obeys the requirements; obviously, the order in which a blank is processed is as given in the program for the blank. Requirements for processing times are also fulfilled (this will be ensured by the executor rule of the schedule to be described in the next section), as are the requirements regarding collision avoidance. Finally, the maximal residence time of the blank in the system will not be exceeded because this is the quickest possible schedule, and we assume that the quickest possible schedule fulfills the residence time requirement.

16.8 Executing the Current Schedule

At this point in our design process, we have fixed enough details so that we can make more precise the meaning of rule ExecuteSchedule and of the derived predicate scheduleHasFinished which are used in mode executingSchedule

```
scheduleHasFinished =def isEmpty(currentSchedule)

ExecuteSchedule =def
  IF isEmpty(currentSchedule)
  THEN SKIP
  ELSE LET s=first(currentSchedule),
           t=rest(currentSchedule)
       IN
          IF isActuator(s)
          THEN || ActivateActuator(s))
               || currentSchedule := t
          ELIF isSensorPredicate(s)
          THEN IF sensorPredicateIsTrue(s)
               THEN currentSchedule := t
               ELSE SKIP
          ELSE IF waitUntilMoment = ⊥
               THEN waitUntilMoment := now + s
               ELIF now ≥ waitUntilMoment
               THEN || currentSchedule := t
                    || waitUntilMoment := ⊥
               ELSE SKIP
```

Fig. 16.8. Rule and predicate controlling the execution of a schedule.

of rule TPSystem as given in Fig. 16.4. Figure 16.8 presents our approach. is-
Actuator and isSensorPredicate tell if a schedule element is an actuator
or a sensor predicate, respectively; a schedule element which is neither of
these is a real number representing a delay. If an actuator has been recognized, it is activated (rule scheme ActivateActuator is assumed to do
this), and the first element of the current schedule is removed. If a sensor
predicate has been recognized, it is checked if it is true (via the predicate
sensorPredicateIsTrue); if it is, the entry is removed from the schedule;
otherwise, nothing is done, i.e., the controller just waits. Finally, i.e., if the
first element of the schedules says that the controller should wait for some
time, it is checked if the moment when the waiting should end (waitUntil-
Moment, initialized with ⊥) has already been computed or not. If it has not
yet been computed, the computation is performed; and if it already has been
computed, it is checked if the control program already waited long enough;
when this is the case, i.e., when the current time is at least as large as the
moment up to which the system should wait, the entry is removed from the
schedule; otherwise, the system does nothing, i.e., it just waits.

Note that the STASM semantics of these rules fulfill the timing requirements quite obviously. In the NTASM semantics of the rule, waiting times
might be by an infinitesimal longer than given in the program, because of
the infinitesimal discretization, and because of the fact that activating an
actuator or evaluating a sensor predicate takes at least time dt. We deem
such an infinitesimal deviation from the specified timing acceptable, which

should not be a problem in practical situations. If the maximal processing times in processing units or the maximal total residence time of a plate are not by a standard margin larger than the minimal times, this might become a problem, but this case is very unrealistic. Thus, under plausible assumptions, also the NTASM semantics will fulfill the requirements.

Some other derived symbols and rules used in TPSystem could also be defined at this spot, but since they are fairly obvious, we do not give the definitions here. Thus, we just assume that the meanings of the symbols blank-InSystem, CleanUp, MoveCraneOneToFeedBelt and nextProgramAvailable are appropriately fixed.

16.9 Two Cranes, Order of Processing Units Fixed

Only one omission of our design now remains to be filled in: we have to define a function mkScheduleForFixedOrder_twoCranes(p) which yields a two-crane schedule for a program p.

In our interpretation of the task description, we promised to find a schedule for a blank if there exists one. Specifically, this means that if there is a schedule so that the maximal residence requirement of the blank in the system is obeyed, the control program will use it. For programs with a variable order of processing units, we reduced the problem in a simple way to the problem for programs with a fixed order of processing units, as described in Sect. 16.6. For a system with one crane and a program with a fixed order of the processing units, the computation of the schedule with minimal residence time is fairly easy, as described in Sect. 16.7.

The case with two cranes is more complicated than the one with one crane because the residence time of a blank in the system depends (a) on the order in which cranes are used for the transports of a blank between belts and processing machines, (b) on the initial positions of the second crane, and (c) on the speeds of the cranes in the different directions and the geometry of the production cell.

16.9.1 Splitting a Schedule into Segments

We approach the problem by considering the schedule by which a new blank is transferred from the feed belt through the processing system to the deposit belt to be split into *segments*. During one segment of a schedule, the same crane is responsible for moving the blank between belts and processing units, and a segment ends if a crane loses this responsibility, either to the other crane, or because the blank has been put on the deposit belt. During a segment, the blank is moved from one defined position (feed belt, deposit belt or one of the processing units) to another, until the last position of the segment is reached, which is the first position of the next segment (if there is one), or the deposit belt in the other case.

In a two-crane system, a schedule has at least two segments, since without collision, only the first crane can fetch a blank from the feed belt and only the second crane can put the blank to the deposit belt. Since we have at most four steps in a blank program, there are at most four segments during the processing of a program, but we will abstract from this later. Since only an even number of segments transfer a blank from the feed belt to the deposit belt, two and four segments are the only possibilities in the system considered.

Our global strategy for scheduling is similar to (but more involved than) the strategy used for constructing a variable-order schedule from a solution to the fixed-order schedule problem: We simply consider all possible splits of the movements of the blank into segments, develop a maximal speed schedule for each segmentation, and finally select a schedule which fulfills the timing conditions with respect to oven-type processing units and the total residence time. The way of constructing the schedules ensures that the other conditions are fulfilled, only the total residence time might be longer than allowed because of an badly chosen segmentation, or the upper time of residence in an oven-type processing unit might be exceeded if a change of cranes takes place while the blank is located in an oven-type processing unit, since there is some minimal time which is needed for a change of responsibility. Since we require that for each program, a possible schedule exists, and we construct, for each segmentation, a schedule with a minimal total residence time and minimal residence times in oven-type machines, an admissible schedule will be found. This idea is expressed in the function given in Fig. 16.9. A segmentation is a list of non-empty lists of program steps where the concatenation of the smaller lists yields almost the program step list of the original program, with the only difference that the first step in all but the first smaller lists is a repetition of the last step of the previous list, and the last step of the last segment is the position of the deposit belt. Each smaller list in a segmentation, i.e., each segment, represents a sequence of movements between positions which is to be performed by the same crane. EvenPUSegmentations(p) is the set of segmentations of program p into an even number of segments. The only symbol needing more elaboration is the function mkScheduleForSegmentation, which yields a quickest schedule for a segmentation given as argument.

16.9.2 The Active and the Passive Crane and Their Tasks

We call the crane which is responsible for moving the blank during a segment the *active* crane of the segment. The other crane is called *passive*. The latter

```
mkScheduleForFixedOrder_twoCranes(p)  =_def
  LET S = {s|∃(q : EvenPUSegmentations(p)) :
          s = mkScheduleForSegmentation(q)
       }
  IN ε({s ∈ S : processingTimeOk(s,p) ∧ ovenTimesOk(s,p)})
```

Fig. 16.9. Computing the schedule for a program with a two-crane system.

term is slightly misleading because also the passive crane has specific tasks, as will be described shortly. In order to be specific, let us say that a segment ends precisely in the moment the active crane drops the blank at the last position of the segment.

Let us now consider the tasks of the two cranes during a segment.

During a segment, the active crane (which, at the beginning of the segment, has not yet gripped the blank) is responsible for moving to the place where the blank will be taken up, for taking up the blank from its place, for moving it to its first destination, and for putting it down at its destination; if the segment has not yet ended, the active crane then waits for the processing of the blank being finished, picks up the blank again and continues as before. After the transport of the blank to the place marking the end of a segment has been accomplished and there is another segment in the schedule, the responsibilities change. Altogether, during a segment, the behavior of a crane is similar to the case with one crane; a difference is that possibly, the other crane is not yet far enough out of the way, so that before the active crane starts a movement into the direction of the passive crane, it has to be ensured that the distance to the other crane will not become too small. This can be done during the planning phase, since we assume that the system runs error free.

A formerly active, now passive crane has two tasks: Firstly, it has to get out of the way so that the formerly passive, now active crane can do its work without collision. Secondly, it has to assume a sequence of positions during its waiting time so that it can resume responsibility again quickly, as soon as it should be required to do so. Thirdly, if (and when) its time has come to become active again, it has to move towards the processing unit from where it has to take up the blank, i.e., to the first position of the segment in which it is (or will be) again active.

Before work on a blank starts, the passive crane might have to assume a special position or even start moving from there in order to take over its responsibility from the other one quickly enough when the residence time of the blank is running, i.e., before the active crane picks up the blank from the feed belt.

16.9.3 Resting Position, Target Position and Initialization

The resting position of a passive crane is a position which is out of the range which the active crane will need to do its work during the work on the current segment, but which is as near as possible to the next position at which the now passive crane will be needed again; the latter is called the "target position". Both the resting position and the target position are only computed for passive cranes, i.e., for crane two for odd-numbered segments, and for crane one for even-numbered segments. Since only segmentations with an even number of segments are considered, the functions are for the last segment, i.e., if the segmentation considered contains only one more

```
mkTargetPosition(q) =def
  IF length(q) = 1
  THEN mkFeedBeltPosition
  ELSE mkPosition(xIdx(lastPU(first(q))),
                  yIdx(lastPU(first(q))))

mkRestingPosition(q,crane) =def
  IF length(q) = 1
  THEN mkFeedBeltPosition
  ELSE mkPosition(xIdx(lastPU(first(q)))+(crane=1 ? -1 : 1),
                  yIdx(lastPU(first(q))))
```

Fig. 16.10. Computing a resting position and a target position.

segment, always called with crane one. The computation of the two positions is different if we deal with the last segment in a segmentation or with another segment. In the first case, we are computing the positions for crane one at the end of a schedule; it seems sensible to use the position over the feed belt for both. In the other case, the positions are defined by the position of the last element of the currently executed segment in the segmentation: this is the target position, and for the resting position, the y index is the same, and the x index is, for crane one, by one less than the index of the last processing unit in the current segmentation, and by one larger than this in the other case. Figure 16.10 defines the functions.

The resting position is assumed by the passive crane before a fresh blank is picked up from the feed belt, and after a crane has dropped the blank at the end of its activity during a segment and the other has taken over. A special case is crane two after it has completed the last segment for a blank: In this case, there is no resting position defined for the crane, and it just moves its gripper up and waits until a next blank reaches the end of the feed belt.

As soon as a segmentation to use has been determined, a resting position is defined and crane two will move there during the initialization of the system for the work on the next segmentation, before the new blank to be processed is picked up. The initialization of the transport-and-processing system consists just of crane two moving to its resting position for the first segment (see Fig. 16.11). The global controller rule TPSystem deals with the requirement that crane one moves to the feed belt before a schedule starts.

```
mk2CranesInitialization(q) =def
  LET r = mkRestingPosition(q,2) IN
    list(
      moveCrane(2,xPos(r)), moveCrane(2,yPos(r)),
      isCraneAt(2,xPos(r)) ∧ isCraneAt(2,yPos(r))
    )
```

Fig. 16.11. Initialization schedule for the two-crane system.

16.9.4 Specifics of Crane Behavior

The main features of the behavior of the cranes in a two crane system is described in the flow diagram in Fig. 16.12. This diagram describes the states through which a crane goes during its work on a segmentation, starting after the initialization has been finished. We will describe the meanings of the nodes of the diagrams.

- **down1** is the state in which a crane which just starts its activity moves down towards the blank. Before this state is entered, the crane must have reached the position over the blank. When this state is entered, the gripper

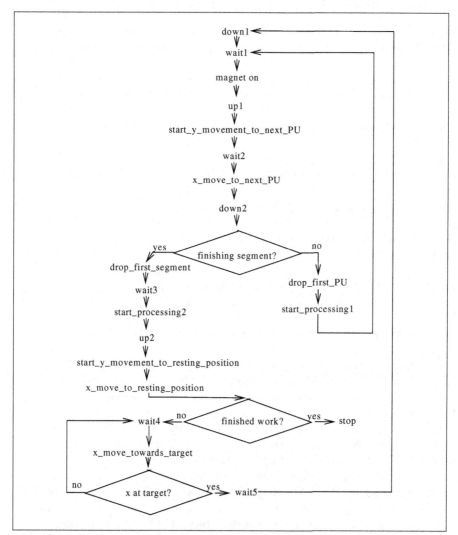

Fig. 16.12. Behavior of cranes in the two-crane system.

is moved downwards. The state is left when the gripper has reached the lower position.

This is also the state in which crane one starts its work after the initialization.

— When the gripper has reached the lower position, the crane must possibly wait before it may pick up the blank. This phase is represented by state **wait1**. There are three reasons why it might be necessary to wait: (a) If the blank is in an oven-type processing unit, the minimal processing time might not yet have been reached. In this case, the crane waits until the minimal processing time has been reached. (b) If the blank is in a drill-or-press type processing unit, the work of the processing unit might not yet have been finished. In this case, the cranes waits until the processing unit has finished its work. (c) If the blank is located on the feed belt (then the active crane is necessarily crane one), it might be necessary to wait until crane two has reached a position from where it can pick up the blank after the first segment has ended as quickly as possible. If the second crane needs more time from its resting position to its target position than is needed for the first segment of the current segmentation, the second crane might come later than necessary; to avoid that the total residence time is already counting in such a case, crane one will wait until crane two is near enough.

— After the crane has waited long enough, it picks up the blank by switching its **magnet on**, and then moving the loaded gripper up in state **up1**.

— When the gripper has reached the upper position, the movement in the y-direction which is necessary in order to reach the position of the next processing unit of the first segment of the segmentation is initiated. State **start_y_movement_to_next_PU** represents this; this state is immediately left for state wait2.

— Before the crane can start its x-direction movement into the direction of the next position it has to check if the passive crane, which is currently moving to its resting position, is far enough out of the way. If it is not, it has to wait. This happens in state **wait2**.

— When it is ensured that the passive crane is far enough out of the way, the active crane moves in the x-direction to the next position in the currently executed segment. This movement happens in state **x_move_to_next_PU**.

— After the crane has reached its target position (both its x- and its y-coordinate), it moves the gripper down again. State **down2** represents this phase.

— What happens next depends on the case if the current is the last transport of the current segment, i.e., if the active crane is just finishing the current segment. If this is not the case, no change of responsibilities has to take place: The current program step is just stripped from the current segment (in state **drop_first_PU**), the magnet is turned off, and possibly, the processing unit is turned on. The latter happens in state **start_processing1**. After this, the computation continues in state **wait1**, which has already been discussed.

– If the current transport is the last in a segment, a change of responsibilities takes place. First, the current segment (the transports for which have now been processed) is removed from the segmentation (**drop_first_segment**). Normally, the crane would now just proceed to drop the blank in order to start its processing; but there is a case in which it has to wait with this: If the current processing unit is an oven-type machine, the other crane, which must pick up the blank before the upper limit of the processing time has been reached, might be too slow. If this situation is possible, the currently active crane might have to wait some time with dropping the blank on the oven so that the currently passive crane will come soon enough. This waiting phase is denoted by **wait3**.

– When the crane has waited long enough, the crane will drop the blank by switching the magnet off, and if the processing unit is of the drill-or-press type it will be switched on. This happens in state **start_processing2**.

– After the crane has dropped the blank, it has now changed its role: It is passive. It first moves up (start **up2** represents this phase), initiates the y-movement to the resting position (in state **start_y_movement_to_resting_position**), and then moves to the x-coordinate of the resting position (in state **x_move_to_resting_position**). It stays in this state until the x-coordinate of the resting position has been reached. Since the resting position is always in the direction away from the other crane, no collision can occur because of this movement. A collision could only happen if this movement towards the resting position is not quick enough and the other, now active crane has picked up the blank and moves it into the same direction, but quicker. In order to deal with this possibility, the other crane would have to wait in the already discussed state **wait2**.

– After the now passive crane has reached its resting position, its task changes: Either it has finished its task for the current segmentation; then it just stops (state **stop**), and the whole process will be started afresh by the main driver program when the next two-crane-schedule has to be executed for the next blank.

– If there will be a segment in the current segmentation in which the crane will become active again, it has to be ensured that the crane is always as near to the position where it is next needed as is possible without risking collision with the active crane. This is done by first waiting until it is ensured that the other crane will have left the region of the next x-index in the direction of the target position when the current crane reaches that region. This waiting is done in state **wait4**.

wait4 is also the state in which crane two starts after the initialization: After initialization, crane two is located at its resting position for the first segment.

– When the crane has waited long enough, the crane moves one x-position towards its next target, i.e., the next position where it will be needed again

(in state **x_move_towards_target**). This state is left if that x-position
isreached.

– After the crane has reached the next position, it is checked if this is already
the x-coordinate of the target. If it is not, we might have to wait again until
the other crane leaves the next position where we have to go (again in state
wait4). If the target x-coordinate has been reached, we have to wait until
also the y-coordinate has been reached (state **wait5**), and then, the gripper
of the crane which now is becoming active again can start moving down
again (in the already discussed state **down1**).

This interpretation fixes most features of the schedule for a single crane
to be constructed. Only the waiting times to use in states **wait1**, **wait2**,
wait3 and **wait4** deserve more discussion (see Sect. 16.9.5). Let us assume that this problem has been solved; then, the derivation of a schedule
for a single crane from the flow diagram specification is straight forward,
but tedious. We will not do this here, but simply assume that a function
`mkOneCraneScheduleForSegmentation(q,crane)` has been defined which,
for a segmentation q and a crane number, yields the schedule for this crane.
It remains to be shown how these two schedules can be combined into one.

Our strategy is to insert, in each of both schedules, in front of each Boolean
expression on the sensors of the system, which implies a waiting time for the
schedule, this implied delay. These waiting times can be computed because
(a) the initial configuration (the one assumed by the system after the initialization of the system for a blank program) is known, (b) the speeds of all
movements and the processing times in drill-or-press type processing units
are known, and (c) no sensors which are controlled from outside the system
occur in the constructed schedule for the cranes; the only sensors for which
such times could not have been computed are the ones of the feed belt and the
deposit belt, and both do not have to be dealt with by the work on a segmentation – they are dealt with by the enclosing abstract control program. We
assume that a function `addExplicitDelays(schedule1,schedule2,conf)`,
invoked with two schedules for the two cranes and the configuration of the
system from where to start, and yielding a pair of two schedules for the two
cranes, but without sensor occurrences, implements this strategy.

Note that ideally, i.e., if we assumed that the processing times and speeds
of the system components are exactly known, we could just drop the sensor
expressions from the schedules and get the same total behavior. The decision
not to remove the sensor expressions from the schedules reflects our decision
that this assumption would be too ideal.

The second (and last) step then consists of combining the two schedules.
Figure 16.13 describes how the pieces fit together. `combineSchedules` computes the combination in a recursive fashion, by using any non-delay at the
start of one of the argument schedules first, and by using the minimum delay
if both schedules start with a delay step.

```
combineSchedules(s₁,s₂)  =def
  IF isEmpty(s₁)
  THEN s₂
  ELIF isEmpty(s₂)
  THEN s₁
  ELSE
    LET f₁=first(s₁), r₁=rest(s₁),
        f₂=first(s₂), r₂=rest(s₂)
    IN
      IF ¬isExplicitDelay(f₁)
      THEN list(f₁) . combineSchedules(r₁,s₂)
      ELIF ¬isExplicitDelay(f₂)
      THEN list(f₂) . combineSchedules(s₁,r₂)
      ELIF f₁ ≤ f₂
      THEN list(f₁) . combineSchedules(r₁,list(f₂ − f₁).r₂)
      ELSE list(f₂) . combineSchedules(list(f₁ − f₂).r₁,r₂)

mkScheduleForSegmentation(q)  =def
  LET schedPair
      = addExplicitDelays(
          mkOneCraneScheduleForSegmentation(q,1),
          mkOneCraneScheduleForSegmentation(q,2),
          mkInitialConfiguration(q)
        )
  IN combineSchedules(first(schedPair),second(schedPair))
```

Fig. 16.13. Computing the schedule for a given segmentation.

16.9.5 Waiting Times in a Two-Crane System

The only thing that remains to be determined are the waiting times in the single-crane schedules for the two-crane system as defined in Sect. 16.9.4. We use the state names from the diagram in Fig. 16.12 again and repeat, for convenience, the reasons for the waiting times:

- Crane one might have to wait in state **wait1** until crane two is near enough before the blank is picked up from the feed belt and total residence time starts running).
- A loaded crane might have to wait in **wait2** some time before it transports the blank to the next processing unit because the passive crane might not yet have moved far away enough.
- A crane which is about to drop the blank at the end of a segment might have to wait in state **wait3** if the blank is to be dropped on an oven-type processing unit and the other crane might be too slow to pick up the blank again before the maximal processing time has been reached.
- A passive crane will typically have to wait in state **wait4** before it may start the movement to the next x-position in the direction of the processing unit where it has to become active again.

Note that when the waiting time computed for a state is negative (which is not uncommon, as will be seen), the value zero has to be put into the single-crane schedule, since the function `combineSchedules` does not handle negative delays properly.

It is most convenient to start with discussing the waiting time in **wait4**. How long must a passive crane wait until it may move one x-position in the direction of its target? To be specific, let us assume that crane two is the passive crane for which we compute the waiting time; the other case can be reasoned about analoguously. Let us call the x-position of crane two x_i; since its target position must be to the left, the next x-position to head for on its way to the target is x_{i-1}; we call this x-coordinate the intermediate target of the passive crane (which before the last movement is at the same time the final target). After it is started, the movement can not be stopped until that x-position is reached. In order to avoid a collision with crane one, crane two must wait so long that crane one will be on its way away from x_{i-1} when crane two reaches that region, and will never come back again during its work on the current segment.

In order to compute the time until crane one is far enough out of the way up to the end of the work on a segment, we use a function `timeUntilLeft(q,crane,x,conf)`. For a segment q, a crane number, an x-coordinate and a current configuration (`conf`), this function computes the time up to the first moment in which the crane will start leaving the x-coordinate given into the direction away from the other crane and never come back again until it reaches the resting position to be assumed after the work on the current segment, all this under the assumption that the waiting times in states **wait1**, **wait2** and **wait3** are zero. For example, `timeUntilLeft(q,1,x_{i-1},conf)` is the time after which crane one will have left the intermediate target if started from the configuration `conf` and will not come back again until it has reached its resting position, and `timeUntilLeft(q,1,x_{i-1} - min_x_dist,conf)` is the time after which crane one will be far enough away from the intermediate target position so that a collision with crane two at that position is avoided.

The time until the active crane has left some area is computed under the (in general wrong) assumption that in the waiting states of an active crane **wait1**, **wait2** and **wait3**, no time is spent. We have to discuss why this can not lead to problems:

- First, note that the value of the function is only relevant when the passive crane is far enough out of reach, i.e., after the passive state has reached its resting position, and during its careful approach to its target position; this means that ignoring the waiting time in state **wait2** can not lead to problems, since also in a proper computation of waiting times, this situation would lead to a waiting time of zero in this state.
- Second, note that not waiting in states **wait1** and **wait3** will not lead to collisions, only to the possibility that the total processing time for a blank

will be longer than strictly necessary (for **wait1**), or that a blank is processed longer in an oven than allowed (for **wait3**). These two problems will be dealt with later, when the waiting times for these states are computed.

Let us now consider the case that crane two is slower than or as quick as crane one in its x-movements. Then the optimal waiting time, i.e., the time so that crane two reaches the target as quickly as possible without danger of collision, is so that crane two reaches the x-coordinate $x_{i-1} + min\_x\_dist$ exactly when crane one leaves from x_{i-1}: in this moment, we have the minimal allowed distance; earlier during the movement towards the intermediate target, the distance was larger; and later during this movement, it will not be smaller, because crane one leaves the intermediate target at least as quickly as crane two approaches it.

If crane two is quicker than crane one, the described waiting time would be too short because crane two would approach the intermediate target position quicker than crane one would move away from it. In this case, the time of nearest approach should be when crane two reaches the intermediate position and crane one is moving away from $x_{i-1} - min\_x\_dist$.

Function wait4time in Fig. 16.14 expresses the result of this reasoning for the general case, i.e., without restriction to the case that crane two is passive. First, the special case is handled that the passive crane is crane one and we deal with the last segment. In this case, the crane does not have to wait, because the target is to the left of the crane, away from the other crane, so no collision can occur because of the next movement. Otherwise, we use a LET-phrase for computing the waiting time. First, the number of the other crane is computed. sign is used for determining the intermediate target position intmdtTarget one index position from the current x position into the direction of the target, where we have to deal with the special case

```
wait4Time(q,conf,crane) =def
  IF crane=1 ∧ lastSegment(q)
  THEN 0
  ELSE
    LET otherCrane = (crane=2 ? 1 : 2),
        sign = (crane=2 ? -1 : +1),
        intmdtTarget = xCoord(xPos(crane,conf)+sign),
        slower = (VXcrane < VXotherCrane),
        refCrane = IF slower
                      THEN intmdtTarget
                      ELSE intmdtTarget - sign*min_x_dist,
        refOtherCrane = refCrane + sign*min_x_dist
    IN
      timeUntilLeft(q,otherCrane,refOtherCrane,conf)
        - abs(refCrane-xCoord(crane,conf))/VXcrane
```

Fig. 16.14. Waiting time before the passive crane does the next x-movement towards its target position.

that during the last segment, the target of crane one is to the left, not to the right. `slower` is a Boolean variable recording if the passive crane is slower than its counterpart. It is used in the case distinction for the computation of the x-coordinate of the crane for the moment of nearest aproach between the two cranes. This coordinate is assigned to `refCrane`, and it is used in the computation of the position of the other crane at the moment of nearest approach (`refOtherCrane`). Finally, the waiting time is computed as difference from the time until the other crane has left the x-coordinate of the point of nearest approach, and the time the passive crane needs to reach its position for the moment of nearest approach.

Note that the time computed by `wait4time` might be negative. This means that the passive crane might even have started its movement earlier (by the absolute value of the computed time) than the current moment without that a collision would have occurred. But since we assume that the waiting time is checked as early as possible, i.e., as soon as the passive crane has reached the x-coordinate from which it can start the next move, it is not possible for the passive crane to use this extra time. But there are situations in which the other crane might use this time: Instead of moving as quickly as possible, it might wait exactly this time before it starts its movement without, and yet, collisions will be avoided. This feature is used in the computation of the waiting times in states **wait1** and **wait3**.

Figure 16.15 presents the function for computing the waiting time for crane one before it picks up the blank from the feed belt. If the waiting time of the then passive crane, i.e., of crane two, is negative in the initial situation, this means that the total residence time of the blank in the system can me reduced when the blank is picked up by crane one after this amount of time.

Figure 16.16 presents the function computing the waiting time for a crane before it drops the blank onto an oven at the end of a segment. Here again, the crane may only wait if its passive counterpart has a negative waiting time (otherwise, a collision would occur), and the waiting time again may be at most as long as the absolute value of this negative waiting time, similar to the case for state **wait1**. But since the total residence time is already running when a crane is in this state, the crane should move as early as possible without endangering that the blank stays too long in the oven. For this, we compute the oven time which would ensue if the blank would be dropped immediately (we assume that this is determined by the function

```
wait1Time(q) =def
  LET t=wait4Time(q,mkInitialConfiguration(q),2)
  IN IF t < 0
     THEN −t
     ELSE 0
```

Fig. 16.15. Waiting time before blank is picked up for the first time.

```
wait3Time(q,conf,crane)  =def
  LET t=wait4Time(q,conf,3-crane) IN
    IF t ≥ 0
    THEN 0
    ELSE
      LET s=defaultOvenTime(q,conf,crane),
          m=maxOvenTime(q,conf)
      IN IF s ≤ m
         THEN 0
         ELSE min(s − m,−t)
```

Fig. 16.16. Waiting time before the blank is dropped in an oven at the end of a segment so that a slow different crane can be near enough to pick the blank up in time.

defaultOvenTime), and we determine the maximal oven time (via the function maxOvenTime). If the default oven time is smaller than or equal to the maximal oven time, we do not have to wait. Otherwise, we either wait for the difference between the default oven time and the maximal oven time or the absolute value of the waiting time of the passive crane, whichever is smaller. In this case, collisions are avoided, but maximal oven times are not necessarily obeyed. If a constructed schedule does not fulfill the oven-time condition (because the difference $s − m$ is larger than $−t$ at the end of some segment), it will be sorted out from the set of considered schedules in mkScheduleFor-FixedOrder_twoCranes by the predicate ovenTimesOk (see Fig. 16.9).

Figure 16.17 presents the last function, that for waiting time in state **wait2**. The case is very similar to the one with state **wait4**, only the roles are exchanged: Now the active crane is the one which possibly has to wait before it can start its movement towards its next target, because perhaps, the passive crane is not yet far enough out of the way. Now, we do not deal with intermediate targets: When the movement starts, it goes directly to the x-coordinate of the next processing unit (**target**). In this case, a problem can only ensue if the crane is quicker than its counterpart, and if the next x-coordinate lies to the same side as the other crane; otherwise, the crane does not have to wait. If it might have to wait, the reference point for the other crane is computed analoguously to the case for state **wait4**, but the waiting time can be computed simply by dividing the distance to travel to the reference point by the traveling speed and subtracting from this the time which the current crane will need to reach its target when it has been started.

16.10 Are the System Properties Ensured?

In Sect. 16.3, several properties are which should be proved of the system under consideration. We will now go through this list, shortly explaining how a proof would proceed in each case.

```
wait2Time(q,conf,crane) =def
  LET otherCrane = (crane=2 ? 1 : 2),
      sign = (crane=2 ? -1 : +1),
      target = xCoord(xPos(nextPU(q))),
      quicker = (vx_crane > vx_otherCrane),
      refOtherCrane = target + sign*min_x_dist
  IN
    IF quicker ∧ sign*(target - xCoord(crane,conf))>0
    THEN sign*(refOtherCrane-xCoord(otherCrane,conf))/vx_otherCrane
         - sign*(target-xCoord(crane,conf))/vx_crane
    ELSE 0
```

Fig. 16.17. Waiting time before a loaded crane can move to the next processing unit when the other crane might not yet be far enough away.

- *The two cranes may never be nearer that* min_x_dist *on their x-coordinates.*
  This holds in the initial case, and the waiting times for states **wait1**, **wait2**, **wait3** and **wait4** were carefully chosen to ensure that this also holds during the processing. An induction will show that this invariant will hold, only possibly allowing infinitesimal errors.
- *A blank may only be put into a processing unit if it is not occupied by some other blank, and it may only be put onto the deposit belt if the sensor does not report that the start of the belt is occupied.*
  This is obviously fulfilled by the system, since a blank is only picked up from the feed belt if there is no blank in the rest of the system, including the deposit belt.
- *The feed belt must be switched off when a blank arrives at its end, and a gripper magnet may only be switched off if the gripper is in the lower position above a processing unit or a belt.*
  Both invariants are obviously fulfilled by the control program; for the latter, this can be seen be inspecting the schedules for the crane or cranes.
- *Every blank taken from the feed belt will eventually be put on the deposit belt.*
  Since a blank is only taken from the feed belt when the whole system is free, and the sum of processing times, transport times and (possibly) crane change times is finite, the computed schedule will lead to the blank being dropped on the deposit belt after some finite amount of time.
- *Blanks go through the processing units given in their programs; if the program specifies that the order of the program list has to be respected, this is the order used for the blank.*
  This is obviously fulfilled by the computation of the schedules for the crane(s).
- *Between the moment when a blank is picked up from the feed belt and the moment it is put on the deposit belt, no more than the maximal allowed system processing time as specified in its program may be spent.*

Since each crane starts all its movements as early as is possible considering the other restrictions (collision avoidance, maximal oven times), a minimal time schedule for a program or a segmentation will be constructed. And if several possibilities for the order of the program steps or the split of the program into segments exist, for each of them a minimal time schedule is computed; if a schedule fulfilling this condition exists (which we assume), it will thus be found. This holds for both the one-crane system and the two-crane system.

— *The minimal and maximal processing times in oven-type processing units must be respected.*
For the one-crane system, this is trivial. For the two-crane system, the waiting time in **wait1** if the current processing unit is an oven will ensure that the minimal processing time is respected, and the waiting time in **wait3** is computed so that the maximal oven processing time is respected during the work on the current segmentation, if this is possible obeying the no-collision requirement (which need not be the case for some segmentations).

16.11 Summary

This chapter presents a larger case study, which is inspired by an industrial application. The task description had been designed to show how different formalisms can deal with timing requirements and variants of a system.

The timing requirements pose no special problems for our approach to modelling timed systems; the STASM semantics allows a quite straightforward implementation of the requirements, and for the NTASM semantics, plausible assumptions are necessary.

Our solution for the two-crane case is of considerable complexity, but this does not seem to have to do with shortcomings of the formalism we used. Rather, the problem itself seems to be difficult and to need an inconveniently large number of case distinctions, so it is expected that also the formalization of the approach has to reflect this.

The flexibility in the architecture for the systems which have to be dealt with can quite nicely be dealt with in the ASM approach because of the freedom to choose the abstraction level as one wants to. Thus, the differences between variants for the system architecture do not have to be dealt with everywhere in the model: these spots where the variants play a role are clearly localized.

Part IV

Summary

17. Summary

The main result of this work is that there exists a model of quantitative linear time which is both discrete and dense in the real numbers, and which can be used for the description and analysis of algorithms which make use of quantitative properties of a linear dense model of time with purely discrete means.

During the development and use of this model, the concepts of well-behavedness and strong well-behavedness arise naturally for the characterization of dense-time algorithms which lend themselves to infinitesimal discretizability. Because of the choice of the very flexible ASMs as base formalism it is possible to transfer these concepts to more specific machine models.

Looking more specifically at the goals described in Sect. 2.7, we conclude:

- Timing enhanced Petri nets and timed automata are modelled quite directly by our approach: the data-part of the models can be expressed without overhead induced by the formalism. The same holds for Fischer's synchronization protocol. It might sensibly be expected that this would also work for other formalisms or applications to be modelled.
- The discreteness of the time model has made it possible that Fischer's protocol can be proved with purely discrete means. We think that this discrete method can be used for proving safety properties of timed systems in general.
- The formalism is quite flexible in that it does not fix the abstraction level at which an algorithm is to be described. An example is given in the definition of timed automata where an abstract definition has been made concrete in two different ways, and in the production cell case study where the common features of the variants of the system could be dealt with at an abstract level.

Chapter 3 gave an overview of problems of different models of time. Let us sum up if our approach can solve them:

- A problem of classical discrete models of time is that the unit must be fixed beforehand; this means that there is a lower bound on the time distance of events. This bound also exists in our approach, but it is smaller than any strictly positive classical real number, and its exact value is not supposed to be known.

- The intuitive choice of $\mathbb{R}$ as the time domain of densely linearly timed algorithms can *almost* be preserved.
- Composition of modules designed with different step widths is a problem in classical approach to discrete time. We avoid this by assuming a constant but unknown infinitesimal step width.
- Refinement of discrete steps is no problem because in any non-empty standard interval there is an unlimited number of opportunities for steps; thus, as long as the system has limited activity also after the refinement, there is enough room for the extra steps possibly introduced by the refinement.
- There is always a next point in time of the system, and in each non-empty set of moments there is a first moment. Both is not necessarily the case in dense models of time. A drawback of our approach is that not every predicate can be used to define sets of moments; this follows from the restriction that predicate "st" is in general not set-forming.
- There are no Zeno runs, but this is no real win, since the underlying problem of unlimited activity of a system in limited time can occur.
- Our model of time is uniform. Discrete steps and time steps do not have to be dealt with differently.
- If in a composition of two modules, considered at standard-$\mathbb{R}$-resolution, two events from different modules occur at the same time, then the $d \times \mathbb{N}$-resolution is fine enough to see if they happen at the same time or, if not, which happens before the other. But nondeterminism with respect to this order must be made explicit, whereas in the classical model, it was implicit.

On our way to the major results just mentioned, we collected some minor ones.

- We define the semantics of our variant of ASMs as action systems and add special consideration for the description of effective systems. Action systems contain enough structure to express synchronous as well as asynchronous composition.
- On the basis of the semantics just mentioned, we describe a convention for the formalization of the interaction of a system with its environment in ASMs which is easily used in refinements.
- We dwell on an aspect of Gurevich's thesis which might be misunderstood (the claim that ASMs can be used for "coding free" description of algorithms on any abstraction level): The exact tuning of intuition and formalization means that what can be described as one intuitive step can also be described as one step of the algorithm; we do not have to refine the intuitive steps just because the formalism does not admit steps of the abstractness headed for. This does not mean that we do not have to make some features explicit in the control- and data-part of the algorithm which in other formalism can stay implicit.
- We describe differences of ASMs as base formalism for the description of discrete systems in comparison to other base formalisms.

– We develop an interpretation for ASMs which encodes the timing of an algorithm in the framework of an interval-sequence semantics (the STASM interpretation of ASM rules). The timing is encoded in the rules, it is not described independently of the rules as is done in other approaches to the description of timing-based systems with ASMs. The formalism-induced artifacts of infinite activity and hesitation are described.

– We develop the NTASM interpretation of ASM rules and relate it with a standard model of timed systems (STASM interpretation) by the definition of a simulation relation, and well-behavedness and strong well-behavedness. The latter two concepts are formalizations of the idea that an algorithm can be both interpreted as description of an STASM system and as an NTASM system, i.e., that it admits infinitesimal discretization of the time domain.

– A notation for a temporal logic has been developed which allows the concise expression of specifications of requirements for timed systems and the expression of formalism-specific artifacts (mainly, this is unlimited activity).

– We give expositions of the main ideas used for asynchronous and synchronous models of concurrency in the untimed ASM framework. This forms the basis for the later discussion of timing-dependent features of STASMs and NTASMs and can serve as a basis for ASM-models of other formalisms. We discuss main problems of the two approached induced by the formalization, i.e., fairness for asynchronous and causality for synchronous composition.

– It is described how deadlines can be implemented in the synchronous (simple) and the asynchronous framework (more complicated).

– We describe how the concept of receptivity, which is the concept of unlimited activity as applied to open systems, is vastly simplified in our framework in comparison to frameworks based on a non-uniform model of time, and we define the practically more relevant concept of (m, n)-receptivity.

– We describe how different magnitudes of the non-standard reals can be used for making explicit that the timing of some components can be neglected in comparison to that of others.

– We formally characterize commonly occurring conditions under which cycle counting is not necessary in order to prove timing properties at a higher abstraction level.

– We describe a meta-model for doubly timed Petri nets, showing the differences between time nets and timed nets by their expression in a common framework and exposing an ambiguity in the original definition of Merlin and Farber's time nets.

– Some conditions for ensuring well-behavedness of doubly timed Petri nets are analyzed, showing that the concept of infinitesimal discretizability can be lifted from ASMs to Petri nets.

- We give a description of timed and hybrid automata, organized in two abstraction levels which makes common features of the formalisms stand out, and we again analyze the condition for well-behavedness.
- We present a solution to a task description which is meant, by their authors, as a benchmark for formalisms with respect to their capabilities of dealing with timing requirements and variants of a reactive system. Our formalism does not seem to induce extra complications in addition to those present in the task description, and specifically, both the timing requirements of the task and the need to describe variants pose no problems at all.

There are some inherent problems of our approach, i.e., problems which we do not expect to be solvable without considerable changes in the underlying framework:

- We use concepts from nonstandard analysis. The gain in understandability of our system descriptions resulting from the choice of a discrete and uniform base model for time might thus be offset by the use of concepts which are not very common in computer science.
  Perhaps the main problem resulting from this point is that if an invariant to be checked is non-standard (for example: "the standard part of the value of term t is always greater than or equal to zero"), it can *not* be checked by simple induction on the positions in system behaviors.
- In our approach, one intuitive step of an algorithm can not necessarily be expressed as one step of the formalism – single intuitive time steps have in general to be expressed by an unlimited number of steps. This is an unavoidable consequence of the use of a uniform model of time.
- The timing of an algorithm is encoded in the rules, not given independently of them. Thus, one is less flexible in describing systems behaviors using this approach than in other approaches using ASMs for the description of timing-based algorithms. Only experience can show if this really is a problem, or if for more involved uses of the independence of the descriptions of rules and timing, this just comes down to having to encode control structure in ASMs explicitly, which *is* accepted for untimed uses of the formalism. We suspect this to be the case.
- The constancy of the step width in NTASM systems might not always be convenient.
- Simulation of an NTASM system is in general difficult. It can not be done step-by-step, since in order to simulate an appreciable amount of time, an unlimited number of steps have to be performed. If the execution of some discrete step can depend on general functions of **now**, the length of the next time step might be impossible to compute; restrictions for the use of **now** in conditions are necessary.

Finally, we describe some work which could be done for building on the current approach:

- More case studies could help to show the range of the approach (and its limitations).
- The temporal logic might be axiomatized, a proof system might be investigated, and heuristics for its use might be developed.
- We did not yet investigate the possibility to describe system behaviors as solutions of differential equations. The base idea would be to describe the change of a continuously changing quantity y by an assignment of the form `y:=y+dt*y'`. This would mean that `now` is not the only non-derived symbol any more which changes its value continuously and where we have to deal with infinitesimal errors when compared with a classical description of the system. We did not yet explore in detail which problems arise from this approach to system description.
- Since the formalism is very general, for practical use it would be helpful to develop more conventions for the expression of different concepts of timing-based systems in this framework (i.e., in NTASM rules and the associated logic). This can make the missing guidance resulting from generality of the formalism less urgent.
- Tool support, and specifically the possibility for simulation is missing. As already described, simulation can not be done step-by-step. We expect that the formalization of the concept of simulability of an NTASM interpretation of an ASM rule will yield important insights into restrictions which are sensible to effectiveness of descriptions of timing-based algorithms.

A. Common Notation

A.1 Non-standard Quantifiers and Predicates

To express non-classical predicates with functors concisely, we introduce some abbreviations:

$\forall^{\text{st}} x P$ abbreviates $\forall x : st(x) \to P$

$\exists^{\text{st}} x P$ abbreviates $\exists x : st(x) \land P$

$\forall^{\text{fin}} x P$ abbreviates $\forall x : \text{finite}(x) \to P$

$\exists^{\text{fin}} x P$ abbreviates $\exists x : \text{finite}(x) \land P$

$\forall^{\text{st fin}} x P$ abbreviates $\forall^{st} x : \text{finite}(x) \to P$

$\exists^{\text{st fin}} x P$ abbreviates $\exists^{st} x : \text{finite}(x) \land P$

We use the predicates infinitesimal($\cdot$), appreciable($\cdot$) and limited($\cdot$) to characterize elements of $\mathbb{R}$ with these non-standard properties.

For reals x, x', $x \simeq x'$ is defined to hold if and only if $|x-x'|$ is infinitesimal, and $x \sim x'$ is defined to hold if and only x and x' belong to the same magnitude, i.e., $\frac{x}{x'}$ is defined and appreciable.

A.2 Various Kinds of Expressions

tt and ff denote the Boolean values "true" and "false".

For a finite set A, $|A|$ is the cardinality of A.

$\aleph_0$ is the cardinality of $\mathbb{N}_0$.

For a boolean expression b and two expressions x_1 and x_2, the expression $(b \ ? \ x_1 : x_2)$ represents x_1 if b is true and x_2 otherwises.

A.3 Various Expressions for Functions and Sets of Functions

Functional values are sometimes expressed by lambda expressions, i.e., by expressions of the form $\lambda(x : A)(e)$, where x is a new variable, A is a set expression (might be missing if it is understood over which set x ranges), and e is an expression in which x might occur. A is the domain of the function. The range is the set of values e can assume for x ranging over A.

A restriction of a function f to the intersection of its domain and a set D is written $f \downarrow D$.

For two sets A and B, $A \rightarrow B$ represents the set of functions with domain A and range B.

For a non-empty set S, $\epsilon(S)$ is Hilbert's choice function yielding an element of S.

The domain of a function f is denoted $\mathrm{dom}(f)$ and the range is denoted $\mathrm{ran}(f)$.

For a function f the expression $f[a \mapsto b]$ is a function mapping elements $x \in \mathrm{dom}(f) - \{a\}$ to $f(x)$ and mapping a to b.

Finite functions may be given as sets of mappings, written like $\{x \mapsto 0, y \mapsto 1\}$.

Two functions f and g are *consistent* if they agree on common arguments. Note that disjointness of domains implies consistency.

For two functions f and g, $f[g]$ denotes the function $\lambda(e : \mathrm{dom}(f) \cup \mathrm{dom}(g)) : (e \in \mathrm{dom}(g) ? g(e) : f(e))$, i.e., f is extended and overridden by g. Note that for consistent f and g, $f[g] = g[f]$.

A.4 Some Common Sets

For a set S, $\mathcal{P}(S)$ is the set of subsets of S.

$\mathbb{N}_0$ represents the set of natural numbers including zero. $\mathbb{N}$ represents the set of natural numbers excluding zero. $\mathbb{Z}$ is the set of integers.

$\mathbb{R}$ represents the real numbers, $\mathbb{R}_0^+$ represents the nonnegative real numbers, and $\mathbb{R}^+$ represents the positive real numbers, i.e., $\mathbb{R}_0^+ - \{0\}$.

An interval I of $\mathbb{N}_0$ is a convex subset of $\mathbb{N}_0$, i.e., a set of elements of $\mathbb{N}_0$ such that for $i, j, k \in \mathbb{N}_0$ with $i < j < k$, $i \in I \wedge k \in I$ implies $j \in I$. Intervals may be empty or total. The set of intervals over $\mathbb{N}_0$ is denoted as $\mathrm{intervals}(\mathbb{N}_0)$. An initial interval of $\mathbb{N}_0$ is an interval which is empty or the minimal element of which is 0.

For some set A, $\boldsymbol{A}$ is the set of sequences of elements of A, which are represented as functions $f \in A^I$ for initial intervals I of $\mathbb{N}_0$ such that the ith letter of such a sequence is $f(i-1)$.

ω is the first transfinite ordinal.

For some strictly ordered set M not containing ∞ and two elements $a, b \in M$, (a, b) denotes $\{m \in M : a < m < b\}$, $[a, b]$ denotes $\{m \in M : a \leq m \leq b\}$, $[a, b)$ denotes $\{m \in M : a \leq m < b\}$, $(a, b]$ denotes $\{m \in M : a < m \leq b\}$, (a, ∞) denotes $\{m \in M : a < m\}$, and $[a, \infty)$ denotes $\{m \in M : a \leq m\}$.

A.5 Some Definitions

A *partial order* on a set S, typically written as $\leq$, is a binary relation which is transitive ($s \leq s' \wedge s' \leq s'' \rightarrow s \leq s''$), reflexive ($s \leq s$) and antisymmetric ($s \leq s' \wedge s' \leq s \rightarrow s = s'$). We write $s \geq s'$ for $s' \leq s$, $s < s'$ for $s \leq s' \wedge s \neq s'$, and $s > s'$ for $s' < s$.

We call a relation $R \subseteq A \times B$ **bi-total** if for each $a \in A$, there is a $b \in B$ with $(a, b) \in R$ and vice versa. The set of bi-total relations over sets A and B is denoted as $\text{bitotal}(A, B)$.

The operators $\lfloor \cdot \rfloor$ and $\lceil \cdot \rceil$ represent the functions "round a real down to the next integer" and "round a real up to the next integer".

The semantics of a syntactical object t in a context c will typically be denoted $[\![t]\!]_c$. Most often, c will be a first-order structure assigning meanings to the symbols occurring in the first-order term t.

References

[ACD93] R. Alur, C. Courcoubetis, and D. Dill. Model-checking in dense real-time. *Information and Computation*, 104:2–34, 1993.

[ACH⁺95] R. Alur, C. Courcoubetis, N. Halbwachs, T. A. Henzinger, P.-H. Ho, X. Nicollin, A. Olivero, J. Sifakis, and S. Yovine. The algorithmic analysis of hybrid systems. *Theoretical Computer Science*, 138:3–34, 1995.

[ACH97] L. O. Arkeryd, N. J. Cutland, and C. W. Henson, editors. *Nonstandard Analysis: Theory and Applications*. Kluwer Academic Publishers, Dordrecht, Boston, London, 1997.

[AD94] R. Alur and D. L. Dill. A theory of timed automata. *Theoretical Computer Science*, 126:183–235, 1994.

[AH97] R. Alur and T. A. Henzinger. Modularity for timed and hybrid systems. In *Proceedings of the 8th International Conference on Concurrency Theory (CONCUR'97)*, LNCS 1243, pages 74–88, Berlin, 1997. Springer-Verlag.

[AL92] M. Abadi and L. Lamport. An old-fashioned recipe for real time. In J. de Bakker, C. Huizing, W. de Roever, and G. Rozenberg, editors, *Real Time: Theory in Practice*, LNCS 600, pages 1–27, 1992.

[AL95] M. Abadi and L. Lamport. Conjoining specifications. *ACM Transactions on Programming Languages and Systems*, 17(3):507–534, 1995.

[AS85] B. Alpern and F. B. Schneider. Defining liveness. *Information Processing Letters*, 21:181–185, 1985.

[BB03] T. Bolognesi and E. Börger. Abstract state processes. In E. Börger, A. Gargantini, and E. Riccobene, editors, *Abstract State Machines – Advances in Theory and Applications (ASM2003)*, LNCS 2589. Springer-Verlag, 2003.

[BD91] B. Berthomieu and M. Diaz. Modelling and verification of time dependent systems using time petri nets. *IEEE Transactions on Software Engineering*, 17(3):259–273, 1991.

[BdS91] F. Boussinot and R. de Simone. The Esterel language. *Proceedings of the IEEE*, 79(9):1293–1304, September 1991.

[Ben98] F. Benjes. *Verfeinerung in verschiedenen Modellen für Paralleles Rechnen*. PhD thesis, Universität Mannheim, 1998.

[Ber99] G. Berry. The constructive semantics of pure ESTEREL. Draft Version 3.0. Technical report, Centre de Mathématiques Appliquées, Ecole des Mines de Paris, 1999.

[Bey01] D. Beyer. Rabbit: Verification of real-time systems. In P. Pettersson and S. Yovine, editors, *Proceedings of the Workshop on Real-Time Tools (RT-TOOLS 2001, Aalborg)*, pages 13–21, Uppsala, 2001.

[BG92] G. Berry and G. Gonthier. The ESTEREL synchronous programming language: Design, semantics, implementation. *Science of Computer Programming*, 19(2):87–152, 1992.

[BH98]   E. Börger and J. K. Huggins. Abstract state machines 1988-1998: Commented ASM bibliography. *Bulletin of the EATCS*, 64, 1998.

[BLL⁺96]   J. Bengtsson, K. Larsen, F. Larsson, P. Petersson, and W. Yi. Uppaal – a tool suite for automatic verification of real-time systems. In R. Alur, T. A. Henzinger, and E. D. Sontag, editors, *Hybrid Systems III*, LNCS 1066, pages 232–243, Berlin, 1996. Springer-Verlag.

[Bör98]   E. Börger. High level system design and analysis using abstract state machines. In Hutter, Stephan, Traverso, and Ullmann, editors, *Current Trends in Applied Formal Methods (FM-Trends 98)*, LNCS, 1998.

[BR98]   D. Beyer and H. Rust. Modeling a production cell as a distributed real-time system with cottbus timed automata. In H. König and P. Langendörfer, editors, *FBT'98: Formale Beschreibungstechniken für verteilte Systeme*, pages 148–159. Shaker Verlag Aachen, 1998.

[BR99]   D. Beyer and H. Rust. Concepts of Cottbus Timed Automata. In K. Spies and B. Schätz, editors, *FBT'99: Formale Beschreibungstechniken für verteilte Systeme*, pages 27–34. Herbert Utz Verlag München, 1999.

[BR00a]   D. Beyer and H. Rust. Modular modelling and verification with Cottbus Timed Automata. In C. Rattray and M. Sveda, editors, *Proceedings of the IEEE/IFIP Joint Workshop on Formal Specifications of Computer Based Systems (FSCBS 2000)*, pages 17–24, Edinburgh, 2000.

[BR00b]   D. Beyer and H. Rust. A tool for modular modelling and verification of hybrid systems. In A. Crespo and J. Vila, editors, *Proceedings of the 25th IFAC Workshop on Real-Time Programming (WRTP 2000)*, pages 181–186, Oxford, 2000. Elsevier Science.

[BR01]   D. Beyer and H. Rust. Cottbus timed automata: Formal definition and semantics. In C. Rattray, M. Sveda, and J. Rozenblit, editors, *Proceedings of the 2nd IEEE/IFIP Joint Workshop on Formal Specifications of Computer-Based Systems (FSCBS 2001, Washington, D.C., April 2001)*, pages 75–87, Stirling, 2001.

[BS97a]   D. Beauquier and A. Slissenko. On semantics of algorithms with continuous time. Technical Report 97-15, Université de Paris 12 – Val de Marne, October 1997.

[BS97b]   D. Beauquier and A. Slissenko. The railroad crossing problem: Towards semantics of timed algorithms and their model checking in high level languages. In M. Bidoit and M. Dauchet, editors, *Proc. of TAP-SOFT'97: Theory and Practice of Software Development, 7th Int'l Joint Conference CAAP/FASE*, LNCS 1214, pages 202–212, 1997.

[BS03]   E. Börger and R. Stärk. *Abstract State Machines. A method for high-level system design and analysis*. Springer-Verlag, 2003.

[CHR91]   Z. Chaochen, C. Hoare, and A. P. Ravn. A calculus of durations. *Information Processing Letters*, 40:269–276, 1991.

[Dij65]   E. W. Dijkstra. Programming considered as human activity. *Proc. IFIP-Congress 1965:New York*, pages 213–217, May 1965.

[Dij75]   E. W. Dijkstra. Guarded commands, nondeterminacy, and formal derivation of programs. *Communications of the ACM*, 18(8):453–457, 1975.

[DLP79]   R. A. DeMillo, R. J. Lipton, and A. J. Perlis. Social processes and proofs of theorems and programs. *Communications of the ACM*, 22(5):271–280, May 1979.

[DOTY96]   C. Daws, A. Olivero, S. Tripakis, and S. Yovine. The tool KRONOS. In R. Alur, T. A. Henzinger, and E. D. Sontag, editors, *Hybrid Systems III*, LNCS 1066, pages 208–219, Berlin, 1996. Springer-Verlag.

[dR98]   W.-P. de Roever. The need for compositional proof systems: A survey. In W.-P. de Roever, H. Langmaack, and A. Pnueli, editors, *Compositionality: The Significant Difference*, LNCS 1536, pages 1–22, Berlin, 1998. Springer-Verlag.

[DS94]   M. Diaz and P. Sénac. Time stream petri nets, a model for timed multimedia information. In *Proc. 15th Int. Conf. Application and Theory of Petri Nets 1994*, LNCS 815, pages 219–238, Berlin, 1994. Springer-Verlag.

[FMM94]   M. Felder, D. Mandrioli, and A. Morzenti. Proving properties of real-time systems through logical specifications and petri net models. *IEEE Transactions on Software Engineering*, 20(2):127–141, February 1994.

[FP78]   N. Francez and A. Pnueli. A proof method for cyclic programs. *Acta Informatica*, 9:133–157, 1978.

[Fra86]   N. Francez. *Fairness*. Springer-Verlag, New York, Berlin, Heidelberg, Tokyo, 1986.

[GH96]   Y. Gurevich and J. K. Huggins. The railroad crossing problem: An experiment with instantaneous actions and immediate reactions. In H. Kleine-Büning, editor, *Computer Science Logics. Selected Papers from CSL'95*, LNCS 1092, pages 266–290. Springer-Verlag, 1996.

[GM95]   Y. Gurevich and R. Mani. Group membership protocol: Specification and verification. In E. Börger, editor, *Specification and Validation Methods*, pages 295–328. Oxford University Press, 1995.

[GMM99]   A. Gargantini, D. Mandrioli, and A. Morzenti. Dealing with zero-time transitions in axiom systems. *Information and Computation*, 150:119–131, 1999.

[Gor95]   M. Gordon. The semantic challenge of verilog hdl. In *Proceedings of the Tenth Annual IEEE Symposium on Logic in Computer Science*, 1995.

[Gur88]   Y. Gurevich. Logic and the challenge of computer science. In E. Börger, editor, *Current Trends in Theoretical Computer Science*, pages 1–57. Computer Science Press, 1988.

[Gur93]   Y. Gurevich. Evolving algebras: An attempt to discover semantics. In G. Rozenberg and A. Salomaa, editors, *Current Trends in Theoretical Computer Science*, pages 266–292. World Scientific, 1993.

[Gur95a]   Y. Gurevich. Evolving algebras 1993: Lipari guide. In E. Börger, editor, *Specification and Validation Methods*, pages 9–36. Oxford University Press, 1995.

[Gur95b]   Y. Gurevich. Platonism, constructivism, and computer proofs vs. proofs by hand. *Bulletin of the EATCS*, 57:145–166, October 1995.

[Gur97]   Y. Gurevich. May 1997 draft of the ASM guide. Technical Report CSE-TR-337-97, University of Michigan, EECS Department, 1997.

[Gur99]   Y. Gurevich. Sequential ASM thesis. Technical Report MSR-TR-99-09, Microsoft Research, Redmond, 1999.

[GY76]   S. L. Gerhart and L. Yelowitz. Observations of fallibility in applications of modern programming methodologies. *IEEE Transactions on Software Engineering*, 2(3):195–207, September 1976.

[Hal90]   A. Hall. Seven myths of formal methods. *IEEE Software*, pages 11–19, September 1990.

[Hal93]   N. Halbwachs. *Synchronous Programming of Reactive Systems*. Kluwer Academic Publishers, 1993.

[Har87]   D. Harel. Statecharts: A visual formalism for complex systems. *Science of Computer Programming*, 8:231–274, 1987.

[HCP91]   N. Halbwachs, P. Caspi, and D. Pilaud. The synchronous dataflow programming language lustre. *Proceedings of the IEEE*, 79(9):1305–1320, September 1991.

[HG92]   C. Huizing and R. Gerth. Semantics of reactive systems in abstract time. In J. de Bakker, C. Huizing, W. de Roever, and G. Rozenberg, editors, *Real Time: Theory in Practice*, LNCS 600, pages 291–314, 1992.

[HHWT95]   T. A. Henzinger, P.-H. Ho, and H. Wong-Toi. A user guide to HyTech. In *Proceedings of the First Workshop on Tools and Algorithms for the Construction and Analysis of Systems (TACAS)*, LNCS 1019, pages 41–71. Springer-Verlag, 1995.

[Hoa85]   C. Hoare. *Communicating Sequential Processes*. Prentice Hall, Hemel Hempstead, 1985.

[Hoo92]   J. Hooman. Compositional verification of real-time systems using extended hoare triples. In J. de Bakker, C. Huizing, W. de Roever, and G. Rozenberg, editors, *Real Time: Theory in Practice*, LNCS 600, pages 252–290, 1992.

[HP85]   D. Harel and A. Pnueli. On the development of reactive systems. In K. R. Apt, editor, *Logics and Models of Concurrent Systems*, pages 477–498. Springer-Verlag, Berlin, 1985.

[HPZ97]   M. Heiner and L. Popova-Zeugmann. Worst-case analysis of concurrent systems with duration interval petri nets. In E. Schieder and D. Abel, editors, *Entwurf komplexer Automatisierungssysteme 1997, Proc. 5. Fachtagung EKA'97, IfRA 1997*, pages 162–179, Braunschweig, May 1997.

[HU79]   J. E. Hopcroft and J. D. Ullman. *Introduction to Automata Theory, Languages, and Machines*. Addison Wesley, Reading, 1979.

[Jos92]   M. Joseph. Problems, promises and performance: Some questions for real-time system specification. In J. de Bakker, C. Huizing, W. de Roever, and G. Rozenberg, editors, *Real Time: Theory in Practice*, LNCS 600, pages 315–324, 1992.

[Koy92]   R. Koymans. (real) time: A philosophical perspective. In J. de Bakker, C. Huizing, W. de Roever, and G. Rozenberg, editors, *Real Time: Theory in Practice*, LNCS 600, pages 353–370, 1992.

[Lam87]   L. Lamport. A fast mutual exclusion algorithm. *ACM Transactions on Computer Systems*, 5(1):1–11, 1987.

[Lam94a]   L. Lamport. Introduction to TLA. Technical Report 1994-001, Digital Systems Research Center, 1994.

[Lam94b]   L. Lamport. The temporal logic of actions. *ACM Transactions on Programming Languages and Systems*, 16(3):872–923, May 1994.

[Lam97]   L. Lamport. Composition: A way to make proofs harder. Technical Report SRC Technical Note 1997-030a, digital Systems Research Center, 1997.

[LBBG85]   P. LeGuernic, A. Benveniste, P. Bournai, and T. Gautier. SIGNAL: A data-flow oriented language for signal processing. Technical Report RR 378, INRIA, 1985.

[LGLL91]   P. LeGuernic, T. Gautier, M. LeBorgne, and C. LeMaire. Programming real time applications with signal. *Proceedings of the IEEE*, 79(9):1321–1336, September 1991.

[LL95]   C. Lewerentz and T. Lindner, editors. *Formal Development of Reactive Systems*. LNCS 891. Springer-Verlag, Berlin, Heidelberg, 1995.

[LM96]   A. Lötzbeyer and R. Mühlfeld. Task description of a flexible production cell with real time properties. FZI Technical Report, 1996.

[LMS86]   R. Lipsett, E. Marschner, and M. Shahdad. VHDL–the language. *IEEE Design and Test*, pages 28–41, 1986.

[LR94]   D. Landers and L. Rogge. *Nichtstandard Analysis*. Springer-Verlag, Berlin, 1994.

[LSVW96]   N. Lynch, R. Segala, F. Vaandrager, and H. Weinberg. Hybrid I/O automata. In R. Alur, T. A. Henzinger, and E. D. Sontag, editors, *Hybrid Systems III*, LNCS 1066, pages 496–510, Berlin, 1996. Springer-Verlag.

[LT87]   N. A. Lynch and M. R. Tuttle. Hierarchical correctness proofs for distributed algorithms. In *Proceedings of the 6th Annual ACM Symposium on Principles of Distributed Computing*, pages 137–151. ACM, August 1987.

[Lyn96]   N. Lynch. *Distributed Algorithms*. Morgan Kaufmann Publishers, San Francisco, 1996.

[Mar89]   F. Maraninchi. Argonaute: Graphical description, semantics and verification of reactive systems by using a process algebra. In *International Workshop on Automatic Verification Methods for Finite State Systems*, LNCS 407. Springer-Verlag, 1989.

[Mar90]   F. Maraninchi. Argos, une langage graphique pour la conception, la description et la validation des systèmes réactives. Master's thesis, Université Joseph Fourier, Grenoble, 1990.

[McM93]   K. McMillan. *Symbolic Model Checking*. Kluwer Academic Publishers, 1993.

[MF76]   P. M. Merlin and D. J. Farber. Recoverability of communication protocols – implications of a theoretical study. *IEEE Trans. Comm.*, 24(9), 1976.

[Mil75]   H. D. Mills. How to write correct programs and know it. *Int. Conf. on Reliable Software:Los Angeles*, pages 363–370, April 1975.

[Mil89]   R. Milner. *Communication and Concurrency*. Prentice Hall, 1989.

[MMS90]   L. E. Moser and P. M. Melliar-Smith. Formal verification of safety-critical systems. *Software – Practice and Experience*, 20(8):799–821, August 1990.

[Mos85]   B. C. Moszkowski. A temporal logic for multilevel reasoning about hardware. *IEEE Computer*, 18(2):10–19, 1985.

[Mos90]   P. D. Mosses. Denotational semantics. In J. van Leeuwen, editor, *Handbook of Theoretical Computer Science, Vol. B*, pages 575–631. Elsevier, Amsterdam, 1990.

[MP92]   Z. Manna and A. Pnueli. *The Temporal Logic of Reactive and Concurrent Systems: Specification*. Springer-Verlag, New York, 1992.

[MP95]   Z. Manna and A. Pnueli. *Temporal Verification of Reactive Systems: Safety*. Springer-Verlag, New York, 1995.

[Nau82]   P. Naur. Formalization in program development. *BIT*, pages 437–453, 1982.

[Nau85]   P. Naur. Intuition in software development. *Proc. TAPSOFT: Formal Methods and Software Development*, 2:60–79, March 1985.

[Nel77]   E. Nelson. Internal set theory, a new approach to nonstandard analysis. *Bulletin American Mathematical Society*, 83:1165–1198, 1977.

[NS92]   X. Nicollin and J. Sifakis. An overview and synthesis on timed process algebras. In J. de Bakker, C. Huizing, W. de Roever, and G. Rozenberg, editors, *Real Time: Theory in Practice*, LNCS 600, pages 526–548, 1992.

[ORSvH95]   S. Owre, J. Rushby, N. Shankar, and F. von Henke. Formal verification for fault-tolerant architectures: Prolegomena to the design of PVS. *IEEE Transactions on Software Engineering*, 21(2):107–125, February 1995.

[Par72]   D. L. Parnas. On the criteria to be used in decomposing systems into modules. *Communications of the ACM*, 15(12):1053–1058, December 1972.

[Pet62]   C. A. Petri. *Kommunikation mit Automaten*. PhD thesis, Institut für Instrumentelle Mathematik, Bonn, 1962.

[Pnu77]   A. Pnueli. The temporal logic of programs. In *Proceedings of the 18th Annual Symposium on Foundations of Computer Science*, pages 46–57. IEEE Computer Science Press, 1977.

[Pop91]   L. Popova. On time petri nets. *J. Inform. Process. Cybernet. EIK*, 27(4):227–244, 1991.

[Ram74]   C. Ramchandani. Analysis of asynchronous concurrent systems by timed petri nets. Technical Report TR 120, MIT, 1974. Project MAC.

[Rei86]   W. Reisig. *Petrinetze*. Springer, Berlin, 1986.

[Rob88]   A. Robert. *Nonstandard Analysis*. Wiley and Sons, New York, Chichester, Brisbane, 1988.

[Rob96]   A. Robinson. *Non-standard Analysis*. Princeton University Press, Princeton/New Jersey, 1996.

[Rus94]   H. Rust. *Zuverlässigkeit und Verantwortung*. Vieweg, Braunschweig, Wiesbaden, 1994.

[Sko34]   T. Skolem. Über die Nichtcharakterisierbarkeit der Zahlreihe mittels endlich oder abzählbar unendlich vieler Aussagen mit ausschließlich Zahlvariablen. *Fund.Math.*, 23:150–161, 1934.

[TM95]   D. E. Thomas and P. R. Moorby. *The Verilog Hardware Description Language*. Kluwer Academic Publishers, 1995.

[Tur37]   A. M. Turing. On computable numbers with an application to the Entscheidungsproblem. *Proc. London Math. Soc.*, 2(42):230–265, 1937.

[vdB94]   M. von der Beeck. A comparison of statecharts variants. In H. Langmaack, W.-P. de Roever, and J. Vytopil, editors, *Formal Techniques in Real-Time and Fault-Tolerant Systems*, LNCS 863, pages 128–148, Berlin et al., 1994. Springer-Verlag.

[vN66]   J. von Neumann. *The Theory of Self-Reproducing Automata*. University of Illinois Press, 1966.

[Vol79]   R. Vollmar. *Algorithmen in Zellularautomaten*. B. G. Teubner, Stuttgart, 1979.

[Win88]   G. Winskel. An introduction to event structures. In J. de Bakker, W. de Roever, and G. Rozenberg, editors, *Linear Time, Branching Time, and Partial Orders in Logics and Models of Concurrency*, LNCS 354, pages 364–397. Springer-Verlag, Berlin, 1988.

[Win90]   J. M. Wing. A specifier's introduction to formal methods. *Computer*, pages 8–24, September 1990.

[Wir71]   N. Wirth. Program development by stepwise refinement. *Communications of the ACM*, 14(4):221–227, April 1971.

[Zei76]   B. P. Zeigler. *Theory of Modelling and Simulation*. Wiley, New York, 1976.

Index

Lecture Notes in Computer Science

For information about Vols. 1–3351

please contact your bookseller or Springer

Vol. 3399: Y. Zhang, K. Tanaka, J.X. Yu, S. Wang, M. Li (Eds.), Web Technologies Research and Development - APWeb 2005. XXII, 1082 pages. 2005.

Vol. 3398: D.-K. Baik (Ed.), Systems Modeling and Simulation: Theory and Applications. XIV, 733 pages. 2005. (Subseries LNAI).

Vol. 3397: T.G. Kim (Ed.), Artificial Intelligence and Simulation. XV, 711 pages. 2005. (Subseries LNAI).

Vol. 3396: R.M. van Eijk, M.-P. Huget, F. Dignum (Eds.), Agent Communication. X, 261 pages. 2005. (Subseries LNAI).

Vol. 3395: J. Grabowski, B. Nielsen (Eds.), Formal Approaches to Software Testing. X, 225 pages. 2005.

Vol. 3394: D. Kudenko, D. Kazakov, E. Alonso (Eds.), Adaptive Agents and Multi-Agent Systems III. VIII, 313 pages. 2005. (Subseries LNAI).

Vol. 3393: H.-J. Kreowski, U. Montanari, F. Orejas, G. Rozenberg, G. Taentzer (Eds.), Formal Methods in Software and Systems Modeling. XXVII, 413 pages. 2005.

Vol. 3392: D. Seipel, M. Hanus, U. Geske, O. Bartenstein (Eds.), Applications of Declarative Programming and Knowledge Management. X, 309 pages. 2005. (Subseries LNAI).

Vol. 3391: C. Kim (Ed.), Information Networking. XVII, 936 pages. 2005.

Vol. 3390: R. Choren, A. Garcia, C. Lucena, A. Romanovsky (Eds.), Software Engineering for Multi-Agent Systems III. XII, 291 pages. 2005.

Vol. 3389: P. Van Roy (Ed.), Multiparadigm Programming in Mozart/OZ. XV, 329 pages. 2005.

Vol. 3388: J. Lagergren (Ed.), Comparative Genomics. VII, 133 pages. 2005. (Subseries LNBI).

Vol. 3387: J. Cardoso, A. Sheth (Eds.), Semantic Web Services and Web Process Composition. VIII, 147 pages. 2005.

Vol. 3386: S. Vaudenay (Ed.), Public Key Cryptography - PKC 2005. IX, 436 pages. 2005.

Vol. 3385: R. Cousot (Ed.), Verification, Model Checking, and Abstract Interpretation. XII, 483 pages. 2005.

Vol. 3383: J. Pach (Ed.), Graph Drawing. XII, 536 pages. 2005.

Vol. 3382: J. Odell, P. Giorgini, J.P. Müller (Eds.), Agent-Oriented Software Engineering V. X, 239 pages. 2005.

Vol. 3381: P. Vojtáš, M. Bieliková, B. Charron-Bost, O. Sýkora (Eds.), SOFSEM 2005: Theory and Practice of Computer Science. XV, 448 pages. 2005.

Vol. 3380: C. Priami, Transactions on Computational Systems Biology I. IX, 111 pages. 2005. (Subseries LNBI).

Vol. 3379: M. Hemmje, C. Niederee, T. Risse (Eds.), From Integrated Publication and Information Systems to Information and Knowledge Environments. XXIV, 321 pages. 2005.

Vol. 3378: J. Kilian (Ed.), Theory of Cryptography. XII, 621 pages. 2005.

Vol. 3377: B. Goethals, A. Siebes (Eds.), Knowledge Discovery in Inductive Databases. VII, 190 pages. 2005.

Vol. 3376: A. Menezes (Ed.), Topics in Cryptology - CT-RSA 2005. X, 385 pages. 2005.

Vol. 3375: M.A. Marsan, G. Bianchi, M. Listanti, M. Meo (Eds.), Quality of Service in Multiservice IP Networks. XIII, 656 pages. 2005.

Vol. 3374: D. Weyns, H.V.D. Parunak, F. Michel (Eds.), Environments for Multi-Agent Systems. X, 279 pages. 2005. (Subseries LNAI).

Vol. 3372: C. Bussler, V. Tannen, I. Fundulaki (Eds.), Semantic Web and Databases. X, 227 pages. 2005.

Vol. 3371: M.W. Barley, N. Kasabov (Eds.), Intelligent Agents and Multi-Agent Systems. X, 329 pages. 2005. (Subseries LNAI).

Vol. 3370: A. Konagaya, K. Satou (Eds.), Grid Computing in Life Science. X, 188 pages. 2005. (Subseries LNBI).

Vol. 3369: V.R. Benjamins, P. Casanovas, J. Breuker, A. Gangemi (Eds.), Law and the Semantic Web. XII, 249 pages. 2005. (Subseries LNAI).

Vol. 3368: L. Paletta, J.K. Tsotsos, E. Rome, G.W. Humphreys (Eds.), Attention and Performance in Computational Vision. VIII, 231 pages. 2005.

Vol. 3367: W.S. Ng, B.C. Ooi, A. Ouksel, C. Sartori (Eds.), Databases, Information Systems, and Peer-to-Peer Computing. X, 231 pages. 2005.

Vol. 3366: I. Rahwan, P. Moraitis, C. Reed (Eds.), Argumentation in Multi-Agent Systems. XII, 263 pages. 2005. (Subseries LNAI).

Vol. 3365: G. Mauri, G. Păun, M.J. Pérez-Jiménez, G. Rozenberg, A. Salomaa (Eds.), Membrane Computing. IX, 415 pages. 2005.

Vol. 3363: T. Eiter, L. Libkin (Eds.), Database Theory - ICDT 2005. XI, 413 pages. 2004.

Vol. 3362: G. Barthe, L. Burdy, M. Huisman, J.-L. Lanet, T. Muntean (Eds.), Construction and Analysis of Safe, Secure, and Interoperable Smart Devices. IX, 257 pages. 2005.

Vol. 3361: S. Bengio, H. Bourlard (Eds.), Machine Learning for Multimodal Interaction. XII, 362 pages. 2005.

Vol. 3360: S. Spaccapietra, E. Bertino, S. Jajodia, R. King, D. McLeod, M.E. Orlowska, L. Strous (Eds.), Journal on Data Semantics II. XI, 223 pages. 2005.

Vol. 3359: G. Grieser, Y. Tanaka (Eds.), Intuitive Human Interfaces for Organizing and Accessing Intellectual Assets. XIV, 257 pages. 2005. (Subseries LNAI).

Vol. 3358: J. Cao, L.T. Yang, M. Guo, F. Lau (Eds.), Parallel and Distributed Processing and Applications. XXIV, 1058 pages. 2004.

Vol. 3357: H. Handschuh, M.A. Hasan (Eds.), Selected Areas in Cryptography. XI, 354 pages. 2004.

Vol. 3356: G. Das, V.P. Gulati (Eds.), Intelligent Information Technology. XII, 428 pages. 2004.

Vol. 3355: R. Murray-Smith, R. Shorten (Eds.), Switching and Learning in Feedback Systems. X, 343 pages. 2005.

Vol. 3354: M. Margenstern (Ed.), Machines, Computations, and Universality. VIII, 329 pages. 2005.

Vol. 3353: J. Hromkovič, M. Nagl, B. Westfechtel (Eds.), Graph-Theoretic Concepts in Computer Science. XI, 404 pages. 2004.

Vol. 3352: C. Blundo, S. Cimato (Eds.), Security in Communication Networks. XI, 381 pages. 2005.